CRIMINAL PROCEDURE

Judy Hails Kaci J.D., LL.M.

COPPERHOUSE PUBLISHING COMPANY

1590 Lotus Road
Placerville, California 95667
(916) 626-1260

Your Partner in Education
with
"QUALITY BOOKS AT FAIR PRICES"

CRIMINAL PROCEDURE

Library of Congress Catalog Number 94-69409
ISBN 0-942728-66-1 Paper Text Edition

Printed in the United States of America.

About the Author

Author Judy Hails Kaci has taught criminal law and procedure for over 20 years. She is currently a Professor in the Department of Criminal Justice at California State University, Long Beach and has also been a Visiting Assistant Professor at Illinois State University (1981-83) and an adjunct professor at John Jay College in New York City (1978-80). Dr. Kaci is a former sergeant with the Los Angeles County Sheriff's Department. Her education includes: B.S. in mathematics from Loma Linda University; M.S. in criminology from CSU Long Beach; J.D. from Southwestern University School of Law and an LL.M. in criminal justice from New York University School of Law. She has published two other books, *Criminal Evidence* and *Criminal Procedure: A Case Approach* (both by Copperhouse Publishing Company) and numerous articles in professional journals on criminal procedure, prisoner's rights, and domestic violence. She is a past president of both the California Association of Administration of Justice Educators and the Western and Pacific Association of Criminal Justice Educators; she also served a three year term as trustee for Region V of the Academy of Criminal Justice Sciences. She is an inactive member of the California State Bar.

Dedication

Miriam and Kahina

My twin inspirations

Contents

Chapter 9

Chapter 10

Preface

Criminal Procedure is designed to help students/officers understand how activities in both law enforcement and corrections interface with court proceedings. It will de-mystify the judicial process and help the reader understand the importance of collecting evidence and documenting facts that may not appear relevant to the crime being investigated. A knowledge of the lengthy court process that follows the arrest makes it easier for officers to prepare to testify and assist the prosecutor. Obtaining convictions will be easier because officers can efficiently focus on what needs to be done. Study questions at the end of each chapter are designed to develop a better understanding of the process in your local area.

Chapters 1 and 2 place the police role in the larger context of American government. Chapter 3, which relies heavily on the Fourth Amendment warrant clause, discusses arrest and search warrants. It provides a detailed discussion of how to prepare affidavits, obtain warrants from a judge and execute them. Chapter 4 discusses many of the agencies that local law enforcement interacts with at the local, state and federal level.

The remaining chapters of this book follow the chronological order of court proceedings. Chapter 5 covers the first steps in the journey through the court system. It discusses interaction with the prosecutor in order to obtain a criminal complaint. Detailed information is given on what facts must be included in this legal document. The arraignment that follows formally launches the criminal case. Felonies are screened by a judge at the preliminary hearing or by grand jurors when an indictment is sought. Chapter 6 discusses these two processes in detail.

Many behind-the-scene activities precede the start of a criminal trial. These are discussed in Chapters 7 and 8. While the prosecutor is officially in charge at this stage, it is important for law enforcement officers to be familiar with the issues involved because they may be called to testify at pre-trial hearings. Investigators must understand what they are expected to do to prepare the case for trial and the types of information the prosecutor will need to effectively question each witness. All officers involved should review the case focusing on what questions are likely to be asked when they are testifying.

No two trials are alike, but there are many similarities. Chapter 9 follows the presentation of evidence at a typical trial. Officers need to understand the rules on direct and cross examination and what can be done on rebuttal. Several special mini-trials are discussed in Chapter 10: evaluation of the defendant's mental competency; adjudication of the defendant's plea of not guilty by reason of insanity; and determination if the death penalty should be imposed. Juvenile Court hearings are also discussed in this chapter.

The sentencing hearing, discussed in Chapter 11, follows a conviction. In nearly all cases the judge may consider facts in addition to those used to establish the defendant's guilt when sentencing. Presenting appropriate evidence at this hearing may have a major impact on the length of the defendant's sentence. The case is not final until the appeal is over. Chapter 12 reviews the appellate process and discusses direct appeals as well as avenues used to reach the state's highest court and the United States Supreme Court.

Most decisions related to the defendant's punishment and/or rehabilitation are not made in the courtroom. Chapter 13 looks at the various hearings involved in the correctional system and the due process requirements for each. Both institutional hearings, such as those to impose discipline or set parole dates, and proceedings related to community based corrections, such as probation revocation hearings, are discussed.

Civil suits play an increasingly large role in our lives. Chapter 14 discusses various forms of litigation that result from on-duty activities of law enforcement and correctional officers. Suits typically filed in state courts and under the federal Civil Rights Act are covered. Forfeiture proceedings used to attach a defendant's property are also discussed.

Ideally a student should complete an introductory course in criminal justice prior to taking this class. There is sufficient material in the book, however, to provide necessary background information for those who have not and to refresh the memories of those who have not reviewed the topic recently. While a course in evidence is recommended for all students planning careers in law enforcement, it is not required in order to comprehend this material.

JHK

Chapter 1

Criminal Justice as Part of the American Legal System

Learning Objectives

After reading this chapter, the student will be able to:

- Explain six sources of criminal law.
- Explain how a bill becomes a law.
- Describe the structure of the judicial system.
- Explain the authority of federal and state courts.
- Describe the roles of the following participants in the criminal justice system: law enforcement, prosecutor, defendant, defense attorney, judge, and jury.

Key Terms

bench trial
bills of attainder
common law
cruel and unusual punishment
defendant
double jeopardy
due process
equal protection
ex post facto
exclusionary rule
freedom of speech
geographic jurisdiction
jury nullification
precedent
self-incrimination
state constitution
subject matter jurisdiction
sunset laws
U.S. Code
U.S. Congress
U.S. Constitution
U.S. Courts of Appeals
U.S. District Courts
U.S. Supreme Court
unreasonable search and seizure
venue
writ of certiorari
writ of habeus corpus

1.1 Sources of Law

No single code book contains all the laws. Due to the federal system of government used in the United States there are at least two layers of laws: state and federal. Cities and other municipal agencies also enact laws.

Federal Laws

There are two distinct types of federal law: the United States Constitution and the United States Code. The Constitution is binding on all levels of government in the United States. The U.S. Code has provisions that apply to the entire nation and others that are only used in federal territories such as Washington D.C. and the national parks.

U.S. Constitution

A few provisions of the Constitution apply to criminal laws. **Ex post facto** laws are prohibited. Laws that make conduct criminal that was legal at the time it was done are ex post facto. So are laws that make the penalty more severe than was authorized at the time the crime was committed. A law which changes the rules of evidence to make it easier for the prosecution to obtain a conviction than it was at the time the crime was committed would also be ex post facto.

No **bills of attainder** may be passed by the legislature. A bill of attainder was used by the British Parliament to impose the death penalty and required that the person's property be forfeited to the government. The constitutional prohibition also includes bills of pains and penalties which were used to impose criminal penalties without trials for non-capital crimes. These bills were passed by the legislature and there was no trial. The key is that individuals are either named, easily identified members of a group or described in terms of conduct.

The ***writ of habeus corpus*** is used by a person to challenge illegal confinement. The Constitution prohibits suspension of the *writ of habeus corpus* except when required due to rebellion or invasion.

The majority of what we call "constitutional rights" come from the Bill of Rights and the Fourteenth Amendment. While the Bill of Rights was originally enacted to prevent oppressive conduct by the federal government, the U.S. Supreme Court has used the due process clause of the Fourteenth Amendment as a vehicle for applying many, but not all, the provisions of the Bill of Rights to state actions.

The following is a brief summary of the constitutional amendments that apply to local law enforcement. An in-depth study of these principles is required to function effectively as a police officer. These topic are covered in a separate course.

First Amendment

The First Amendment provides for **freedom of speech**, freedom of assembly, freedom of the press, freedom of religion and the right to petition the government for redress of grievances.

Nearly all speech is protected by the First Amendment. A few categories, such as obscenity (pornography, not profanity) and "fighting words" are not protected. The key to freedom of speech is that the minimum restraint necessary must be used and that the law must be "content neutral." A law is unconstitutional if it forbids both legally protected speech and speech that is not protected. It is also impermissible to base decisions on the content of the speech. For example, a law prohibiting speeches in the park would be "overbroad" because it would cover both protected and unprotected speech. Refusing to give a parade permit to a racist group because the town does not approve of the opinions expressed would violate the "content neutral" requirement.

Freedom of the press is a difficult issue in criminal cases because the defendant has the right to trial by an impartial jury. Inflammatory media coverage may make it impossible to find jurors who are not already prejudiced against the defendant. The press has access to any court hearing that is open to the public and may publish any information it discovers on its own. The court may be closed to the press only if there is a specific, compelling reason for closure, such as emotional trauma to a young child who is testifying regarding being molested. The judge may issue gag orders which forbid disclosure of information to the press by prosecutors and defense attorneys. When used, such "gag orders" must be very limited in scope.

Criminal laws may not be designed to interfere with a person's exercise of religion. Laws, such as bigamy and a prohibition on possession of peyote, that have a purpose other than deterring religious activities are allowed. The government cannot establish religion. Conditions of probation that include attending church are forbidden.

Fourth Amendment

The Fourth Amendment prohibits **unreasonable searches and seizures**. A "reasonable expectation of privacy" test has been used instead of restricting the amendment to "persons, houses, papers, and effects" (the words used in the amendment). The Fourth Amendment is violated if a person's reasonable expectation of privacy is invaded by government agents. A person who does not take reasonable steps to protect his/her privacy cannot complain that the Fourth Amendment has been violated.

Probable cause is defined as a group of facts that would convince a reasonable person that an event occurred. The Fourth Amendment sets probable cause as the minimum standard for issuing warrants. Probable cause must be established under oath or affirmation. This is usually done by a written affidavit signed under penalty of perjury. Specific facts must be given which, under the totality of the circumstances, establish probable cause to arrest an individual for a specified crime (arrest warrant) or to search a specific location for items of evidence listed in the warrant (search warrant). A neutral magistrate or judge must review the facts and determine that probable cause exists to issue the warrant.

Probable cause is mentioned in the "warrant clause" of the Fourth Amendment, but the Supreme Court has also used this standard for making warrantless arrests. A full search of the person and area under his/her immediate control is permitted whenever there is a legal custodial arrest. Some other searches may also be done on probable cause even though no warrant has been obtained.

Only unreasonable searches or seizures are prohibited. The Court has attempted to set standards that fit the circumstances. Items left where they can be seen by an officer who is legally at the location are considered in "plain view" and no unreasonable search has occurred. Cars on a public roadway are subject to many vehicle code regulations and, due to their windows, have a lesser expectation of privacy than houses or other enclosed areas. Therefore, the Court has relaxed the warrant requirement in many instances where vehicles are involved.

The Court also recognized law enforcement's need to investigate suspicious conduct when there is no right to make an arrest. The "reasonable suspicion" standard, which requires less certainty of criminal activity than probable cause, can be used for this purpose.

Fifth Amendment

The Fifth Amendment applies to **self-incrimination**: any testimonial communication that can be used to incriminate a person. It is personal: a person can only claim its protection if he/she would face criminal charges based on what he/she said. The *Miranda* warnings have made this amendment famous. *Miranda* warnings must be given prior to custodial interrogation. A suspect may waive these rights if the waiver is knowing, intelligent and voluntary.

The Fifth Amendment also prohibits **double jeopardy**. This applies whenever a person is tried for the same crime after being acquitted or convicted except when the defendant successfully appealed and had the conviction reversed. It also prohibits conviction (either at one trial or sequential trials) on a crime and lesser included offenses.

Sixth Amendment

Numerous rights related to criminal trials are listed in the Sixth Amendment: speedy trial, public trial, impartial jury, being informed of the charges prior to trial, right to cross-examine witnesses who testify for the prosecution, right to subpoena witnesses for the defense, and assistance of counsel. These rights will be covered in considerable detail later in this book.

Eighth Amendment

This amendment prohibits excessive bail and fines. It also forbids **cruel and unusual punishment**. In 1976 the Supreme Court held that the death penalty is not cruel and unusual punishment if appropriate procedural safeguards are used to prevent arbitrary jury decisions.

Due Process

While due process consists of both substantive due process and procedural due process, the majority of the cases applying to criminal law are procedural. Laws that are vague violate due process. So do laws that give police too much discretion.

Equal Protection

Equal protection is used to prohibit racial discrimination. Newer cases involve sexual discrimination. Discrimination on the basis of ability to pay also violates equal protection in some circumstances. The poor must be provided with attorneys at government expense during court proceedings from arraignment through sentencing and the first appeal. Jail sentences, either directly or due to revocation of probation, cannot be imposed for failure to pay fines if the defendant has made bona fide efforts but is unable to pay.

United States Code

The U.S. Code contains laws enacted by the United States Congress. There must be some power delegated to the federal government in the Constitution or its amendments as a basis for each law. Some federal powers, such as regulation of interstate commerce, have been interpreted broadly enough to allow federal laws on interstate car theft, kidnapping and other crimes. The Civil Rights Act is an example of laws passed to enforce an amendment to the constitution.

Congress serves as the legislature for federal territories such as Washington D.C., national parks, military bases, and post offices. This results in sections of the U.S. Code which cover criminal offenses ranging from petty theft to murder. Laws passed for this purpose are not binding on the states.

State Laws

State Constitutions

Each state has its own constitution. Some are extremely long, others quite brief. The state constitution establishes the framework for the state's government. Terms of office for the governor and other officials are usually set in the constitution. How the legislature is elected and the length of their terms are specified. Judicial selection procedures and the length of the terms for judges are usually included in state constitutions.

Many other items may be included in a state's constitution. Most include a "Bill of Rights" which guarantees certain rights for people living in the state. States that allow constitutional amendment by the initiative process frequently have amendments on subjects normally handled by the legislature.

The state constitution and its Bill of Rights must give residents all the rights afforded by the U.S. Constitution and Bill of Rights. This is the minimum acceptable standard. Each state can give its residents more rights than are mandated by the federal constitution. For example, a state can require police to obtain arrest warrants under circumstances where warrants were not required under the Fourth Amendment. This does not violate the U.S. Constitution because it gives residents more rights.

State Statutes

The process for enacting new laws and amending old ones is set out in the state constitution. This usually involves a simple majority vote of both houses of the state legislature, but each state is free to establish different procedures. For example, a two thirds majority may be required to raise taxes.

Each state is free to decide what acts are criminal provided the laws do not violate the U.S. Constitution or Bill of Rights. There is no requirement that state criminal laws be the same. This results in a wide variety of crimes and punishments. Two states may use the same name, such as burglary, for crimes that do not have similar elements. Actions that are criminal in one state, such as gambling, may be legal in another. A criminal act may be a felony in one state and a misdemeanor in another.

Local Law

Each state delegates authority to local entities such as counties, cities, and townships. This is usually specified in the state constitution. The local entities have the right to enact laws, frequently called ordinances. It is not uncommon to find enforcement of city ordinances restricted to law enforcement officers employed by the city which enacted the ordinance.

Statewide laws, such as those in the penal code, usually preempt local ordinances. This means that if there is a conflict between the state law and the local law, the state law is considered the only valid law on the subject. Sometimes a state law is written specifically authorizing municipalities to enact ordinances for more complete coverage of special problems. When this happens, the state laws will not preempt local ordinances on the same subject.

Common Law

"Common law" has a variety of meanings depending on the context in which it is used. The common law system refers to the legal system of England. Most of the American colonies derived their legal systems from English common law. Some of its characteristics in criminal cases include the presumption that a person is innocent until proven guilty, the requirement that a case be heard before a neutral magistrate, and the stipulation that a jury is composed of lay people rather than professional jurists.

Common law is also used to refer to the body of law that was brought to this country from England in the seventeenth century. "Common law burglary" refers to the definition of burglary that was used in England at that time. Many states now have statutes which say that the common law no longer applies. The intent of these code sections is to emphasize that the laws enacted by the legislature rather than the traditional definitions are to be used . Even so, if a statute uses common law terms and the legislature did not define them, the courts will look to the common law when applying the statute.

Another feature of common law is heavy reliance on **precedent**. When judges apply the law, they are supposed to follow the decisions already issued by higher courts. A court has the authority to reverse itself, and thus change the rule, but it does not have the authority to make a rule inconsistent with prior opinions of higher courts. When a new issue arises, the judge should review the precedents that exist for similar issues and try to apply law in a manner consistent with existing precedent.

1.2 Structure of Legislative System

Federal

The **United States Congress** is divided into the Senate and the House of Representatives. Each state, regardless of population, has two senators, each of whom is elected by the entire state. Senators serve six year terms with one third of the seats up for election every two years.

There are 435 seats in the House of Representatives. Seats are allocated based on population. Boundaries are redrawn every ten years after the national census in an attempt to keep the population in each district approximately equal. Each state has a minimum of one seat in the House but there is no upper limit on how many representatives a state may have. Members of the House of Representatives serve two-year terms; all seats are up for election every other year.

Any legislator may introduce a bill in the house in which he/she is a member. Many more bills are introduced than are passed into law. Special interest groups, including law enforcement, labor unions, business and professional organizations, as well as private individuals ask their representatives to "carry" bills. They frequently draft the bill and try to find other legislators who will co-author the bill. Once the bill is introduced, these groups lobby other legislators to support the bill; opposing interest groups lobby for negative votes. Lobbying efforts range from contacting the legislators (in person, by mail, telephone and FAX) to campaign contributions or providing volunteer staff to help with the campaign. After passage of the bill, there may be lobbying to have the president sign or veto it.

A bill must be passed by both houses of Congress. If amendments change the bill after it has been approved by one branch of Congress, a conference committee is formed to try to reconcile the differences and then both the House and Senate must vote to approve the resulting bill. Bills that are not passed by the end of the two year congressional session die. If they are reintroduced in the next session, the process starts over.

The final step is approval by the president. The president can either sign the bill, veto it, or leave it unsigned. If the president vetoes a bill while Congress is in session, it can still become law if two thirds of both houses vote to override the veto.

STATE

There are no restrictions in the U.S. Constitution on how the individual states operate their legislatures. Nearly all have established bicameral (divided into two houses) legislatures similar to the House and Senate. One house may have more members than the other. For example, the state senate may have 40 members while the assembly has 80. To do this, a senate district would have twice the population of an assembly district.

The Supreme Court has ruled that state legislative districts must be divided so that each elected representative is from a district of approximately the same population as other members in the same house. This applies to both houses in a bicameral system even though the U.S. Senate is allowed to operate under a different system.

The process of enacting a law in the state legislature is similar to that used in Congress. A bill is introduced into one of the legislative bodies and, if passed there, goes to the other. Only after passage by both does it go to the governor. The governor has the power to veto legislation. Some states give the state legislature the power to override a veto. A bill that does not become law can be introduced in the next legislative session.

The process of asking a legislator to introduce a bill and lobbying is similar at the state and federal levels. There is a greater opportunity for individuals and civic groups to try to influence the process at the state level due to the fact that each legislator represents fewer people. The wider range of activities the state controls also results in more interaction with local groups. Mothers Against Drunk Drivers (MADD) is a good example of a group which has been very successful in lobbying state legislatures.

Most criminal laws become effective on January 1 of the year following passage rather than the date the governor signed the bill. Sometimes the effective date is sooner; most states provide for this if special procedures are followed. Occasionally a law will not become operative for two or more years. This is usually done so that necessary equipment purchases and training can be completed before the law goes into effect. If the bill does not follow the normal rule, the bill must state the date it will take effect.

Legislation usually remains in effect until repealed or amended. A recent trend has been to make **"sunset" laws**. These laws are enacted with an end date stated in the bill. State laws may mandate that all laws on certain topics take effect for only a limited period of time. For example, the California law authorizing electronic surveillance warrants expired after five years. This gave the legislature the chance to review the use of wiretaps and decide whether it should make the law permanent, change it, or discontinue authorization for wiretaps.

1.3 Structure of Judicial System

The structures of the federal and state judicial systems for handling criminal cases are similar. Two exceptions are noted: state courts typically have more layers in order to facilitate handling of misdemeanors and other minor crimes; the federal system has separate courts for special purposes, such as bankruptcy courts. Each level of court must follow precedent. The courts are organized geographically with appeals going up the organization chart in a predetermined order.

Federal

Criminal charges are filed and trials held at the **U.S. District Court**. There is at least one district court in each state. States generating large case loads will have more than one district, each using the state's name, for example, the Southern District of New York. Where the district covers a large land mass, there may be courthouses at several cities; each is called an office.

Appeals are heard by the **United States Courts of Appeal** (circuit courts). These are organized geographically in circuits. There are currently 11 circuits which handle the 50 states plus one for cases

Geographic Organization of United States Circuit Courts of Appeals

First Circuit	Maine, Massachusetts, New Hampshire, Puerto Rico, Rhode Island
Second Circuit	Connecticut, New York, Vermont
Third Circuit	Delaware, New Jersey, Pennsylvania
Fourth Circuit	Maryland, North Carolina, South Carolina, Virginia, West Virginia
Fifth Circuit	Louisiana, Mississippi, Texas, Virgin Islands
Sixth Circuit	Kentucky, Michigan, Ohio, Tennessee
Seventh Circuit	Illinois, Indiana, Wisconsin
Eighth Circuit	Arkansas, Iowa, Minnesota, Missouri, Nebraska, North Dakota, South Dakota
Ninth Circuit	Alaska, Arizona, California, Guam, Hawaii, Idaho, Montana, Nevada, Northern Mariana Islands, Oregon, Washington
Tenth Circuit	Colorado, Kansas, New Mexico, Oklahoma, Utah, Wyoming
Eleventh Circuit	Alabama, Florida, Georgia
Federal Circuit	Matters related to federal government
District of Columbia Circuit	Acts similar to a state court for crimes and civil matters arising in the District of Columbia

Table 1.1

regarding the federal government and another for the District of Columbia. For example, the proper designation for the federal appellate court for Pennsylvania, New Jersey and Delaware is the United States Third Circuit Court of Appeal.

Appeals are usually heard by a panel of three appellate judges. A majority vote is required. The number of panels of judges in each circuit is usually determined by the workload. In special circumstances a rehearing can be requested *en banc*. This means that a larger panel, sometimes all the justices of the circuit, will hear the case.

Each circuit has equal standing. Circuit courts must follow precedent established by the United States Supreme Court. They are not bound by decisions of other circuits, but they may use them as a basis for decisions if they agree with the legal reasoning used.

The **United States Supreme Court** is at the top of the federal judicial system. Cases are heard by a panel of nine justices. Federal law requires that the Supreme Court hear some cases, such as border disputes between states. Most cases come by ***writ of certiorari*** (frequently called *cert*). This writ requests that the court accept the case. Four of the nine justices must vote to grant the writ before a case will be scheduled for a hearing. Granting the writ does not indicate the Supreme Court will reverse the lower court's decision: some of the justices may have voted to grant *cert* because they favor reversing the lower court decision while the remaining justices may want to affirm it. Oral arguments are held a few months after *cert* is granted and an opinion is usually issued six to nine months later.

STATE

While the basic structure of the state courts closely resembles the federal system, the names used may be different. Most states call the highest court the Supreme Court, but some do not. New York designates it the Court of Appeals; the Supreme Court in New York conducts felony trials. A few states, such as Texas, have specially designated courts which only hear criminal appeals.

Most state courts separate felony and misdemeanor trials. Typically all cases start in the same courts. These courts are frequently called municipal court or justice courts although numerous other titles are used. Many states transfer felonies to a higher court for trial. The case stays in the trial court through sentencing.

The use of two separate courts results in different appellate procedures for misdemeanors and felonies. The basic rule is that an appeal goes to the next higher court on the organization chart. A state may have misdemeanor appeals heard by judges who normally preside over felony trials. Felony appeals are more likely to be heard in the intermediary level court equivalent to the federal court of appeal (names vary from state to state).

The highest court in each state functions much like the United States Supreme Court: cases are usually heard only if the justices grant a hearing. The most frequent exception is for cases in which the death penalty has been imposed: the state Supreme Court may be required to hear these cases instead of the lower level appellate courts.

1.4 Authority of Courts

Courts can only make binding decisions if they have authority over the case. This is called **jurisdiction**. An individual court must also have authority to hear the case. This is called **venue**.

Jurisdiction

The jurisdiction of a court is based on two things: whether there is authority over the place where the crime occurred; and whether there is authority over the subject matter involved.

Geographic Jurisdiction

A state has jurisdiction over all crimes committed within its geographical boundaries. Sometimes there is also jurisdiction for acts that occur out of state. A simple example would be a person who stood ten feet from the state line and shot someone in another state. The state where the injury occurred would have jurisdiction even though the defendant never set foot in the state. Crimes occurring through the mail, telephone, FAX, etc. would also result in jurisdiction if there was harm within the state.

Federal jurisdiction is somewhat similar. It covers acts done inside the United States or its territories (including overseas military bases and embassies). In some situations it also covers injuries to United States citizens that occur while they are overseas.

Typical

State Court Organization

Subject Matter Jurisdiction

Subject matter jurisdiction means that the court has the authority to hear cases on this subject. State courts cannot try cases based on another state's criminal laws.

A court of general jurisdiction usually can hear any felony under that state's laws. It can also hear cases in which the charges include both felonies and misdemeanors. If a state has a separate level of courts that conduct arraignments and misdemeanor trials, they are said to be of limited jurisdiction because they cannot hear felony trials. Cases involving only misdemeanors must be tried in these courts.

In criminal cases, federal courts only have subject matter jurisdiction over crimes in the United States Code. An indictment cannot contain both federal and state charges.

Venue

Venue divides cases between courts within the state or federal system. The legislature draws geographic boundaries for each court. If a case is filed in the wrong court, it may be dismissed for lack of venue. The prosecution usually has the right to refile the case in the correct court district. For example, a robbery that occurs in Cook County must be filed in that county's courts. The prosecutor may need to check the map to determine which court to use if the crime occurred near the boundary line.

Either side may request a change of venue after the case has been correctly filed. One reason for a change of venue is to find an impartial jury when there has been inflammatory media coverage before the trial. When a change of venue is granted, the case will be moved to a different county and heard by a jury from the new location. The prosecutor will be from the original locale.

Exclusionary Rule

In 1961 the United States Supreme Court expanded the exclusionary rule to cover state courts. Since then, both state and federal judges have been required to exclude evidence obtained in violation of the Fourth and Fifth Amendments. Over the years, exceptions have been made so that some unconstitutionally seized evidence can be used at trial. The basic rule remains that unconstitutionally seized evidence, and evidence obtained as the result of the original action (fruit of the poison tree) cannot be used by the prosecution in state or federal trials.

States have the authority to make their own exclusionary rules as long as the constitutionally required rule is followed. State policy may dictate that there is a greater expectation of privacy in certain situations, such as booking people arrested for the most trivial offenses, which mandate more protections for the person than found in the United States Constitution. Our federal system of government allows states to do this. The reverse is not true: states may not give the police authority to act in violation of the Fourth Amendment as interpreted by the United States Supreme Court.

1.5 Roles of Participants in the Justice System

The American legal system assigns distinct roles to the participants in the criminal justice system. Some, such as the roles of the prosecutors and defense attorneys, are in conflict with each other.

Law Enforcement

Law enforcement functions include preventing crime, apprehending criminals, and other activities which protect and serve the community they police. The philosophy of each law enforcement agency is a reflection of the community it serves.

Investigating criminal activity and making arrests are clearly police functions. Patrol officers must carefully observe human behavior and be suspicious when it appears criminal activity is occurring. Officers have the right to make an arrest whenever there is probable cause that the person has committed a crime. In addition to probable cause, the officer may consider other factors when deciding to make an arrest. These include: is there a need to arrest the suspect in order to prevent further violence? will the victim prosecute? how serious is the crime? will warning the suspect, rather than making an arrest, sufficiently deter future violations? are there other more serious calls that need to be handled immediately?

The Supreme Court has characterized law enforcement as being involved in the "often competitive job of ferreting out crime." Pressures to make arrests, either due to a public outcry or the officer's desire to further his/her own career, may influence the actions taken. The Court has been reluctant to view police officers as acting objectively. Requiring judicial review of warrant applications is a buffer in the process designed to insert an impartial observer between the police and the suspected criminal.

Investigations done after an arrest may show that the suspect is not the person who committed the crime. The police have a duty to release the person under these circumstances unless there is probable cause that the suspect committed some other crime. The police function is to find the truth, not merely to obtain convictions. All information discovered by the police, whether it shows guilt or innocence, must be made available to the prosecutor.

Prosecutor

The prosecutor, like the police, is part of the executive branch of government. The prosecutor serves as a gatekeeper of the judicial process. Cases are reviewed and decisions made on what charges, if any, will be filed. The prosecutor does not have to file the same charges the police used when making the arrest.

While probable cause is sufficient to file the case, the prosecutor always keeps in mind that it takes proof beyond a reasonable doubt to obtain the conviction. A more legalistic approach is taken when reviewing the case: is there admissible evidence which will result in a conviction? are the eyewitnesses credible? have the defendant's Fourth and Fifth Amendment rights been violated?

Other factors also influence the prosecutor's decision. One is workload. Minor charges may be rejected if there are already more cases awaiting trial than the prosecutor can handle. Cases may be rejected if there is doubt that they can be "won" even though the prosecutor personally believes the suspect is guilty.

Another consideration is public attitudes. These attitudes will likely be reflected in the minds of the jurors who will be selected for the trial. Judicial attitudes also influence the prosecutor. If the local judge has a reputation for giving extremely light sentences for some cases, such as minor batteries, the prosecutor may decide it is not worthwhile to even file the charges.

Plea bargaining also reflects these considerations. Plea bargaining is one device used to reduce the workload. The prosecutor is in charge of making a "deal" which is just — the defendant should receive a sentence that appropriately reflects the seriousness of the offense(s). Prosecutors may tip the scales by overcharging in order to be able to offer the defendant a good "bargain." Overcrowded court calendars and sentencing practices of local judges also influence the final decision.

The prosecutor is charged with seeking justice. Any evidence indicating the defendant's innocence must be disclosed to the defense attorney. The prosecutor also has a duty not to introduce perjured testimony and not to seek inflammatory pre-trial publicity that could bias potential jurors. The prosecutor has the power to ask the court to dismiss charges "in the interest of justice" even though the defendant may be believed to be guilty. This power can be used to drop charges when a defendant has agreed to cooperate with the prosecution or become a police informant. Sometimes it is used because the defendant is suffering from a terminal illness.

Defendant

A criminal suspect is considered a defendant once the charges have been filed in court. The defendant is presumed innocent until proven guilty. This gives the defendant the right to refuse to cooperate with the police. The Fifth Amendment protects the defendant from being forced to make incriminating statements. It also prohibits the inference that the defendant's silence is an admission of guilt.

Defense Attorney

The role of the defense attorney is to protect the defendant. Constitutionally, this is based on a combination of: Fifth Amendment right not to incriminate self; Sixth Amendment right to counsel; due process right to be convicted by proof beyond a reasonable doubt. Added to this is the traditional attorney-client privilege covering confidential communications. Confessions by the defendant to his/her attorney or the defense attorney's personal belief that the client is guilty do not change the duties of the defense attorney.

The defense attorney is charged with doing everything in his/her legal power to defend the accused. The defense attorney should seek an acquittal or dismissal. When plea bargains are possible, the attorney has the responsibility to use his/her best legal judgment in advising the client on the available options. Motions should be filed to suppress any evidence that the police obtained in violation of the defendant's Fourth and Fifth Amendment rights. At trial, the defense attorney should make appropriate objections to evidence the prosecution tries to admit and aggressively cross-examine witnesses and attempt to impeach them. The Sixth Amendment right to counsel includes all of these tactics which force the prosecution to meet its burden of proof.

The attorney must not resort to illegal tactics, such as introducing testimony known to be false or tampering with the evidence, in order to gain the client's freedom. Conduct in court should not be designed to threaten and intimidate witnesses beyond the scope of legitimate cross-examination. During opening statements, cross-examination, and closing arguments the defense attorney should not allude to evidence that is inadmissible or use unfounded innuendos to infer that witnesses have been untruthful or have withheld facts.

JUDGE

The judge serves as a neutral referee in the American criminal justice system. A judge who has a personal stake in a case is required to recuse (remove) him/herself from the case. This would occur if the judge or a member of the judge's immediate family is a defendant, victim, or witness in the case. It also applies if the judge previously was a member of the law firm which is representing one side in the case. Sometimes judges are removed from cases because they have made statements indicating personal biases about the case or similar cases.

Judges in nearly all states are now required to have experience as members of the state bar. The legal training and experience gained prior to taking the bench give them background in both the rules of law and the practical application of law to courtroom situations.

In a jury trial the judge acts as a referee. The judge listens to objections and makes rulings on the admissibility of evidence. He/she controls the tenor of the courtroom by cautioning the attorneys and witnesses about their emotional outbursts and flamboyant conduct. The judge can control the line of questioning to avoid harassment of the witness. Rulings the judge makes on the jury instructions control the law of the case. Jury instructions related to particular defenses have decisive impacts on many cases.

There is no jury in a **bench trial**. The judge decides both the law and the facts. In addition to the normal judicial function of ruling on the admissibility of evidence and objections to questions, the judge personally evaluates the evidence and decides the guilt or innocence of the defendant. This unique combination of roles is used only if both the prosecution and defense agree to waive a jury trial.

JURY

The jury listens to the evidence that is admitted at trial and applies the law given in the jury instructions. The collective opinions of the jury should equate to the judgement of a "reasonable person." The jury's function is also to serve as a jury of the defendant's peers. This implies that they are the conscience of the community. While they are given instructions on what the law is, they also have the authority to temper their decision as they believe justice requires.

The jury may totally reject the jury instructions and acquit a person. This is called **jury nullification**. The opposite is not true: the conviction will be reversed if the jury convicts the defendant of a crime not included in the jury instructions. Jury nullification occurs most often when community standards do not parallel the letter of the law. Double jeopardy prevents the prosecution from refiling a case under these circumstances. An example would be acquitting an elderly person who had killed a terminally ill spouse who was in excruciating pain and was begging to die.

SUMMARY

The criminal justice system is governed by a combination of federal and state laws. Small portions of the U.S. Constitution apply to criminal justice but the First, Fourth, Fifth, Sixth and Eighth Amendments plus the due process and equal protection clauses of the Fourteenth Amendment have major impacts. A few sections of the U.S. Code apply to criminal conduct in the states.

Most laws directly affecting local law enforcement are either in the state constitution or enacted by the state legislature. The U.S. Constitution gives the states a great deal of leeway in making criminal laws. There is no requirement that states have the same crimes, that punishment for the same crimes be equal, or that crimes with the same names have similar definitions. States usually give local municipalities authority to enact laws on some issues.

The American legal system is largely based on the British common law model. Many of our crimes started with the definition in use at the time settlers came to America from England. Statutes enacted by state legislatures have largely replaced common-law crimes. The old definitions are still used if new laws use the old terms but fail to define them.

Federal laws are enacted by the U.S. Congress. A bill can be introduced into either house of Congress but must be passed by both houses. It then goes to the president who may either sign it or veto it. State laws follow similar paths through the state legislature and then to the governor.

The state and federal legal systems consist of three or more tiers. Criminal arraignments are held at the lowest tier and the case works its way up the organizational chart. The courts are organized geographically: which court the case goes to depends on where the crime occurred.

A court can act only if it has jurisdiction. Federal courts have jurisdiction over crimes described in the U.S. Code. State courts have jurisdiction over crimes committed in the state. A court must also have venue over a case; this means the crime occurred within the geographical boundaries of the judicial district.

The role of law enforcement is to enforce laws by making arrests. Officers have discretion not to arrest even though there is probable cause. The prosecutor screens cases prior to filing them. In addition to deciding if there is probable cause, the prosecutor considers a variety of other factors including the admissibility of evidence, workload, and community attitudes.

Our legal system presumes the defendant innocent until proven guilty. The Fifth Amendment gives the defendant a privilege against self-incrimination. The defense lawyer's duty is to protect the defendant's rights. He/she is to be considered innocent unless the prosecution has established guilt beyond a reasonable doubt at trial. The defense attorney has the duty to represent the defendant whether or not he/she personally believes he/she is guilty. There is no right to use illegal tactics, such as introducing perjured testimony, to accomplish this goal.

The judge presides over the trial and makes rulings on the admissibility of evidence. He/she also controls the demeanor of the courtroom and rules on jury instructions. In a bench trial, the judge also weighs the evidence to determine guilt.

The jury hears the evidence at trial and decides whether the prosecution has established guilt beyond a reasonable doubt. The jury is sworn to follow the jury instructions but has the authority to ignore the instructions and vote for acquittal. In this way, the jury acts as the conscience of the community.

STUDY QUESTIONS

1. Explain which provisions of the U.S. Constitution apply to a state's authority to enact criminal laws.
2. Explain how the following amendments to the U.S. Constitution apply to a state's criminal justice system:
   a. First Amendment
   b. Fourth Amendment
   c. Fifth Amendment
   d. Sixth Amendment
   e. Eighth Amendment
   f. Fourteenth Amendment (due process and equal protection clauses)
3. Explain how laws in the United States Code apply to criminal acts in a state.
4. Describe the interaction between the U.S. Constitution and state constitutions.
5. Describe the ways state laws may provide different rights than those in the U.S. Constitution and Bill of Rights.
6. How does English common law affect the American criminal justice system?
7. Describe the structure of the federal legislative system; of the legislative system in the state and city where you live.
8. Diagram the process used to enact a law in the U.S. Congress; in your state legislature.
9. Describe the structure of the federal judicial system; of your state's judicial system.

10. How are jurisdiction and venue determined in federal courts? in the courts in your state?
11. Explain the role of precedent in judicial opinions.
12. Explain the exclusionary rule.
13. Describe the role of law enforcement in making arrests and obtaining convictions in the criminal justice system.
14. Describe the roles of the prosecutor and defense attorney in the criminal justice system.
15. Describe the roles of the judge and jury in the criminal justice system.

Chapter 2

Police Function

Learning Objectives

After reading this chapter, the student will be able to:

- Explain who has the legal status of a peace officer.
- Explain the jurisdiction of a peace officer.
- Explain the authority of a peace officer to stop a person when there is no authority to make an arrest.
- Describe the arrest powers of a peace officer.
- Describe the procedures that may be used to identify a suspect.
- Explain what procedures can be employed when a suspect is booked into jail.

Key Terms

arrest warrant required
booking search
consent to search
custodial interrogation
deadly force
felony arrest
frisk
Interstate Agreement on Detainers
jurisdiction of peace officers
lineup
Miranda warnings
misdemeanor arrest
non-deadly force
out-of-state warrants
pat-down
peace officer
photographic lineup
plain view doctrine
probable cause
reasonable suspicion
request identification
right to counsel at lineup
search incident to arrest
showup
Terry v. Ohio
unduly suggestive
Uniform Fresh Pursuit Act
waiver of *Miranda* warnings
warrantless vehicle searches

2.1 Role of Police

The local police have a variety of functions: protection of life and property; crime prevention; enforcement of laws; detection and apprehension of criminals; and other miscellaneous duties. The emphasis placed on each of these functions varies among police departments. It is the result of both formal and informal political processes.

The role of police in a community is complex because it is strongly influenced by social, legal and political factors. The Bill of Rights of the U.S. Constitution provides legal boundaries on what the police can do. State laws also regulate the police. These laws are enacted through the political process. Within the community, individuals and groups interact with city government and exert influence on how their police department is run. All of these forces shape the duties and attitudes of local law enforcement. On a larger scale, the same can be said for agencies operating at the state and national levels.

City officials are elected through formal political processes. Police responsiveness to local needs may be a campaign issue. Candidates may promise stricter enforcement of the laws, a crackdown on drugs, or a reduction in the crime rate. In most cities, the police chief serves at the will of the city council (or equivalent body). A majority vote of the city council is all that it takes to fire the chief. Elected officials have a direct impact on law enforcement agencies due to their control of the budget.

The police may use their discretion by strictly enforcing laws or by being more public service oriented. Pressures on city officials by residents and businesses are an informal political process which have a major impact on how the police utilize discretion and allocate resources. For example, if there is a public outcry about drug dealers or prostitutes in one part of the city, the police may shift personnel so that more arrests can be made for these crimes. On the other hand, if the police enforce the law too rigidly, such as issuing traffic citations for minor violations, public pressure may result in less police activity.

2.2 Peace Officers

All citizens have the right to arrest for crimes that occur in their presence and to use appropriate levels of force in defense of themselves, others, their homes and property. Peace officers have these powers plus authority that is granted to them by the laws of the state in which they are employed.

Peace Officer Defined

State law defines who is a peace officer and what authority he/she can exercise. The test of who a peace officer is is based on two criteria: who the employer is; and in what capacity the person is employed. Many states mandate specific training courses be completed within the first year of employment in order to maintain peace officer status.

Police departments, highway patrol, and sheriffs' departments are the best known local law enforcement agencies. A wide variety of others exist: transit authorities, airports, regulatory agencies, such as department of motor vehicles and alcoholic beverage control, park rangers, fire wardens, probation and parole officers, correctional officers, etc. There are also peace officer positions within agencies not thought of as law enforcement agencies, such as consumer affairs, children's protective agencies, and professional licensing agencies. States may designate some law enforcement positions as peace officers for all purposes while restricting others to on-duty activities within the jurisdiction that employs them.

Not everyone who works for a law enforcement agency is a peace officer. Clerical personnel are not peace officers; neither are a variety of other service positions, such as field evidence technicians and community service officers. State law may designate some jobs as non-peace officer positions. Local agencies may also decide that some jobs do not require the powers of a peace officer. Converting peace officer positions to "civilian" positions generally adds specialized personnel to the department and reduces salary expenses.

Authorization to carry a firearm typically is part of peace officer status. A state may restrict this right to on-duty hours for some positions, such as correctional officers. It may even designate some positions as unauthorized to carry weapons at all. Local agencies may have more restrictive policies than the state law.

Jurisdiction

Peace officers are charged with enforcing the laws of the state in which they are employed. This jurisdiction is usually based on geographical boundaries. A peace officer acts under the same authority as does a non-peace officer when out of the jurisdiction. Two exceptions apply: fresh pursuit which goes out of the jurisdiction; and arrests and detainers for crimes committed outside the state.

Within the State

Officers employed by a city police department usually are authorized to act as peace officers within their city both on- and off-duty. They can act as peace officers in other jurisdictions within the state if this is necessary in the performance of their primary duties (e.g., a detective going to another city to make an arrest). They may also make arrests anywhere in the state for crimes occurring in their presence or if there is an immediate danger to life or property. Mutual aid agreements between cities are also a basis for authorizing officers to exercise their peace officer powers outside the jurisdiction where they are employed.

More limited authority is given to some peace officers, particularly reserve officers and those who work as investigators for agencies which are not primarily enforcement agencies. For example, California designates investigators of the Department of Toxic Substance Control as peace officers only for enforcement of laws related to their primary duty; for other crimes, they have the same powers as a private citizen.

Uniform Fresh Pursuit Act

Each state's laws, and the authority of its peace officers, extend only to its geographical boundaries. Criminals fleeing the police do not respect state lines. The Uniform Act on Fresh Pursuit was enacted to allow officers to go into an adjoining state to make an arrest. It only applies to felony arrests. The key provision is:

> Any peace officer of another State, who enters this State in fresh pursuit, and continues within this State in fresh pursuit, of a person in order to arrest him on the ground that he has committed a felony in the other State, has the same authority to arrest and hold the person in custody, as peace officers of this State have to arrest and hold a person in custody on the ground that he has committed a felony in this State (Calif. Pen.Code Section 852.2).

There is no restriction on how far the officers may go into the state. What is mandatory is that the pursuit started in the state where the crime occurred and continued until the arrest was made.

Once a fleeing felon has been arrested in another state, he/she must be taken without unnecessary delay to the local magistrate in the state where the arrest was made. A hearing is held to determine the lawfulness of the arrest. If the magistrate rules the arrest was legal, the person arrested is remanded to custody so that an extradition warrant can be prepared by the state where the crime occurred. The person is released if it is determined that the arrest was not lawfully made.

Detainers and Out-of-State Warrants

The mobility of criminals necessitates procedures to arrest criminals after they have left the state under circumstances that do not amount to hot pursuit. Similar legislation enacted by nearly all the states covers two possibilities: authorizing local officers to make arrests on out-of-state warrants; and placing a hold on the release of a person who is serving a sentence in another state.

Out-of-State Warrants

Authority to make arrests based on out-of-state warrants is found in the Uniform Criminal Extradition Act. The key provision reads:

> . . . it is the duty of the Governor of this State to have arrested and delivered up to the executive authority of any other State any person charged in that State with treason, felony, or other crime, who has fled from justice and is found in this State.

The extradition process requires that the state in which the crime occurred send a copy of an indictment, information, or arrest warrant with accompanying affidavits to justify the return of the person arrested.

A court hearing is held in the state where the arrest was made. Its purpose is to inform the person arrested of the extradition request and to verify that the documents provided establish probable cause. The state requesting extradition must show that the suspect was in their state when the crime occurred. If the person arrested wishes to object to the extradition, he/she should file a *writ of habeas corpus*.

Detainers

Detainers are used to prevent the release of an inmate after he/she completes the jail or prison sentence currently being served. It is used because there are other criminal charges pending against that inmate. The agency that filed the retainer takes custody of the inmate at the time the inmate is due to be released.

The **Interstate Agreement on Detainers** is used when a detainer has been filed against an inmate by an out-of-state agency. It applies if any of the following court documents have been filed in a case —

indictment, information, or complaint. The purpose of the uniform act is to allow the inmate to have pending charges tried while he/she is serving the current sentence.

An inmate must be notified if a detainer has been filed. The inmate may then demand a trial on the charges. Once the demand has been made, the state filing the detainer has 180 days, plus necessary continuances, to bring the case to trial. The inmate is transported to the location where the trial will be held but remains in custody throughout the proceedings. Failure to bring the case to trial within the time limits specified results in dismissal of the charges without the right to refile them.

The inmate is returned to the state where he/she was serving sentence at the end of the trial or when charges are dismissed. Sometimes the two sentences can be served concurrently even though the convictions occurred in two different states. The inmate will be returned to the state that filed the retainer, if necessary, after the original sentence is served in order to serve any remaining time on that state's conviction.

Authority of Peace Officers

State law establishes the authority of peace officers to act. This authority must be exercised in a manner consistent with the Bill of Rights. The Fourth and Fifth Amendments must be considered in many contexts. Officers may act upon less suspicion than constitutionally mandated if the suspect consents to the detention or questioning.

This section contains a brief review of the most common situations encountered by patrol officers. Each police officer needs to take a course emphasizing the application of the Fourth and Fifth Amendments in order to learn the full scope of these constitutional rights.

Stop for Questioning

Police frequently observe something that indicates that further investigation is needed. Many times the initial observation does not give the officer enough information to arrest someone, but there is definitely something going on that needs to be checked out. The Supreme Court has agreed that the police should have the power to stop a suspect for brief questioning in these situations. In ***Terry v. Ohio***, the leading case, the Court authorized temporary detention for questioning if there are specific articulable facts which lead a reasonable police officer to believe that criminal activity is occurring. Information from victims, witnesses and informants may be used to establish reasonable suspicion.

This standard is frequently called **reasonable suspicion**. It differs from probable cause to arrest in several ways. Reasonable suspicion does not require as many facts as are needed to make an arrest. The officer must be able to cite specific facts that led to the belief that criminal activity was present, but it is not necessary to identify a specific crime believed to be in progress. To make an arrest, the officer must believe that it is more probable than not that the suspect committed a crime. Reasonable suspicion only requires that a reasonable officer would believe that some criminal activity is occurring. The officer may not stop a person based only on a hunch or the fact that the person is associating with "known criminals."

The Supreme Court, recognizing that it is frequently necessary to search a suspect in order to protect the officer, authorized protective searches during a temporary detention if the officer has a reasonable suspicion that the suspect is armed or dangerous. This limited search permitted in *Terry* is designed solely for the protection of the officer. There is no automatic right to search every person stopped. Officers must have a reasonable suspicion that the search is needed for their protection. If a person is stopped, for example, because there is reasonable suspicion that a violent crime has just been committed or is in progress, the right to search logically follows. If the situation involves a non-aggressive person believed to be preparing to commit a property crime, there may be no right to search.

The officer may **pat-down ("frisk")** the suspect's outer clothing for weapons. If the officer feels an object believed to be a weapon, he/she may retrieve the suspicious object. If, in fact, the object seized is not a weapon, whatever was seized will still be admissible. On the other hand, if the officer feels something in the suspect's pocket that does not resemble a weapon, there is usually no right to retrieve it.

One exception to this rule is the case where contraband is "plainly detected through the sense of touch" during a pat-down for weapons. This is a very limited exception: the officer must be able to determine that an item is contraband during the course of a normal pat-down. The Court pointed out that examination of a suspicious but unidentified object, in order to identify it as contraband, is not allowed. The Court rejected a seizure made after an officer discovered a small lump in a suspect's pocket during a legal pat-down and determined it was cocaine after "squeezing, sliding, and otherwise manipulating the contents of the defendant's pocket."

Request Identification

The Supreme Court recognized a legitimate need for police to stop individuals and demand identification if there is reasonable suspicion of criminal activity. State laws authorizing such stops must set specific standards for determining what type of identification is acceptable.

Use of Force

Anytime an officer has the right to detain someone, the officer has the right to use force to prevent that person from leaving. This applies to both temporary detentions and arrests. The force used must always be reasonable under the circumstances. **Deadly force** is justified only if a life is in danger.

Non-deadly force must also be used in a reasonable manner. The rationale for using force is to detain and subdue the suspect. Only tactics reasonably necessary to achieve these objectives are allowed. The amount of force allowed changes as the suspect's actions change; more force is permitted if the suspect becomes combative; less force is authorized as the suspect's resistance diminishes. No force is authorized once the suspect is passive.

Investigate

Many situations occur during a criminal investigation that require the officer to determine whether a search warrant is required. The basic rule is that a warrant is required unless there is an exception to the Fourth Amendment that applies. This section will mention a few of the most common exceptions to the warrant requirement. Officers working the field need to take a complete course and frequent refresher courses on search and seizure.

There is no special right to enter or remain at a location merely because it is a crime scene. In most cases, the crime victim will ask the police to investigate. A search warrant is required if no one consents. Emergencies, such as looking for victims who need immediate medical attention, temporarily excuse compliance with the warrant requirement. Conducting an investigation on private property after medical aid has been rendered requires consent or a search warrant.

Consent allows officers to proceed without search warrants. The Supreme Court ruled that a person does not need to be advised of his/her right to withhold consent. The test is whether **consent to search** was voluntarily given. Consent can only be obtained from a person with apparent authority over the area to be searched. The person giving the consent controls the area that may be searched and the time allowed for the search. Consent can be withdrawn at any time.

The **plain view doctrine** is one of the most useful exceptions to the warrant requirement. It covers any item left in plain view of an officer who is legally in the position to observe it. No warrant is required if the officer can tell by looking at the item that it is something than can be legally seized. Plain view does not allow the officer to move the item in order to look for identification numbers or indications that the item is contraband.

The Supreme Court views vehicles as having a much lower expectation of privacy than houses and other buildings. Their mobility creates a need to act more rapidly than required for stationary structures. The following **warrantless vehicle searches** are permitted: (1) if a vehicle is stopped based on reasonable suspicion and the officer reasonably believes that a weapon is in the vehicle, the passenger compartment may be searched for weapons whether or not the suspect will be released at the scene; (2) incident to the arrest of an occupant, the entire passenger compartment may be thoroughly searched; (3) based on probable cause to believe that there is evidence in a vehicle, the portion of the vehicle where the evidence is believed to be may be searched at the scene or later at an impound lot or police station; and (4) the contents of any vehicle legally impounded for storage may be inventoried. Closed containers found in a vehicle under any of the above situations may be opened and inspected.

Arrest

Traditionally, the authority of a peace officer to make an arrest was different for misdemeanors and felonies. In addition to these distinctions, the Supreme Court has required arrest warrants under some circumstances.

Felony Arrest

A peace officer is authorized to make a felony arrest whenever he/she has probable cause to believe that a felony has been committed.

Probable cause is defined as sufficient facts to make a reasonable person more certain than not that the event occurred. A peace officer also needs probable cause that the person to be arrested committed the crime; absolute certainty is not required. Peace officers have the power to make legal arrests even though no felony actually occurred as long as there were sufficient facts to support probable cause.

Misdemeanor Arrest

The traditional rule is that a peace officer may make a misdemeanor arrest ***only if*** the offense occurred in his/her presence. As with felonies, probable cause is all that is necessary when determining whether the misdemeanor occurred and whether the suspect committed the crime. Some state statutes modify this rule, mainly in authorizing arrests of juveniles and anyone suspected of misdemeanor drunk driving or battery of a spouse, even though the offense was not committed in the officer's presence.

When Arrest Warrants Are Required

The United States Supreme Court requires a warrant to make an arrest in a residence unless there is an emergency, such as hot pursuit or someone screaming for help. This rule applies to both felony and misdemeanor arrests. An arrest warrant is sufficient if officers want to enter the suspect's dwelling. A search warrant is needed to enter the home of another person to arrest the suspect.

Officers lack authority to arrest for misdemeanors that occurred when they were not at the scene unless a state law has expanded their authority. In these situations there are three alternatives:

1) have someone who witnessed the misdemeanor make a "citizen's arrest";
2) obtain an arrest warrant based on affidavits containing statements of people who witnessed the offense; or
3) make no arrest.

Search Incident to Arrest

The basic rule is that immediately following a custodial arrest, officers may conduct a thorough search of the person arrested and the area under his/her immediate control. Only searches done at the scene immediately after the arrest qualify. Searches done later must be justified on some other grounds.

Whatever is found on the person or under his/her immediate control is admissible. There are no restrictions on the thoroughness of the search conducted when the suspect is arrested and taken into custody. Only the area searched is restricted. Anywhere the person arrested could "reach" to obtain weapons or destroy evidence can be searched. This "arms reach" rule is applied without considering the fact that the suspect is handcuffed. Anywhere he/she could reach if not restrained is included. Officers may open cupboards, look under the bed or anywhere else that is within reach. Also items seized do not have to be specifically related to the crime for which the person was arrested.

Non-custodial arrests are handled in a different manner. Traffic stops are a typical example of non-custodial arrests. This is a much smaller invasion of the suspect's privacy. Accordingly, intrusive searches are not permitted. If the suspect will be released at the scene, officers may not invade the suspect's privacy by conducting a thorough search. With a non-custodial arrest, the search is similar to what can be done during a field interview (i.e., a protective pat-down for weapons).

Arrests frequently involve either the driver or passenger of a car. The Supreme Court has allowed a search of the entire passenger compartment, including the glove box and console, incident to the custodial arrest of an occupant of the car. The search must be done at the time of the arrest, but the suspect may be removed from the car before the search. The Court authorized an extensive search of anything in the passenger compartment, including luggage and other parcels. Other parts of the car, such as the trunk, require further justification.

Interrogation

The Supreme Court has defined interrogation as the process of questioning or its functional equivalent. Asking questions about a crime is clearly interrogation. So is requesting a narrative statement. The Court has also included indirect attempts to obtain information. For example, if two officers engage in a conversation with the intent of being overheard and eliciting a response, this is the functional equivalent of interrogation.

Miranda v. Arizona is one of the best known Supreme Court cases. Confessions obtained in violation of *Miranda* are inadmissible when offered by the prosecution to prove the defendant's guilt. They can be used for impeachment if the defendant who made the confession takes the witness stand.

When Miranda Warnings Are Required

The key to giving *Miranda* warnings is **custodial interrogation**. The suspect must be in custody at the time ***and*** the police must be interrogating him/her.

Custody, for the purposes of *Miranda*, is the equivalent of a custodial arrest. Custodial arrests do not include traffic stops where citations are issued and the violator is released at the scene. Field interviews based on reasonable suspicion are not covered. In addition, custody does not apply to situations where the suspect is being questioned at the police station but is not under arrest.

On the other hand, it does not matter why the suspect is in custody. Warnings are required if a suspect was arrested for one crime and questioned regarding a different one. Questioning by a different law enforcement agency also necessitates the warnings. *Miranda* warnings are even required if the suspect is questioned while in jail serving time on a totally unrelated offense.

Volunteered statements are admissible even though *Miranda* warnings were not given. As used in this context, volunteered means the suspect came forward on his/her own initiative and made a statement. Detailed questioning that follows the volunteered information is considered interrogation.

Content of Miranda Warnings

The Supreme Court has permitted paraphrasing of the *Miranda* warnings but has been quite intolerant of misleading warnings. Prior to custodial interrogation, the suspect must be warned:

1) You have the right to remain silent.
2) Anything you say can and will be used against you in a court of law.
3) You have the right to have an attorney present during questioning.
4) If you cannot afford an attorney, one will be appointed at no charge to assist you during questioning.

The right to remain silent includes the right to refrain from making both oral and written statements. Even if the suspect agreed to talk at the beginning of the interview, he/she has the right to stop the interrogation at any time.

Second, anything that the suspect says can be used against him/her in court. This includes all admissions that may be incriminating in any way, attempts to incriminate another person, and anything which could be used for impeachment. An attempt to talk to the police "off the record" indicates that the suspect does not understand the warnings.

Third, the suspect has the right to have an attorney present during questioning. Law enforcement officers may not continue questioning a suspect after an attorney has been requested. The police have two alternatives: give the suspect an attorney or stop questioning. Failure to provide an attorney violates the suspect's rights ***only if*** there is further questioning.

Lastly, if the suspect cannot afford an attorney, one will be provided at no cost to the suspect. The purpose of this warning is to inform the indigent suspect that a lack of money will not prevent him/her from having an attorney present during questioning. It is not the duty of the police to review the financial status of the suspect. If the suspect requests an attorney, the police should proceed in the same manner regardless of the suspect's apparent wealth (or lack thereof): questioning must stop.

Merely reciting the Court's language is not enough. The warnings must be given so that the suspect can understand them. This may mean using simplified language or calling for an interpreter. The prosecution bears the burden of convincing the judge that the warnings were correctly explained to the suspect. This must be established by a preponderance of the evidence.

Waiver of Miranda Rights

Once *Miranda* warnings have been correctly given to a suspect who is in custody, the police may try to obtain a waiver of the suspect's rights. The waiver must be knowing, intelligent, and voluntary. To have a knowing waiver, the suspect must have been correctly advised of his/her rights. The courts have uniformly required that the police show that they have done this. It is not presumed that anyone knows the *Miranda* warnings.

Intelligent, as used in this context, means that the person has the basic intelligence necessary to understand his/her rights. This may be in issue if a young juvenile is involved. It also comes up if the suspect is mentally retarded or extremely intoxicated (either due to alcohol or drugs). Only the most extreme cases qualify for suppression due to the lack of an intelligent waiver.

Voluntariness is somewhat hard to define in this context. The police may not use coercion to obtain a waiver of *Miranda* rights. Physical force cannot be used to obtain a confession. Deprivation of food and/or sleep for long periods is not allowed. Neither are false promises of leniency, such as offers to drop charges or assurances that the suspect will get a light sentence if a confession is made.

Miranda Warning Card

"You have the right to remain silent."

"If you give up the right to remain silent, anything you say can and will be used against you in a court of law."

"You have the right to speak with an attorney and to have the attorney present during questioning."

"If you so desire and cannot afford one, an attorney will be appointed for you without charge before questioning."

Some states add the additional statement that, **"You can decide at any time to exercise these rights and not answer any questions or make any statements."**

After the admonition has been given, you need to ask the following questions:

"Do you understand each of these rights I have explained to you?"

"Do you wish to give up the right to remain silent?"

"Do you wish to give up the right to speak to an attorney and have him present during questioning?"

If a suspect then says, "No, I don't want to talk to you," the interview is over. If he waives all his rights, carefully document his responses (tape recorded if possible) and then continue with your interview.

Absent one of these obviously coercive acts, the courts look at the totality of the circumstances. The key concept is that the police are not allowed to overbear the will of the suspect. This balances the acts of the police against the vulnerability of the defendant. What may be coercive when done to a naive teenager may be considered acceptable when applied to a streetwise ex-convict.

Lies and half-truths may be permitted. The police do not have to tell the suspect all of the crimes being investigated. Neither do they have to inform him/her that someone has arranged for an attorney to come to the jail to provide counsel. Statements like, "We found your fingerprints at the scene," or "Your friend confessed and blamed it all on you," have been allowed even though they are not true.

The last issue involving the waiver of *Miranda* rights is the procedure used to obtain the waiver. The Supreme Court has not set a protocol. Express waivers are preferred but in one case the Court found a valid waiver was implied by the suspect's conduct. The suspect had responded in the affirmative when asked if he understood his rights, but did not reply when asked if he wished to waive them. The indication that he understood the warnings, coupled with the fact that he answered the questions the police asked, was enough to convince the Court that a valid waiver had been obtained. In another case, the Court decided that an oral confession was admissible even though the suspect told police that he would talk to them but would not make a written confession without his attorney present.

Subsequent Interrogations

It is not uncommon for the police to interrogate a suspect more than once. The procedures that should be followed at the second interrogation depend largely on what was done at the first.

If the suspect waived his/her *Miranda* rights during the first interrogation, all subsequent interrogations can be conducted rather routinely. The Supreme Court has not required a new set of *Miranda* warnings every time questioning is resumed. The warnings need to be repeated only if the suspect is not likely to remember his/her rights. Interrogation must be stopped immediately if the suspect invokes the right to remain silent. This does not mean, however, that a police officer may never resume questioning. The Supreme Court has insisted that the suspect's rights be scrupulously guarded. Police may not badger the suspect with frequent attempts to get the suspect to talk, but after a reasonable time they may ask the suspect if he/she would like to continue the interrogation. A new waiver of *Miranda* is mandatory prior to resuming questioning. In the leading case, there was a two hour gap between the interrogations; the second interview was conducted by different officers on a different floor of the police building and focused on a different crime.

A different rule applies if the suspect requested to speak to an attorney rather than merely demanding that the questioning stop. In these situations, an attorney must be present at subsequent interrogation sessions unless the suspect voluntarily requests the interview. The fact that the subsequent interrogation is about a different crime does not alter this rule. Having no knowledge of the prior request for an attorney is not an acceptable excuse.

Identification Procedures

There are three basic procedures used to allow victims or witnesses to identify the person who committed the crime: lineup, showup and photographic lineup. Constitutional rights must be protected during these procedures. A **lineup** is a procedure where the victim or eyewitness is asked to view a group of people and select the one who committed the crime. A **showup** is a much simpler procedure. One suspect is shown to the person who is to make the identification. This can be done in the field or at a police facility. A **photographic lineup** involves showing pictures. The suspect is usually not present when this is done. It may involve handing the witness a few carefully selected photographs or allowing him/her to look through mug books.

There is no special exception to the Fourth Amendment which allows police to detain a suspect solely to conduct a lineup or showup. A suspect may be detained briefly based on reasonable suspicion and a showup conducted at the scene of this detention. Probable cause to arrest is necessary in order to transport the suspect to the police station. Once there, either a lineup or showup may be conducted for any crime in which the person arrested is a suspect. The Supreme Court held that a legally arrested suspect has no Fifth Amendment right to refuse to participate in a lineup. The suspect can be required to walk, take a particular stance, wear clothing or disguises, make gestures observed during the commission of the crime or repeat what witnesses reported the suspect said while committing the crime. While none of these procedures violates the Fifth Amendment, due process demands fundamental fairness. Any special effects that are used on one person in a lineup must be applied to all of the participants.

The defendant has the right to have counsel present during in-court identification procedures. This applies whenever a witness is asked if the person who committed the crime is present in the courtroom. It does not matter whether the identification is made before, during, or after the court hearing begins.

The suspect has a **right to counsel** during a lineup or showup ***after*** court proceedings have been initiated by arraignment or indictment. The attorney acts as an observer and does not have the right to tell the police how to conduct the identification procedure. There is no right to counsel during an identification procedure if the suspect is not present. Photographic lineups can be done before or after arraignment without either the suspect or an attorney present.

In the area of identification procedures, due process means that the police must not use **unduly suggestive** techniques. If there is a substantial likelihood of mistaken identification, the evidence will not be admissible in court. Lineups and photographic lineups have many of the same problems. Nothing in the way these procedures are conducted should point to one individual. One of the first rules is that there must be a good selection of individuals with similar characteristics. Five to seven individuals are usually recommended. Each person in the lineup must match the general description of the perpetrator of the crime. The goal is to have participants who are sufficiently similar so that there is no clue as to which one is the suspect. Anything that makes the suspect stand out is unduly suggestive.

Many of the protections against unduly suggestive lineups do not apply to showups because there is usually only one person shown to the witness. In showup cases, the United States Supreme Court has focused on the reliability of the identification. Factors considered include: opportunity of the witness to view the suspect at the time of the crime (including lighting and the length of time the witness was with the suspect); degree of attention the witness paid to the suspect while the crime was in progress; level of certainty of the witness; accuracy of prior description of the suspect; prior inaccurate identifications made by the witness; and length of time between showup and crime.

Booking

Booking occurs when the person who has been arrested enters the jail or a holding facility. It also happens if a person reports directly to the jail to serve all or part of his/her sentence. Inmates who serve weekends or leave the facility daily on work furlough are subject to booking searches each time they re-enter the jail. Whether the person has been searched recently or not, the right to search at the time of booking is the same. It includes a thorough search of the person and any items in his/her possession at that time. Closed containers may be opened and searched. The reason for allowing booking searches is to prevent weapons and contraband from entering the jail.

The **booking search** is usually the most extensive search of the person that occurs. Due to the fact that weapons and drugs can easily be hidden, strip searches and searches of body cavities are permitted. Reasonable attempts to preserve privacy, such as shielding the strip search area from public view and having searches conducted by officers of the same sex as the suspect, are required. Combative inmates who defy control by booking personnel or those who attempt to flee the booking area during a strip search waive protection of their privacy. Several states have restricted the right to conduct strip searches and body cavity searches if a person was arrested for a misdemeanor.

The courts recognize a minor exception to *Miranda* for the booking process. Questions related to name, address, person to notify in case of an emergency, date of birth, and a few other biographical facts are permitted. *Miranda* applies if questioning at booking is extended in order to obtain information for a criminal investigation.

Summary

Society assigns a variety of functions to the police: protection of life and property; crime prevention; enforcement of laws; detection and apprehension of criminals; and other miscellaneous duties. In order to fulfill these duties, peace officers are given more authority than the average citizen to make arrests. Who has peace officer status is determined by the type of agency involved and the job performed. Most, but not all, peace officers are permitted to carry weapons.

Peace officers have authority within the jurisdiction (city, county, etc.) that employs them and while performing their official duties in other parts of the state. They may follow a suspect into another state and make arrests for crimes that occurred in their state. Officers in one state may also make arrests based on warrants issued in the state where the crime occurred. A person serving a sentence in one state may be detained when his/her sentence has expired so that an officer from another state may take custody and transport the suspect for trial.

The traditional rule is that peace officers have the authority to make arrests based on probable cause that a felony has occurred. They may arrest for misdemeanors only if the crime occurred in their presence. Arrest warrants are required for misdemeanors that did not occur in the officer's presence. Warrants are also required to make arrests inside a home except when there is an emergency. An arrest warrant is needed to arrest the suspect in his/her own home; a search warrant is required if the suspect is in another person's home.

The police may constitutionally detain someone for questioning if there is reasonable suspicion that criminal activity is occurring. A pat-down for weapons may be done if there is reasonable suspicion that the suspect is armed. A person may be asked for identification while stopped, but the state must set specific standards for what types of identification may be required.

The basic rule that officers must follow while investigating crime is that a search warrant is required unless there is an established exception to the Fourth Amendment that fits the circumstances. There is no automatic right to enter and/or search a crime scene without consent of the resident. Consent is valid as long as it was voluntarily given by a person with apparent authority over the area. The person giving the consent controls the area that may be searched and the length of time involved. Consent may be withdrawn at any time.

Items left in plain view do not require search warrants if the officer can observe them from a place where he/she has the legal right to be standing. The officer does not have the right to pick things up and examine them in order to determine if they are stolen or contraband.

Numerous exceptions to the warrant requirement exist for vehicles:

1) if a vehicle is stopped based on reasonable suspicion and the officer reasonably believes that a weapon is in the vehicle, the passenger compartment may be searched for weapons whether or not the suspect will be released at the scene

2) based on probable cause to believe that there is evidence in a vehicle, the relevant portion of the vehicle may be

searched at the scene or later at an impound lot or police station

3) the contents of any vehicle legally impounded for storage may be inventoried

4) closed containers found in a vehicle under any of the above circumstances may be opened and inspected.

Officers may search the suspect incident to any custodial arrest. The scope of this search includes the person and anything within his/her immediate control. This search must be done at the time and place of the arrest. The entire passenger compartment may be thoroughly searched.

Miranda warnings must be given prior to custodial interrogation. Questioning may continue only if there is a knowing, intelligent and voluntary waiver. If there is a waiver but questioning is stopped, interrogation may be resumed at any time. Questioning may be started after a suspect invokes the right to remain silent as long as there has been a sufficient time lapse to indicate that the suspect's rights were scrupulously guarded ***and*** there is a new *Miranda* waiver. If the suspect requested an attorney, questioning may be resumed ***only if*** there is an attorney present.

A suspect has the right to have an attorney present at a lineup or showup ***only if*** the event occurs after arraignment or indictment. Due process forbids lineups, whether in person or photographic, that are unduly suggestive. Nothing about the selection of suspects should point to one particular individual. Showups are judged by the credibility of the person making the identification.

A complete search is allowed at the time of booking. This includes strip searches of the person being booked and checking the contents of everything in his/her possession. Some states have restricted strip searches of suspects booked on misdemeanor charges.

Study Questions

1. List four items commonly considered to be part of the role of police in American society.

2. Explain who has peace officer status in your state.
3. What is the authority of a peace officer to act: within the city employing the officer; within the state where employed; to go into another state to make an arrest?
4. Explain the authority of a peace officer to make an arrest under a warrant issued in another state.
5. Explain the process for detaining a person for a prosecution on a crime committed in your state if that person is currently serving a prison sentence in another state.
6. When may a peace officer detain a person for questioning when there is no authority to make an arrest? How extensive of a search may be done under these circumstances?
7. When may a peace officer stop a person and demand identification? What types of identification may be required in your state?
8. Explain the right of a peace officer to use deadly force; non-deadly force.
9. Explain the right of officers to enter a home to investigate a crime.
10. List four situations in which a warrant is not required in order to search a car. Explain how extensive the search may be in each of these situations.
11. Explain the standard for obtaining valid consent to conduct a warrantless search: who can consent? how extensive is the search? when must the search be stopped?
12. Explain the plain view doctrine.
13. State the *Miranda* warnings. Explain: when they must be given; the standard for a valid waiver; when questioning may be resumed if the suspect refused to talk; when questioning may be resumed if the suspect demands an attorney.
14. Explain the appropriate procedures for conducting a: showup; in-person lineup; photographic lineup.
15. How extensive of a search is permitted at booking? If laws in your state restrict this rule, explain the local restrictions.

CHAPTER 3

THE WARRANT PROCESS

LEARNING OBJECTIVES

After reading this chapter, the student will be able to:

- Explain the basic requirements for issuing an arrest warrant and a search warrant.
- Explain what should be in an affidavit used to obtain a warrant.
- Describe the process for obtaining the warrant.
- Describe how a search warrant should be executed.
- Illustrate how an arrest should be made with a warrant.
- Demonstrate the appropriate procedure for entering a residence to serve a warrant.
- Explain what should be listed on the return of a search warrant.

Key Terms

abstract of a warrant
affidavit
affirmation
anonymous informant
bench warrant
confidential informant
electronic surveillance warrant
executing a warrant
Illinois v. Gates
"John Doe" warrant
knock-notice
neutral magistrate
oath
plain view doctrine
probable cause
recalled warrant
return of a search warrant
serve a warrant
stale information
telephonic search warrant
totality of the circumstances test

The processes for issuing arrest warrants and search warrants are similar. Both require probable cause but the factual showing depends on which type of warrant is needed. This chapter discusses the basic requirements for obtaining warrants.

3.1 Basic Requirements

The second half of the Fourth Amendment is referred to as the warrant clause:

> . . . no Warrant shall issue, but upon probable cause, supported by Oath or affirmation, and particularly describing the place to be searched, and the person or things to be seized.

This mandates several things: probable cause; facts supported by Oath or affirmation; particular description of location to be searched; and particular description of what is to be seized.

Warrant Requirements in Fourth Amendment

Probable Cause

Probable cause is defined as the group of facts which would cause a reasonable person to conclude that it is more likely than not that a given fact exists. The Supreme Court has made it clear that the judge must independently determine that there is probable cause to issue the warrant. This can only be done if the judge is given the facts of the case. Section 3.2 addresses this issue in detail.

Oath or Affirmation

This requirement has been interpreted to mean that the person making the statement formally promises to tell the truth. An **oath** is a solemn declaration to God that a statement is true. An **affirmation** is a solemn declaration to tell the truth when no oath is taken. An affirmation is used when the person objects to taking an oath for religious or other conscientious reasons. Most states allow a person to sign a statement under penalty of perjury that the facts contained in the document are true. This is called an **affidavit**. Some states require affidavits to be notarized. An affidavit meets the Fourth Amendment requirements for an oath or affirmation.

One or more affidavits accompany the application for the warrant. Sometimes the judge will have the officer or another person who is present take an oath and answer additional questions. When the judge does this, the dialogue will be transcribed and a copy attached to the warrant application.

Particularly Describing the Location to Be Searched

A warrant authorizes intrusion into another person's privacy. For this reason, the warrant must contain a description of the area where the officers have the right to go. The information contained in the affidavits, plus any sworn oral testimony the judge hears, must establish probable cause that there is evidence at a specific location. The warrant itself must state exactly where the officers will be authorized to search.

Particularly Describing What Is to Be Seized

In addition to stating where the officers may go, the warrant must specify what they are looking for. Officers may only look in places where the items to be seized might be located. If the warrant is for the seizure of large objects, for example 25 inch TV sets, the officers may only look where items this large can be concealed. On the other hand, if the warrant is for stolen coins, the officer may look almost anywhere because the coins can be hidden in very small places. The plain view doctrine goes with the officer as long as he/she is searching in a place permitted by the warrant. This means that items not listed on the warrant may be seized *provided that* the officers can identify the items as either evidence or contraband without moving them to look for identifying characteristics such as serial numbers.

Arrest Warrant

The Fourth Amendment covers an arrest: it is a seizure of the person. To obtain an arrest warrant, the affidavits need to establish two things: probable cause that a specific crime was committed; and probable cause that the person named committed this crime. The warrant is frequently worded in the same manner as the complaint which the prosecutor files to start a criminal prosecution. In many states, the warrant substitutes for the complaint thus avoiding duplicate paperwork.

An arrest warrant needs to specify the person to be arrested in sufficient detail so that the officer serving the warrant can verify that the correct person is being arrested. This is particularly important because many warrants are entered into the national computer network (NCIC) and the arrest made by an officer totally unfamiliar with the case. A detailed description, including as many of the following as possible, should be included: name, aliases, age and/or date of birth, height, weight, ethnicity and social security number. Approximations, such as age 20 to 25, may be used when necessary. An arrest warrant may be issued even though the legal name of the suspect is unknown. These are called **"John Doe" warrants**: they refer to a specific person, whose name is unknown although an alias may be known. "John Doe" warrants should have particularly detailed descriptions of the suspect, along with as many aliases as possible, in order to avoid arresting innocent people.

An arrest under a warrant is valid if the officer uses reasonable care to verify that the person arrested is the same person named in the warrant. The wrong person may be arrested if the suspect has a popular

State of California
County of Los Angeles
AFFIDAVIT IN SUPPORT OF PROBABLE CAUSE ARREST WARRANT

Your affiant, Officer Mary Black, is employed as a peace officer for the Metropolitan Police Department and has attached hereto and incorporates by reference official reports and records of a law enforcement agency. These reports were prepared by law enforcement officers and contain factual information and statements obtained from victims, witnesses, and others which establish the commission of the following criminal offense(s): PC 459 - Residential Burglary, by the following person: John DeHaviland Smith.

WHEREFORE, your affiant prays that a warrant of arrest be issued for said person. (signed) Officer Mary Black.

A typical arrest warrant

name or is using a false ID, but the arrest and subsequent search will be valid as long as sufficient care was taken. Officers are protected from civil liability for false arrest when they exercise due care.

Arrest warrants are usually valid for at least a year. Many states make the warrant valid for a period equal to the statute of limitations on the crime. Some crimes, such as murder, have no statute of limitation; arrest warrants for these crimes remain valid indefinitely. Officers need to be familiar with the rule in their jurisdiction so they can determine if an arrest warrant is still valid. Automated warrant systems need to be programmed to purge warrants that have expired.

Just as the powers to arrest are more limited for misdemeanors than for felonies, the service of misdemeanor warrants may be more restricted than that of felony warrants. Felony warrants can usually be served 24 hours a day. The officer may make the arrest in public or enter private buildings, including houses, at any time. Many states allow service of misdemeanor warrants 24 hours a day in public places; but residences may only be entered to serve the arrest warrant during "daytime." The hours that are "daytime" are specified in the code and usually are not tied to sunrise and sunset. For example, "daytime" may be 6:00 a.m. to 10:00 p.m. An accurate watch is essential if the arrest is to be made near these time limits: an arrest made under a misdemeanor warrant at 10:05 p.m. would be invalid.

The term **bench warrant** is used to refer to an arrest warrant issued by a judge after a conviction. A common reason for issuing a bench warrant is failure to appear in court in response to a citation. State laws govern issuing bench warrants. Usually they can be served by peace officers in the same manner as misdemeanor warrants.

An arrest warrant can be **recalled**. This means that the court which issued the warrant withdraws the warrant. One reason for recalling a warrant is that the person has surrendered voluntarily. Another is that facts discovered after the warrant was issued show that there is no longer probable cause to support a warrant. It is important to establish procedures to identify recalled warrants and remove them from computerized data bases. An arrest based on a recalled warrant is not valid.

Search Warrant

The search warrant must identify the place to be searched and the items to be seized. This information is necessary so that officers executing the search warrant will know what they are allowed to do. The affidavits containing the facts used to establish probable cause become part of the court record but these facts do not need to be stated on the search warrant.

In most urban areas, the address is used to describe the place to be searched. Even so, it is useful to include other descriptive information, such as "the white house on the northeast corner of Third and Spring." The courts have permitted the search of a house even though the street number in the warrant was wrong when the description made it obvious what location was to be searched. In most cases, the description needs to be more specific than just the address: the portion of the building to be searched needs to be stated. For example, if the informant told the police that the suspect keeps a supply of drugs in kitchen cupboards, the warrant should be issued for the search of the kitchen cupboards, not the entire house. Items found while walking to the kitchen will be covered by the plain view doctrine.

Search Warrant No. 8-24

STATE OF CALIFORNIA

COUNTY OF ORANGE

SEARCH WARRANT

PEOPLE OF THE STATE OF CALIFORNIA to any sheriff, police officer or other peace officer in the County of Orange; PROOF by affidavit having been made before me by Investigator James Green, No. 274, Orange County Sheriff's Office, that there is probable cause to believe that the property described herein may be found at the locations set forth herein and that it was stolen or embezzled you are therefore commanded to search (1) the premises at 118 N. Main Street, Cara Linda, California, a one-story brown frame house, being the first house on the northeast corner of Main and 2nd Streets, enclosed by a chain-link fence and identified with the numerals "118" painted on the curb directly in front of the house, including all rooms, attics, basements, garages, outbuildings and trash containers at these premises, and (2) the person of Wanda May Jubal, a female Negro, approximately 22 years, 5'4", 120 lbs., short/curly black hair,

1" scar on left thumb,

///

for the following property: a 16" gold chain with attached gold coin ring in which is mounted a 1905 US $20 gold coin; the letters "TRU" in the motto "In God We Trust" are noticeably worn down as compared with the other letters; and articles of personal property tending to establish the identity of the current resident of the premises, including utility company receipts, rent receipts, canceled mail envelopes, and printed return-address stickers,

///

///

and to seize it if found and bring it forthwith before me, or this court, at the courthouse of this court.

This warrant may be served only between the hours of 7:00 o'clock a.m. and 10:00 o'clock p.m.

///

Given under my hand and dated this 12th day of August, 1980.

____

Judge of the Municipal Court, Central Orange Judicial District.

This is true even though the warrant was originally sought for the items left in plain view but the judge granted a more restrictive warrant.

A search warrant is only valid if the information used to obtain it was obtained recently. Information that was not obtained recently is called stale. **Stale information** cannot be used if the time lapse is such that the item to be seized may have been moved to another location before the warrant was issued. This will depend on the facts of the case and the type of evidence sought. Drugs are highly mobile and dealers are notorious for their evasive conduct. Information on where a dealer is keeping drugs is stale if it is more than a few days old. Some items, such as built-in appliances which have been installed in the kitchen, are rarely moved. Information on the location of these items would not become stale for a long time.

Search warrants are valid for a limited period of time. This is an extension of the staleness concept used to issue a warrant: waiting a lengthy period before conducting the search makes it more likely that the items sought will have been removed from the location. State law sets the maximum time period, frequently 10 days or less. A warrant that is executed after it has expired is not valid and any evidence found while trying to execute it will be inadmissible.

Search warrants may only be executed once. This ordinarily means that once officers enter the location in order to conduct the search, some members of the investigative team must stay until the job is complete. The fact that the warrant would have been valid for a few more days does not give officers the right to return and search the premises again.

State laws vary on when search warrants may be executed. A common practice is to make search warrants valid only in the daytime unless the judge has indicated otherwise when issuing the warrant. To obtain this consent the judge must be given specific facts indicating there is a need to conduct the search at night. State law should be consulted to determine what hours qualify as "daytime." It cannot be automatically assumed that "daytime" is defined the same for misdemeanor arrest warrants and search warrants.

Electronic Surveillance Warrants

The Supreme Court approved **electronic surveillance warrants** but required a more particularized showing of necessity than is needed for other warrants. Congress reacted by passing the Omnibus Crime Control and Safe Streets Act of 1968. Title III of this Act applies to electronic surveillance. Many states have passed laws adopting this federal legislation; others have passed their own laws for this type of warrant. Federal law allows judges to issue warrants for wiretaps and other forms of electronic surveillance. Some state laws are more restrictive.

Electronic surveillance warrants may only be issued for crimes specified in Title III or the equivalent state law. This usually covers only major felonies. To obtain this type of warrant there must be probable cause that specific types of conversations will occur during the surveillance. In addition to the normal showing of probable cause, the affidavits must establish that normal investigative techniques have been tried and do not work or that there is a special reason to believe that they will not work. The warrant application must name all suspects whose conversations are likely to be seized during the surveillance. Unlike normal warrants, the electronic surveillance application must be approved by the head of the prosecutorial agency (attorney general, district attorney, etc.) or a specific designee before submission to a judge. The warrant is valid for a maximum of 30 days. The Supreme Court interpreted Title III as implicitly authorizing whatever actions are necessary to install, maintain and retrieve the necessary electronic equipment. Some state statutes specifically prohibit covert entries.

Officers must take reasonable steps to minimize intrusion into the privacy of non-suspects while conducting the surveillance: once it is determined that a conversation is not related to the crimes under investigation, the conversation should not be monitored. The warrant can be extended only with a showing that probable cause still exists for the wiretap. A transcript of what was seized is submitted to the court after the surveillance is complete; this is much like the return on a search warrant.

3.2 Drafting Affidavits

At one time, warrant applications read: "The undersigned officer has information from a reliable informant that establishes probable cause to believe that . . . ." The Supreme Court has made it clear that this is not acceptable because the judge is the one who must determine whether probable cause exists to issue a warrant. The judge may rely on facts submitted by the officers but must independently conclude that probable cause exists. For the judge to do this, the affidavit must contain detailed facts.

The judge must consider two issues when determining whether probable cause exists: are the facts in the warrant application sufficient to establish probable cause? and is the source of the facts sufficiently reliable? At one time, the Supreme Court required judges to determine these two things independent of each other. In 1983, ***Illinois v. Gates*** changed that rule: judges now consider the issues together using a **totality of the circumstances test**.

Information comes to the police from several avenues: first hand observation by a police officer; statements by victims and eye witnesses; and informants. An affidavit or oral statement under oath made on first hand observations are considered the most reliable: they are stated under penalty of perjury. Statements by victims and witnesses are generally considered reliable unless there is a motive to provide false information. A more common problem, particularly with the victim, is that there is insufficient detail. Robbery victims, for example, may be adamant that the robber had a large gun, but may be unable to give more than sketchy details on what the robber and get-away car looked like. Unfortunately, this lack of detail makes it impossible to establish probable cause unless the police have additional information.

Police informants pose a different problem. Many informants have ulterior motives: gaining their release; negotiating a plea bargain; being paid for information; or seeking revenge on a former partner in crime. An **anonymous informant** is a person whose identity is unknown. When an informant calls the police department, the officers may have no idea who provided the information and no way to ask for more details. Other times there may be a person who calls periodically and whose voice the officer recognizes but whose true identity remains unknown. Police also have **confidential informants**: people who give information after obtaining a promise that their identity will not be revealed. Since the police actually know who these people are, they may be able to vouch for their reliability.

Under the totality of the circumstances test, a judge may consider information from previously untested informants and anonymous informants. The affidavit should identify the source of the information.

The quantity and quality of information provided is crucial for this purpose. Rather than looking for proof that an informant has previously given reliable information, the judge may look at the facts given in the present case. Extensive details that only a person with first hand knowledge of the facts could provide can be used to validate the information even though the source is unknown to the police. Police verification of some of the details given by the informant is required as well. It is not necessary to verify enough facts to establish probable cause. Neither is it mandatory that any single fact that was verified show criminal activity. The cumulative impact of numerous facts, each apparently innocent when viewed in isolation, can be used to corroborate an informant.

The facts from *Illinois v. Gates* demonstrate the Supreme Court's reasoning. On May 3, 1978, the Bloomingdale Police Department received an anonymous handwritten letter in the mail which read:

> This letter is to inform you that you have a couple in your town who strictly make their living on selling drugs. They are Sue and Lance Gates, they live on Greenway, off Bloomingdale Rd. in the condominiums. Most of their buys are done in Florida. Sue his wife drives their car to Florida, where she leaves it to be loaded up with drugs, then Lance flys down and drives it back. Sue flys back after she drops the car off in Florida. May 3 she is driving down there again and Lance will be flying down in a few days to drive it back. At the time Lance drives the car back he has the trunk loaded with over $100,000.00 in drugs. Presently they have over $100,00.00 worth of drugs in their basement.
>
> They brag about the fact they never have to work, and make their entire living on pushers.
>
> I guarantee if you watch them carefully you will make a big catch. They are friends with some big drug dealers, who visit their house often.
>
> Lance & Susan Gates
> Greenway
> in Condominiums

The United States Supreme Court stated that it was inclined to agree with the Illinois Supreme Court that this anonymous letter, standing alone, did not establish probable cause. The application for the warrant to search the Gates' home included the anonymous letter plus the following facts learned during a police investigation of the case:

> An Illinois driver's license had been issued to Lance Gates, residing at a stated address in Bloomingdale; a confidential informant examined financial records and provided a more recent address; L. Gates had a reservation on Eastern Airlines flight 245 from Chicago to West Palm Beach on May 5 at 4:15 p.m.; surveillance of flight 245 revealed that Gates boarded the flight; surveillance in Florida observed Gates arrive in West Palm Beach and take a taxi to a nearby Holiday Inn; Gates went to a room registered to Susan Gates; 7:00 a.m. the next morning Gates and an unidentified woman left the motel in a Mercury bearing Illinois license plates and drove northbound on an interstate frequently used by travelers going to Chicago; the license plate on the Mercury was registered to a Hornet station wagon owned by Gates; driving time from West Palm Beach to Bloomingdale was approximately 22 to 24 hours.

The U.S. Supreme Court, using the totality of the circumstances test, held that the search warrant was valid. Note the amount of detail given in the affidavit.

The judge cannot determine if probable cause exists unless he/she receives detailed information. Drafting a good affidavit is a time-consuming process. Rushing through it may result in the application being rejected or the warrant being declared invalid by an appellate court. The judge's action will be reviewed solely on the facts available to the judge prior to signing the warrant: additional facts known to the officers, but not conveyed to the judge under oath or in an affidavit, may not be considered.

In *Massachusetts v. Upton*, 466 U.S. 727 (1984), the Supreme Court stated that the totality of the circumstances test completely replaced *Aguilar*'s two-pronged test which required proof of the reliability of the informant. The case involved the following facts:

> At noon on September 11, 1980, Lt. Beland of the Yarmouth Police Department assisted in the execution of a search warrant for a motel room reserved by one Richard Kelleher at the Snug Harbor Motel in West Yarmouth. The search produced several

> items of identification, including credit cards, belonging to two persons whose homes had recently been burglarized. Other items taken in the burglaries, such as jewelry, silver and gold, were not found at the motel.
>
> At 3:20 p.m. on the same day, Lt. Beland received a call from an unidentified female who told him that there was "a motor home full of stolen stuff" parked behind #5 Jefferson Ave., the home of respondent George Upton and his mother. She stated that the stolen items included jewelry, silver, and gold. As set out in Lt. Beland's affidavit in support of a search warrant:
>
> "She further stated that George Upton was going to move the motor home any time now because of the fact that Ricky Kelleher's motel room was raided and that George Upton had purchased these stolen items from Ricky Kelleher. This unidentified female stated that she had seen the stolen items, but refused to identify herself because 'he'll kill me,' referring to George Upton. I then told this unidentified female that I knew who she was, giving her the name of Lynn Alberico, who I had met on May 16, 1980, at George Upton's repair shop off Summer St., in Yarmouthport. She was identified to me by George Upton as being his girlfriend, Lynn Alberico. The unidentified female admitted that she was the girl that I had named, stating that she was surprised that I knew who she was. She then told me that she'd broken up with George Upton and wanted to burn him. She also told me that she wouldn't give me her address or phone number but that she would contact me in the future, if need be."
>
> Following the phone call, Lt. Beland went to Upton's house to verify that a motor home was parked on the property. Then, while other officers watched the premises, Lt. Beland prepared the application for a search warrant, setting out all the information noted above, in an accompanying affidavit. He also attached the police reports on the two prior burglaries, along with the lists of the stolen property.

The United States Supreme Court explained its holding that the affidavit was sufficient to justify issuing the search warrant:

> Examined in light of *Gates*, Lt. Beland's affidavit provides a substantial basis for the issuance of the warrant. No single piece of evidence in it is conclusive. But the pieces fit neatly together and, so viewed, support the magistrate's determination that there

> was "a fair probability that contraband or evidence of crime" would be found in Upton's motor home. The informant claimed to have seen the stolen goods and gave a description of them which tallied with the items taken in recent burglaries. She knew of the raid on the motel room — which produced evidence connected to those burglaries — and that the room had been reserved by Kelleher. She explained the connection between Kelleher's motel room and the stolen goods in Upton's motor home. And she provided a motive both for her attempt at anonymity — fear of Upton's retaliation — and for furnishing the information — her recent breakup with Upton and her desire "to burn him."
>
> * * *
>
> In concluding that there was probable cause for the issuance of this warrant, the magistrate can hardly be accused of approving a mere "hunch" or a bare recital of legal conclusions. The informant's story and the surrounding facts possessed an internal coherence that gave weight to the whole. Accordingly, we conclude that the information contained in Lt. Beland's affidavit provided a sufficient basis for the "practical, common-sense decision" of the magistrate. . . . .

In *United States v. Leon*, 468 U.S. 897 (1984), the lower court found that the affidavits contained insufficient evidence to establish probable cause. The United States Supreme Court accepted this finding. The affidavit was based on the following facts:

> In August 1981, a confidential informant of unproved reliability informed an officer of the Burbank Police Department that two persons known to him as "Armando" and "Patsy" were selling large quantities of cocaine and methaqualone from their residence at 620 Price Drive in Burbank, Cal. The informant also indicated that he had witnessed a sale of methaqualone by "Patsy" at the residence approximately five months earlier and had observed at the time a shoebox containing a large amount of cash that belonged to "Patsy." He further declared that "Armando" and "Patsy" generally kept only small quantities of drugs at their residence and stored the remainder at another location in Burbank.
>
> On the basis of this information, the Burbank police initiated an extensive investigation focusing first on the Price Drive residence and later on two other residences as well. Cars parked at the Price Drive residence were determined to belong to respondents Armando

> Sanchez, who had previously been arrested for possession of marihuana, and Patsy Stewart, who had no criminal record. During the course of the investigation, officers observed an automobile belonging to respondent Ricardo Del Castillo, who had previously been arrested for possession of 50 pounds of marihuana, arrive at the Price Drive residence. The driver of the car entered the house, exited shortly thereafter carrying a small paper sack, and drove away. A check of Del Castillo's probation records led the officers to respondent Alberto Leon, whose telephone number Del Castillo had listed as his employer's. Leon had been arrested in 1980 on drug charges, and a companion had informed the police at that time that Leon was heavily involved in the importation of drugs into this country. Before the current investigation began, the Burbank officers had learned that an informant had told a Glendale police officer that Leon stored a large quantity of methaqualone at his residence in Glendale. During the course of this investigation, Burbank officers learned that Leon was living at 716 South Sunset Canyon in Burbank.
>
> Subsequently, the officers observed several persons, at least one of whom had prior drug involvement, arriving at the Price Drive residence and leaving with small packages; observed a variety of other material activity at the two residences as well as at a condominium at 7901 Via Magdelena; and witnessed a variety of relevant activity involving respondents' automobiles. The officers also observed respondents Sanchez and Stewart board separate flights for Miami. The pair later returned to Los Angeles together, consented to a search of their luggage that revealed only a small amount of marihuana, and left the airport.

An experienced narcotics investigator drafted the affidavit and sought a warrant to search 620 Price Drive, 716 South Sunset Canyon, 7901 Via Magdelena, and automobiles registered to each of the respondents for an extensive list of items believed to be related to respondents' drug-trafficking activities.

The lower court judge did not question the reliability and credibility of the informant, but stated:

> Some details given tended to corroborate, maybe, the reliability of [the informant's] information about the previous transaction, but if it is not a stale transaction, it comes awfully close to it; and all the other material I think is as consistent with innocence as it is with guilt.

Note that the one drug sale the informant claimed to have witnessed occurred five months prior to the information being given to the police; the search warrant was issued after an additional month of police investigation. Although numerous people were seen leaving the locations with small packages, there was no verification that any of these packages contained illegal drugs.

The facts in *Massachusetts v. Sheppard*, 468 U.S. 981 (1984) show the type of detailed information the Supreme Court considers adequate in describing the location to be searched. The investigation showed:

> The badly burned body of Sandra Boulware was discovered in a vacant lot in the Roxbury section of Boston at approximately 5 a.m., Saturday, May 5, 1979. An autopsy revealed that Boulware had died of multiple compound skull fractures caused by blows to the head. After a brief investigation, the police decided to question one of the victim's boyfriends, Osborne Sheppard. Sheppard told the police that he had last seen the victim on Tuesday night and that he had been at a local gaming house (where cards games were played) from 9 p.m. Friday until 5 a.m. Saturday. He identified several people who would be willing to substantiate the latter claim.
>
> By interviewing the people Sheppard had said were at the gaming house on Friday night, the police learned that although Sheppard was at the gaming house that night, he had borrowed an automobile at about 3 a.m. Saturday morning in order to give two men a ride home. Even though the trip normally took only fifteen minutes, Sheppard did not return with the car until nearly 5 a.m.
>
> On Sunday morning, police officers visited the owner of the car Sheppard had borrowed. He consented to an inspection of the vehicle. Bloodstains and pieces of hair were found on the rear bumper and within the trunk compartment. In addition, the officers noticed strands of wire in the trunk similar to wire strands found on and near the body of the victim. The owner of the car told the officers that when he last used the car on Friday night, shortly before Sheppard borrowed it, he had placed articles in the trunk and had not noticed any stains on the bumper or in the trunk.

An affidavit was drafted containing these facts. It requested a warrant to search Sheppard's residence for the following items:

> [a] fifth bottle of amaretto liquor, 2 nickel bags of marijuana, a woman's jacket that has been described as black-grey (charcoal), any possessions of Sandra D. Boulware, similar type wire and rope that match those on the body of Sandra D. Boulware, or in the above Thunderbird. A blunt instrument that might have been used on the victim, men's or women's clothing that may have blood, gasoline burns on them. Items that may have fingerprints of the victim.

The following items seized during the search were admissible: a pair of bloodstained boots, blood stains on the concrete floor, a woman's earring with bloodstains on it, a bloodstained envelope, a pair of men's jockey shorts and women's leotards with blood on them, three types of wire, and a woman's hairpiece, subsequently identified as the victim's.

3.3 Obtaining Warrant From Judge

In addition to preparing necessary affidavits, there are usually preprinted forms that must be completed requesting a warrant. In many jurisdictions, the prosecutor's office reviews and screens warrant applications before they are submitted to a judge. The prosecutor's office may also assist with the clerical work involved. Sometimes the local judges will only review applications that the prosecutor has already approved. It is not uncommon for the person seeking the warrant to also prepare the warrant in advance so that it is ready for the judge's signature.

Sometimes there are several different preprinted forms available, each designed for a specific type of case. When this is true, it is important to use the appropriate form or make corrections that delete all references to facts not established in the affidavits. For example, a form designed for a drug case may have a preprinted paragraph describing drug paraphernalia that can be seized. If used for a non-drug case, this paragraph and any other references to seizing drugs must be removed. Leaving them in the warrant would make the warrant invalid because it authorized a search for things for which probable cause had not been established.

Once the paperwork has been completed, the application can be presented to a judge or magistrate. Both local laws and customs should be consulted to determine which judge reviews warrant applications. In most states, an arrest warrant must be obtained in the jurisdiction where the crime occurred. Search warrants are normally issued by judges in the jurisdiction where the search will be conducted. If there is reason to believe that the suspect fled and hid evidence in a different county, it may be necessary to go to two different courts in order to obtain the necessary warrants.

Most states give trial court judges the authority to grant warrants. Where the court system is large, some judges may be assigned to criminal cases while others are in the civil division. Professional courtesy calls for presenting applications to the judges who hear criminal cases. The presiding judge may designate one judge to hear all warrant applications. It is very common to have one judge "on call" for reviewing warrant applications at night and on weekends. Ask the prosecutor's office which judge to see and what local rules apply.

The application may only be submitted once. If the judge refuses to issue a warrant, the officers may not take the same application to a different judge. The officers have the option of continuing their investigation, drafting new affidavits, and seeking the warrant again. Sometimes the officers know of facts that were left out of the original affidavits that can be added for this purpose.

The judge who issues a warrant must be a **neutral magistrate**. Magistrate, as used here, means a judge or person who state law gives the power to issue warrants. Neutral means that the person has no personal interest in the case. If a judge's salary is in any way based on the number of warrants issued, as opposed to the number of applications reviewed or a flat salary, the judge is not neutral. The warrant is not valid even though probable cause was clearly established and any reasonable judge would have granted the warrant. If a state authorizes ranking members of a law enforcement agency to act as a magistrate, that person cannot issue warrants. Again, the potential conflict of interest, not the facts of the individual case, invalidates the warrant. Judges who are personally involved in the case are not considered neutral. This occurs when the judge, or a member of his/her immediate family, is the victim of the crime in the case for which the warrant is being sought.

Once the judge has reviewed the warrant, it is important that the warrant be completed correctly and signed by the judge. If a warrant was prepared before presenting the paperwork to the judge, it is important to review it and make sure that the judge has agreed to everything that is listed. Lines may be drawn through items that the judge has refused to grant.

Some states allow search warrants to be issued over the telephone at night and on weekends. These warrants are sometimes called **telephonic search warrants**. Normally a conference call is set up with the officer, the prosecutor and the judge. The officer is placed under oath and tells the judge the facts that should be in the affidavit. The judge can ask questions. If the judge grants the warrant, the officer or prosecutor fills out the warrant and signs the judge's name. The entire conference call is recorded and a transcript made. The transcript will take the place of the affidavit in the court file.

3.4 Executing Warrants

The process of acting under a warrant to make an arrest or search is called **executing a warrant** or **serving a warrant**. What is done will vary somewhat depending on whether a search or arrest is being conducted.

Copy of the Warrant

The person who is named in the warrant or whose property is to be searched is normally entitled to see a copy of the search warrant at the time it is served. The person who receives the warrant is not allowed to stop the execution of the warrant: legal challenges to the warrant can be made in court at a later time. Presenting a copy of the warrant merely notifies the person that the officers have the legal authority to enter and search. Once this authority has been established, people on the premises do not have a legal right to resist the search.

Officers executing a search warrant take copies with them when they go to the location where the search will be conducted. Search warrants are either printed in duplicate or xeroxed for this purpose. A copy is given to an adult with apparent authority over the premises that are being searched. If no one is present, a copy is left in a conspicuous location.

Arrest warrants are handled differently when the warrant is entered into a computerized data bank. The arrest is frequently made by officers who were not involved in the investigation. An officer has probable cause to make the arrest if the person detained matches the description of the person named in a warrant listed in the computer. A brief statement of the warrant, called an **abstract of the warrant**, will be requested. This is immediately sent by teletype, FAX, or other teleprocessing equipment to the location where the suspect will be booked. A complete copy of the arrest warrant must be filed with the court before arraignment. The suspect will be arraigned in the same manner as other persons arrested by the local police department. If the warrant is not from the local jurisdiction, the case will then be transferred to the court that issued the warrant. For out-of-state warrants, this will require extradition proceedings unless the suspect waives them.

Knock-Notice

Entering a residential unit (home, apartment, motel room, etc.) involves the invasion of someone's privacy. One reason for the warning is to avoid situations where the residents use weapons in the belief burglars or other criminals are breaking into their homes. For this reason many states require that officers announce their presence and intent before entering whether or not officers have a warrant. This is commonly called "knock-notice." The basic requirements are:

Knock

Officers must knock, ring the doorbell or use some other appropriate method to inform people in the residence that they are there.

Announce Identity and Purpose

Officers must in some way announce their official capacity and why they are demanding entry. For example, "Police officers! We have a search warrant." This must be done with appropriate wording and loud enough so anyone inside who wishes to cooperate will be aware of what is going on.

Waiting Period

After making the necessary announcement, officers must wait long enough so a cooperative person could open the door. The length of time required depends on the circumstances. For example: it is very brief if officers at the front door can see into the living room and know that people are only a few feet from the door; a longer wait is required if officers arrive in the middle of the night and a person who is likely to be asleep in a distant bedroom must respond.

Entry

Officers may enter after complying with the above procedures. Force may be used to gain entry to serve a warrant if no one answers the door or someone refuses to open the door.

The fact that no one appears to be home does not excuse compliance with "knock-notice." "Knock-notice" may be excused for any one of the following reasons: serious danger to the officers; high probability of destruction of evidence; or strong possibility that the suspect will escape. Officers should learn local standards for completely avoiding "knock-notice" and when partial compliance is sufficient.

Plain View

The plain view doctrine applies to observations made while executing both search and arrest warrants. Observations officers make from a vantage point where they are authorized to be do not require separate justification. This applies to observations, but not to actions such as examining objects or turning them over to search for serial numbers in order to run a computer check to determine if the items are stolen.

When serving an arrest warrant, the plain view doctrine primarily applies to items discovered while trying to locate the person named in the warrant. Officers may look anywhere a person might be hiding but not in cupboards or other containers too small to conceal a person. With search warrants, the scope of the search is justified based on the size of the items sought. Anything known to be contraband, stolen property or to have other evidentiary value found while looking in areas large enough to hide items listed in the warrant will be admissible. Searching areas too small to conceal the smallest item listed on the warrant is not permitted. Anything found while doing so is inadmissible.

The Supreme Court has recognized the safety needs of the officers while executing warrants. Officers may quickly walk through the building and look for anyone who might attack them. Any place large enough for a person to hide may be checked. Anything found in *plain view* while doing this cursory search will be admissible.

3.5 Return

The **return** on a warrant is basically an inventory which is filed with the court and becomes a permanent part of the case file. It is frequently printed on the back of the warrant. The officers executing the warrant must fill in the information requested by the court: date and time when warrant was executed; officer(s) who executed the warrant; and an itemized inventory of everything seized while executing the warrant. Items found in plain view should also be included in the inventory. A copy of this itemized list usually must be left at the location when the items are seized. If officers were unable to serve the warrant, this fact will be noted on the return.

Summary

The Fourth Amendment requires probable cause for the issuance of a warrant. Facts must be stated under oath or affirmation or in an affidavit. The place to be searched must be precisely described in the warrant. Any items the warrant authorizes the police to seize must also be described in detail. An arrest warrant needs a sufficient description of the person to be arrested so that the officers can verify that the correct person is being detained.

The "totality of the circumstances" test is currently used to determine if probable cause has been established. It is no longer necessary to establish that the informant has previously given reliable information. The judge may consider all facts presented in the affidavits. Sufficient details must be given so that the judge will be convinced that there is enough credible information to establish probable cause. This can be based on a combination of information from informants and facts discovered during police investigations. Stale information may not be used to obtain search warrants. It is important that the facts show the items sought are still at the location the police wish to search.

The affidavits and any forms required by the local court are submitted to a judge. In large courts, there is usually one judge designated to review the warrant applications. Local court rules may require the prosecutor to review the application before it is presented to the judge. A warrant application can only be presented once. If denied, additional facts must be included before another attempt can be made to have the warrant issued.

Officers must comply with "knock-notice" prior to entering residences to serve either an arrest or search warrant unless there is an emergency creating a danger of: harm to the officer, destruction of the evidence; or escape of the suspect. When a search warrant is executed a copy of the warrant must be given to a responsible adult at the location or a copy left in a conspicuous place if no one is present. Plain view accompanies the officers.

An officer in the field needs to confirm that the suspect matches the description of a person who is listed in the computer as having an outstanding arrest warrant. An abstract of the arrest warrant should be obtained immediately. A copy of the actual warrant will be needed in order to arraign the suspect. Arraignment will occur in the court for the district where the arrest was made. The suspect will then be transferred to the court that issued the warrant.

A return of the warrant is filed with the court. It will indicate when the warrant was executed and list anything that was seized. This form is also used to record the fact that the warrant was not served.

Study Questions

1. List four things specifically required by the Fourth Amendment before a search warrant can be issued.
2. Define probable cause. When seeking a warrant, who determines if probable cause exists?
3. Explain probable cause for a search warrant.
4. Explain probable cause for an arrest warrant.
5. Describe the current test judges are required to use to determine if probable cause has been established to issue a warrant.

6. Define the following terms:
   a. oath
   b. affirmation
   c. affidavit
7. According to the law in your state how long is a misdemeanor arrest warrant valid? A felony warrant? Are there crimes for which arrest warrants do not expire?
8. According to the law in your state, what restrictions are placed on the service of:
   a. misdemeanor arrest warrants?
   b. felony arrest warrants?
   c. search warrants?
9. Define:
   a. bench warrant
   b. recall of a warrant
   c. execution (service) of a warrant
10. Clip newspaper articles on a current criminal investigation. Draft an affidavit for:
    a. a search warrant.
    b. an arrest warrant.
11. Explain how the plain view doctrine applies to the execution of:
    a. an arrest warrant.
    b. a search warrant.
12. Explain the process used in your local court for obtaining search warrants and arrest warrants. Include:
    a. role prosecutor plays in the process
    b. necessary paperwork
    c. which judge should be contacted
    d. location and times the judge will review warrant applications
13. Explain "knock-notice." Under the law of your state, when are officers excused from compliance with "knock-notice?"

14. Explain the process for arresting a person based on information in the police computer network that there is an arrest warrant for that person if a warrant was issued:
    a. in your city.
    b. in another part of your state.
    c. in another state.

15. What is the return on a search warrant? Explain the function of the return.

CHAPTER 4

AUTHORITY OF OTHER INVESTIGATIVE AGENCIES

LEARNING OBJECTIVES

After reading this chapter, the student will be able to:

- Explain the types of cases handled by each of the following federal agencies: Federal Bureau of Investigation, Drug Enforcement Administration, Bureau of Alcohol, Tobacco and Firearms, and Secret Service.
- Describe the interaction between local law enforcement and the state agency which regulates sales of alcoholic beverages.
- Describe the interaction between local law enforcement and the state agency which regulates motor vehicle registration and drivers' licenses.
- Describe the interaction between local law enforcement and the state attorney general's office.
- Explain mutual aid agreements.
- Compare and contrast the relationship between city police and the sheriff's department.
- Explain the role of the coroner.
- Explain the role of Children's Protective Services.

Key Terms

administrative hearing
Alcoholic Beverage Control
Alcohol, Tobacco, and Firearms
attorney general's office
Central Child Abuse Index
Children's Protective Services
contract city
coroner
coroner's jury
criminal histories
Department of Justice
Department of Motor Vehicles
Drug Enforcement Administration
exclusive jurisdiction
Federal Bureau of Investigation
implied consent
inquest
joint jurisdiction
mutual aid agreements
"off-sale" license
"on-sale" license
Secret Service
sheriff's department
"wants and warrants"

Local police officers handle a wide variety of cases. Most other law enforcement agencies are more specialized. A police department may seek assistance from the experts in these specialized agencies. Sometimes the law gives only one agency the authority to handle certain types of cases; this is called **exclusive jurisdiction**. When such a crime occurs, the case must be transferred to that agency. More commonly, the law gives two or more enforcement agencies jurisdiction over the same event. This is referred to as **joint jurisdiction**. The people in both agencies must reach an understanding regarding the handling of these types of cases. This chapter describes the roles of a variety of investigative agencies.

4.1 Federal Agencies

There are many federal agencies with law enforcement responsibilities. Some, like the FBI, are widely known. Others, such as the Securities and Exchange Commission, primarily regulate civil transactions but have small law enforcement units which are highly specialized. Good working relationships between federal and local law enforcement are important. All law enforcement officers need to know which crimes are within the exclusive jurisdiction of specialized agencies. Information on these crimes should be transmitted to the appropriate personnel immediately. When two agencies have authority to handle a case, they must be able to reach agreement rapidly on what each will do. Prior arrangements for making these decisions are necessary in order to investigate crime effectively. A poorly coordinated response can result in failure to do a thorough investigation, loss of important pieces of evidence, needless duplication of efforts, and criminals going unpunished.

Federal Bureau of Investigation

The Federal Bureau of Investigation (FBI), which is part of the Justice Department, is the general law enforcement agency for the federal government. All federal crimes not assigned to other agencies are investigated by the FBI. Its jurisdiction over espionage and treason gives it authority to act as an intelligence-gathering agency. The FBI National Academy at Quantico, Virginia, provides management courses for police chiefs and other management personnel as well as classes on specialized techniques for investigators.

The list of crimes it handles changes as Congress enacts new criminal laws and redefines the jurisdiction of other federal agencies. Criminal violations of the federal Civil Rights Act are investigated by the FBI. Some of the crimes handled by the FBI are also covered by state law. For example: robbing a bank is a federal crime if the bank is insured by the Federal Deposit Insurance Corporation (FDIC) and is also robbery under state law; taking stolen vehicles across state lines comes within the FBI's jurisdiction because it violates the Dyer Act but can also be charged as grand theft auto in the state where the vehicle was stolen.

The FBI has offices in most major cities. Resident agents are located in many smaller cities and rural areas. Each police department needs to keep a list of crimes handled by the FBI and know how to contact FBI agents who are assigned to their area. Both patrol officers and detectives should know when to notify the FBI of criminal activity.

Another function assigned to the FBI is operation of the National Crime Information Center (NCIC). This is a computerized data bank on wanted persons, vehicles and other items. Data is forwarded to the

FBI by local agencies for inclusion. Modern communications equipment enables officers in the field and dispatchers to query the system.

The Uniform Crime Report (UCR) system is maintained by the FBI. *Crime in the United States*, a book published annually giving statistics on offenses reported, arrests and clearances by police department, is the main product of this system. Originally, information was submitted to the FBI in tabular form monthly by local agencies. Many states now have a centralized agency which collects the data from the police departments and sends summaries to the FBI. The UCR is not a report on investigations conducted by FBI agents.

Drug Enforcement Administration

The Drug Enforcement Administration (DEA) is responsible for enforcing federal laws regulating controlled substances. The United States is a signatory to the Single Convention on Narcotic Drugs signed in New York on March 30, 1961, and the Convention on Psychotropic Substances signed in Vienna, Austria, on February 21, 1971. Title 21 of the United States Code contains the federal laws restricting controlled substances. Title 21 also mandates that the Attorney General cooperate with local, state and other federal agencies concerning trafficking in controlled substances and drug abuse. Upon request of the Attorney General, it is the duty of all federal agencies to furnish assistance, including technical advice, to drug enforcement activities of the Justice Department. The combination of these laws gives DEA authority to act worldwide and with all levels of law enforcement within the United States.

DEA has authority in two main areas: prevention of controlled substances originating with legitimate pharmaceutical manufacturers from reaching inappropriate distributors; and investigation of traffic in illicit drugs. Many pharmaceutical firms manufacture drugs with legitimate medicinal value which are on the controlled substance list. DEA is authorized to inspect factories, wholesalers, retailers, pharmacies, and doctors' offices where controlled substances are stored. DEA's rights include copying and verifying all records these firms are required to keep, as well as inspecting the premises for finished and unfinished drugs, containers and labels. DEA is not involved with financial records, sales figures unrelated to shipments, or pricing information.

Title 21 provides for the issuing of administrative warrants if necessary to conduct these inspections. No warrant is required if there is imminent danger to health or safety, reasonable cause to believe that the mobility of a vehicle makes it impracticable to obtain a warrant, or other emergency circumstances.

DEA is also heavily involved in preventing sales of drugs that are illicitly manufactured or smuggled into the United States. The international agreements give DEA the authority to enter foreign countries who have signed these Conventions in order to prevent smuggling into the United States. Their authority to request assistance from other federal agencies has been used to involve the military in these activities. Equally important is cooperation with local law enforcement agencies. DEA usually investigates large-scale drug sales and smuggling operations while local law enforcement handles cases involving smaller quantities. Information obtained during any type of investigation should be passed on to the appropriate agency. What initially appears to be a small drug ring may turn out to be an international operation.

Alcohol, Tobacco and Firearms

The Bureau of Alcohol, Tobacco and Firearms (ATF) was originally a unit of the Internal Revenue Service but has been a separate bureau in the Treasury Department since 1972. It enforces the following laws: Title XI (Explosives) of the Organized Crime Control Act of 1970; Gun Control Act of 1968 as currently amended; Anti-Arson Act of 1982; Federal Alcohol Administration Act of 1935; alcohol, tobacco and firearms provisions of Internal Revenue Code; Contraband Cigarette Law of 1978; and provisions of the Arms Export Control Act of 1976 relating to importation of firearms, ammunition, and implements of war.

ATF is concerned with compliance as well as law enforcement. The compliance function is designed to ensure that the firearms, explosive, alcohol and tobacco industries comply with federal law, pay federal excise and occupational taxes, and obtain required licenses and permits. Illicit production of alcohol ("moonshine") is now infrequent, but ATF investigates and prosecutes bribery, kick backs and payoffs within the alcohol industry. False labeling and product contamination in the wine industry are within ATF's jurisdiction. It also assists states experiencing problems with smuggling of cigarettes and counterfeit tax stamps on cigarettes.

ATF investigates criminal bombings and thefts of explosives. Criminal use of explosive materials, as well as unsafe storage, are also their concern. A computerized Explosives Incidents System (EXIS), which contains information on all explosives incidents reported to and/or investigated by ATF, is used to match targets and motives of suspected bombers as well as identify those who use similar explosive devices. ATF shares information from this system with local law enforcement and also has an agreement with the Defense Department for reciprocal exchange of information regarding thefts and recoveries of military ordinances. The National Explosives Tracing Center (NETC), operated by ATF, is used to trace the source of recovered, stolen or abandoned explosives. It can also trace foreign commercial and military explosives.

The National Firearms Act of 1934 regulates machineguns, sawed-off shotguns and some other "gangster-type" weapons. ATF's enforcement powers over firearms has been expanded so that it now has task forces which target armed career criminals and violent gangs for prosecution in federal court. These activities require coordination with a variety of other federal and local agencies, particularly DEA and the FBI. Stolen firearms transported in interstate commerce are under ATF's jurisdiction. ATF also works to combat international traffic in illegal firearms and ammunition. The National Tracing Center is operated by ATF to assist law enforcement authorities from all over the world locate the source of recovered firearms.

Major arson-for-profit crimes involving commercial and industrial interstate activities are investigated by ATF. National Response Teams provide 24-hour response to any major arson, explosive or explosives-related incident in the geographical United States. ATF provides assistance if a major arson problem exists which exceeds the local agency's resources or involves multiple jurisdictions. Laboratories operated by ATF analyze arson debris for local law enforcement agencies and ATF Audit Staff assist in analyzing financial information on suspects in arson-for-profit cases.

Numerous training courses are offered to local law enforcement agencies on arson, explosives, firearms, and smuggling contraband cigarettes. Gang-related information-sharing conferences are hosted yearly. Advanced courses are given at the Federal Law Enforcement Training Center in Glynco, Georgia. A training course on arson-for-profit investigation is offered for insurance investigators.

Secret Service

The Secret Service is a branch of the Treasury Department. It has two distinctly different functions: provide protection for the president of the United States and other dignitaries; and investigate crimes involving federal obligations (currency, bonds, etc.) and certain other crimes assigned to it by Congress.

Secret Service provides protection for: president and vice president of the United States (and president-elect and vice president-elect) and immediate members of their respective families; former presidents and their spouses for life except that protection for a former president's spouse stops if he/she remarries; children of a former president who are under 16 years of age; visiting heads of state or foreign governments; other distinguished foreign visitors to the United States; official representatives of the United States performing special missions abroad when the president directs that protection be provided; major presidential and vice presidential candidates and, within 120 days of the general presidential election, the spouses of such candidates. The Secret Service relies heavily upon local law enforcement and fire departments for assistance whenever any of the people listed above travel. Threats to kill or kidnap the president, president-elect, vice president, or the vice president-elect are investigated by the FBI, not Secret Service.

The best known investigative function of Secret Service involves counterfeit money. Title 18 Section 3056 of the United States Code authorizes it to investigate violations of federal law involving "coins, obligations and securities" of the United States and foreign governments. "Obligations" includes currency, stamps, bonds, passports, immigration papers and food stamps. The same section empowers Secret Service to handle a variety of crimes against the Federal Deposit Insurance Corporation, federal land banks and federal land bank associations.

The most recent additions to Secret Service's agenda involve fraudulent forms of financial transactions: electronic fund transfer, credit and debit cards, and false identification documents or devices. Interaction with other federal agencies, particularly the Postal Inspectors, is common. Secret Service frequently obtains information from local law enforcement to start these investigations. They work closely with local agencies to successfully complete many cases.

Other Agencies

There are many other federal agencies with law enforcement responsibilities. The following list, which in no way covers all the federal agencies and regulatory commissions, illustrates those with investigative powers: Civil Aeronautics Board; Commission on Civil Rights; Commodities Futures Trading Commission; Consumer Product Safety Commission; Environmental Protection Agency; Equal Employment Opportunity Commission; Farm Credit Administration; Federal Communications Commission; Federal Deposit Insurance Corporation; Federal Elections Commission; Federal Trade Commission; General Services Administration; Interstate Commerce Commission; National Aeronautics and Space Administration; National Labor Relations Board; National Transportation Safety Board; Occupational Safety and Health Administration; Securities and Exchange Commission; Small Business Administration; U.S. Postal Service; and Veterans Administration. Some of these agencies do the complete investigation in cases involving laws within their jurisdiction, others use FBI agents if there is evidence of criminal wrongdoing.

4.2 State Agencies

There are many state-level agencies which are involved in law enforcement. Some, such as the Highway Patrol, are very visible. Others, like Fish and Game, may be well known but not generally thought of as law enforcement agencies. A smooth working relationship between each police department and state agencies is important. First, it is necessary to determine what each agency is authorized to do. Laws creating specialized agencies may have a uniform purpose, but the legislative process results in minor differences between the laws of the various states. Officers cannot safely assume that they have the authority to act because police in another state do. For example, in some, but not all states, laws regulating junkyards give the city police the right to inspect junkyards, without probable cause, to look for parts taken from stolen vehicles.

Second, local police departments and state agencies need to establish good working relationships. This is particularly important where the law gives both agencies the authority to act. Patrol officers need to know whether to handle the call or wait for personnel from a state agency to arrive. This involves policies of both agencies. It also requires a cooperative arrangement between the state agency's local office and the police department. Other factors, such as the distance each officer needs to travel to reach the crime scene, may also be important. Coordination of responses is crucial. The case may be lost if officers from both agencies assume the other agency was going to complete important parts of the investigation. Petty jealousies about who will get credit for the case also lead to improperly conducted investigations. The end result of these problems is unprofessional conduct and loss of the public's respect.

Alcoholic Beverage Control

Nearly every state has an agency charged with regulating the sale of alcoholic beverages. The exact name varies from state to state; it will be referred to here as ABC. The functions of this agency usually involve issuing licenses to sell alcohol and conducting inspections of premises which are licensed or should be licensed.

The licensing function is usually performed exclusively by ABC personnel. They verify that the applications have been completed properly. Investigations are usually conducted to determine if the owners have criminal backgrounds or ties to organized crime that would disqualify them. The investigation may be more extensive for **"on-sale" licenses** (bars, etc., where drinks will be consumed at the location where they are sold) than for **"off-sale" licenses** (liquor stores, etc.). State laws may also differentiate between: private clubs and bars open to the public; bars that primarily sell liquor as opposed to "beer bars" and restaurants which serve drinks with meals. Special permits may be available for a limited time, such as for the day of the company picnic. Information on the number of alcohol beverage licenses already issued for the immediate area may be considered. Proximity of the licensed premises to churches and schools is frequently factored in. Sometimes public hearings are held to determine if people in the neighborhood object. If the application successfully passes the investigation, the license is usually issued for a specific length of time, such as five years. An application for renewal must be made when the license expires and another investigation is conducted.

State licensing laws usually provide that establishments serving alcohol may be inspected at any time. Records and other items may be checked to confirm that the establishment is selling only what is allowed by its license. Record inspections are normally done by ABC personnel.

State law usually allows officers to verify that regulations are followed when selling alcoholic beverages. "Bar checks," going into "on-sale" establishments and checking the ages of people present or verifying that drinks are not sold after the legally mandated closing time, are frequently done by local police as well as ABC personnel. This may also be true for conducting surveillance to make sure liquor stores are not selling to minors.

Violations of laws regulating the sale of alcoholic beverages, such as selling beer to a minor, are grounds to revoke or suspend the license. Police officers who observe violations of these laws may be called as witnesses. The licensee is usually entitled to an **administrative hearing** at which ABC officers must present evidence to establish that there are legal grounds for the action. The hearing, which is usually conducted before a hearing officer or administrative law judge, may be slightly less formal than a court hearing. Due process requirements, such as notice prior to the hearing and a chance to respond, are necessary. Administrative hearings frequently use more lenient rules of evidence, particularly as to hearsay. The standard of proof is usually a preponderance of the evidence. Some states make revocation of a license appealable to the civil court system, others require administrative appeals to be taken first. Charging the licensee with violating criminal laws and simultaneously attempting to revoke the license does not violate double jeopardy because license revocation is not a criminal proceeding.

Department of Motor Vehicles

States regulate the registration of vehicles and licensing of drivers. One state agency, referred to here as DMV, usually handles both of these functions. Local law enforcement officers interact with them less directly than with ABC.

DMV handles a complex system of vehicle registration ranging from passenger cars to commercial trucking. It may also license mobile homes and a variety of other conveyances. Part of this function is performed through car dealers who prepare the necessary forms when cars are bought and sold. DMV may make special arrangements so that

Comparison of Criminal Trial and Administrative Hearing

	Criminal Trial	Administrative Hearing
Who files complaint	District attorney or city prosecutor	Agency seeking to enforce its rules
What can be charged	Violation of criminal law	Violation of agency regulations
Where will hearing take place	Courthouse	Hearing room (several agencies may share hearing room)
Who presides over hearing	Judge	Hearing officer or administrative law judge
Who presents case	District attorney or city prosecutor	Officer of agency bringing action
Use of jury	At request of prosecution or defense	No jury
Rules of evidence	Strictly enforced	May admit hearsay and some other types of evidence not allowed in court
Use of precedence	Judge bound by decisions in prior cases	Hearing officer not bound by decisions in prior cases
Atmosphere	Formal	Less formal
Sanctions imposed	Conviction of crime — prison, jail, etc.	Suspend/revoke license, fines
Appeal	Next higher level court	Usually to higher administrative court and then civil court

Table 4.1

dealers collect registration fees and perform other functions. When problems arise, such as failure to forward fees to the state or falsification of registration, DMV personnel usually have sole responsibility for handling them. Local law enforcement rarely becomes involved in the registration functions although they may issue citations for expired registration, take stolen vehicle reports from car dealers, and be called to a dealership when a dissatisfied customer becomes unruly.

Drivers' licenses are normally issued directly from DMV. Testing, whether written or "behind the wheel," is usually done by DMV examiners. Too many traffic tickets for hazardous violations is usually grounds for suspension or revocation of the license. Violation of rules, such as being involved in a collision when not covered by insurance, may also be grounds for suspension or revocation of the license.

Traffic citations written by police are processed through the local court. DMV is notified by the court when a driver is convicted. Data on the conviction is entered into an automated data bank maintained by DMV. The computer generates notices to the driver when a certain quota of convictions has been reached, such as three moving violations in 12 months. The person whose license is about to be suspended or revoked has the right to request a hearing. Sometimes officers who wrote the tickets are called to testify. As with ABC hearings, the revocation or suspension is usually handled through an administrative process rather than the courts. There may be an appeals process within the administrative framework; it may also be possible to make a final appeal to the state's courts. The outcome of the administrative hearing does not change the action taken in traffic court. Double jeopardy is not violated because DMV actions are not considered criminal proceedings.

Most states have "**implied consent**" laws which make a suspected drunk driver's refusal to take a chemical test for intoxication grounds for suspending his/her license. The vehicle code makes consent to take these tests a condition of issuing the driver's license. Specific tests, such as blood alcohol, breathalyzer and urine analysis, are usually specified. Many states require that the driver be given a choice of tests. Procedures for the police to follow are mandated. License suspension is authorized only if the procedures are followed exactly and the driver refuses to take a test. The "implied consent" rule applies to the administrative process used by DMV to suspend licenses.

It does not regulate the admissibility of evidence of intoxication at a trial for driving under the influence (DUI). These separate rules for the two procedures can lead to the following result: a driver can successfully challenge the attempt to suspend his/her license because a blood test was taken without offering the variety of tests specified in the vehicle code; the same driver may be convicted of DUI because the rules at trial permit the test to be used as relevant evidence on the DUI charge.

Attorney General

Each state has an attorney general who normally heads the state's Department of Justice. There is a great deal of variation between states, but the following functions are typically handled by the state Department of Justice: investigate certain types of crimes; provide assistance to local law enforcement agencies; operate a data bank containing names of wanted persons; maintain criminal histories ("rap" sheets); compile statistics on crimes committed in the state; represent the state when defendants appeal felony convictions; and a variety of noncriminal functions. The Department of Justice frequently takes over criminal investigations when there would be a conflict of interest if a local agency handled the case. An example would be allegations that the Chief of Police is involved in criminal activity. The Department of Justice may also have experts available to assist small agencies. Department of Justice personnel may staff criminalistics laboratories. In some states, the Department of Justice operates task forces which investigate drug dealers, gang activity and other problems. Each police department needs to be aware of the services provided by the Department of Justice so it can effectively use them.

Maintaining **criminal history** information is a data base operation. A system is established so that the courts notify the Department of Justice when a person is convicted. Depending on the state's recordkeeping system, arrest information may also be maintained even though a conviction does not occur. Information is entered into a computerized data bank. Police departments query the system to find out if a suspect has prior convictions. Laws regulating the right to privacy have restricted access to this data bank except when necessary as part of a criminal investigation, in the preparation of a probation and sentencing report, or for required records checks prior to employment in specified jobs.

A data base on wanted persons, often called "**wants and warrants,**" is frequently operated at the state level by the Department of Justice in addition to the National Crime Information Center (NCIC) operated by the FBI. The Department of Justice establishes criteria for entering and removing names in the data base. Each police department must pay close attention to the procedures for adding and deleting information in order to keep the system up-to-date. All law enforcement agencies in the state usually have access to this data base. The equipment is now available so officers can query the system directly from their patrol cars. This is invaluable for the officer making a stop of a suspicious person in the field.

Other specialized databases may also be operated by the Department of Justice. A common one is the **Central Child Abuse Index**, which is a key component of many states' mandatory reporting systems. This index provides information on prior reports of physical and sexual abuse as well as criminal neglect. It can usually be searched by either the name of the suspect or the victim. Some states have recently started computerized databases on protective orders issued in domestic violence cases. Any police department in the state can use this system to verify that a valid order is in effect even though they do not have a copy in their own files. Two problems frequently encountered in domestic violence cases make the statewide file particularly important: victims may be accosted by their abusers at unanticipated locations as they travel; verifying the expiration date of the protective order is critical in order to determine whether it can be enforced.

Two types of criminal statistics may be generated by the Department of Justice: incident statistics and offender-based statistics. Incident statistics give the frequency with which specific events (e.g., murders, robberies, rapes, burglaries and grand thefts) are reported to the police. Other information may also be tabulated such as the number of arrests and/or clearances for each crime. Incident statistics are tabulated by the local agency, usually by computer, and forwarded to the Department of Justice either monthly, quarterly or annually. The state Department of Justice forwards copies of some of these reports to the FBI for inclusion in the Uniform Crime Reports. The data may also be used at the state level to generate a variety of reports.

Offender-based statistics are tabulated from information sheets that follow the offender through the system from arrest to sentencing. Law enforcement typically initiates the paperwork on the offender and then forwards it to the courts. After disposition of the case (dismissal, acquittal, or sentencing), the form goes to the Department of Justice where the data is analyzed and reports made available to law enforcement and the public. Offender-based statistics provide better information on how the criminal justice system is operating because they make it possible to see the disposition of cases. Due to delays between arrest, trial and sentencing, the final statistics produced do not match the incident reports for the year in which the crimes occur.

Other State Agencies

Many other state-level law enforcement agencies exist, frequently as small units within departments not usually associated with investigating criminal activity. For example: Bureau of Consumer Affairs; Department of Fish and Game; Board of Medical Examiners; State Bar; Department of Forestry; Insurance Commissioner; Department of Corporations; and many more. It is important that each police agency be familiar with these agencies for two reasons: their investigators frequently have expertise that is invaluable to officers who rarely handle specialized cases; and state law may require participation by state-level investigators in some cases.

4.3 Local Agencies

Cooperation between local agencies is as important, if not more so, than cooperation between federal, state and local agencies. Patrol officers, in many instances, interact with other local agencies on a daily basis. Sometimes the role assigned some of these agencies appears to conflict with that of the police department. This makes it doubly important that personnel on both sides try to understand each other's duties and work together in a professional manner.

Mutual Aid Agreements

State law normally gives local police officers jurisdiction to perform law enforcement functions within the city that employs them and to go to other areas of the state when necessary to investigate a crime that occurred within their city. Unusual events, such as riots and natural disasters (fires, earthquakes, hurricanes, etc.), leave a city in need of additional law enforcement personnel. Many cities enter into mutual aid agreements with other cities and/or counties so that they can ask for help when an emergency arises. In effect, the mutual aid agreement gives the officers sent to help the same powers as police officers employed by the city they assist. Mutual aid agreements are formal documents, similar to contracts, and vary from city to city. They may cover all emergency services (police, fire, ambulance) or be for only one type of service. The agreement may specify the number of personnel who will be sent. More general language calling for "available personnel" is common; this permits a city to refuse to send aid in cases where sending personnel to another city would seriously impair services in the city that employs the officers. Some agreements call for the city requesting assistance to pay for the cost of services rendered; but it is common for the agency which employs the officers to pay the salary. Mutual aid agreements may be more symbolic than truly mutual. For example, an extremely large city may have a mutual aid agreement with a tiny city in its suburbs; it is unlikely that the large agency will benefit from such an agreement although it could be of enormous benefit to the small department.

County Sheriff's Department

The role of the sheriff's department varies a great deal in the United States. Different functions are performed due to state laws that govern the sheriff; duties may also be different within a state due to agreements between local agencies.

One of the most common roles for the sheriff's department is operating the county jail. Officers working at the jail may be sworn peace officers or have correctional officer status. Some cities also operate jails. Usually the city jails are for pre-sentenced inmates while the county jail houses those serving sentences. New York City Department of Corrections, which operates a large jail on Rykers Island, is an example of a city jail which houses both pre-sentenced and sentenced inmates.

Bailiffs (also called "court services officers" and some other titles) maintain order in courtrooms and may be responsible for custody of inmates who are in the building for a court appearance or trial. These services are provided by the sheriff's department in some areas and by separate agencies, sometimes called the Marshal, in other locations. The laws in some states, such as California, allow the local counties or judges to decide which agency will provide these services. Bailiffs are employed directly by the courts in some states.

Other court-related functions may be performed by the sheriff's department. These include serving legal papers, such as subpoenas and civil complaints. They may be responsible for carrying out evictions, garnishments and other court orders.

Many states give the sheriff's department law enforcement duties. Probably the most common is to provide police services for people who live in unincorporated areas. Depending on the size of the county and its population density, this ranges from serving a few people to over a million inhabitants. Agreements between a city and the county may result in the sheriff's department providing the police force for an incorporated city. Cities which do this are frequently called "**contract cities**." Depending on state law, a contract city can purchase all or part of its police services from the sheriff's department. Contracts may also be permitted between two or more cities.

Larger sheriff's departments provide specialized services such as a centralized records bureau, criminalistics laboratory or bomb squad, to cities within their jurisdiction. Sometimes these must be contracted for. Less formal arrangements also exist, such as calling someone in the homicide bureau and asking for advice.

CORONER

The basic role of the coroner is to determine when deaths are the result of criminal conduct. Autopsies are performed for this purpose. Some coroners also have investigators who look for clues outside the medical realm; others rely on local law enforcement agencies for these duties. State laws identify the types of cases which must be referred to the coroner. Deaths under the following circumstances usually require notification of the coroner: deceased has not seen a doctor recently (law usually states a specific period, such as within 10 days); deceased's personal physician unable to state cause of death; suspected homicide or suicide; death following accident or from gunshot, stabbing or poison; deaths occurring shortly after the patient entered the hospital or while patient under anesthetic; deaths in prisons and other custodial facilities; and deaths of unidentified persons. Patrol officers and hospitals need to be familiar with the exact list in their state.

The coroner's office must be called when death occurs under the circumstances listed in the local state's laws. What the coroner will do varies with state law and local practice. The coroner's pathologist usually performs the autopsy if criminal activity is suspected. Consent of the deceased's family is not required. Some states permit the coroner to authorize another person, such as the hospital's pathologist, to perform the autopsy if no suspicious circumstances are evident.

Coroners are usually authorized to hold an **inquest**. This is a hearing, similar to a trial, to determine whether the death was by criminal means. The focus of the inquest is on *whether* a criminal homicide occurred, not who committed it or the type of offense (first degree murder, voluntary manslaughter, etc.). The prosecutor is responsible for filing charges and handling the criminal case after the coroner has ruled that the death was by criminal means. The law may also provide for an inquest to determine whether a person committed suicide. This ruling may be important in determining how much beneficiaries may collect under the deceased's life insurance policies.

Many states allow the coroner to empanel a jury, commonly referred to as a **coroner's jury**, for the inquest. A preponderance of the evidence is usually required for a finding of death by criminal means. Whether an inquest will be held is determined by local policy and state law. Some states make the inquest mandatory while others leave it to the discretion of the coroner's office. The result of this discretion is that inquests are very common in some locales and done only rarely in others.

Children's Protective Services

All states now have laws mandating reporting of child abuse. This includes physical abuse, sexual abuse and neglect. Law enforcement officers, probation officers, teachers, day care workers and medical personnel are usually required to report suspected abuse. Other people may report but will not be held criminally liable for failing to do so. Each police officer should know the local law on what must be reported, when, to whom and on what forms. Typically a report must be made by telephone immediately with a written report following within one or two days.

Children's Protective Services (referred to here as CPS although the exact name varies from state to state), is the social welfare agency that handles abuse cases. Local policing agencies frequently work with CPS if there is suspicion of criminal activity. The goals of law enforcement and CPS are not the same. Police focus on arresting and prosecuting the abuser. CPS's duties center on protecting the abused child. Keeping the family intact is usually a high priority with CPS. In many states CPS handles the civil court proceedings to remove a child from an abusive home. In these cases, CPS functions as a placement agency and is usually responsible for locating and overseeing foster care and/or adoption. It is important to coordinate the responses between the police department and CPS. State law may require sharing reports.

Other

A wide variety of enforcement agencies exists at the local level. For example, some prosecutors employ investigators to help prepare cases for court; airports and school districts may have their own police forces; consumer fraud may be investigated by a local agency. Each police department needs to have a complete list of the investigative agencies that operate within its jurisdiction; policies should be developed so that officers know when to notify these agencies of possible criminal activity. The police department's job is made easier if there is a coordinated response; failure to work harmoniously can result in criminals eluding apprehension and conviction.

Summary

The structure of American government has resulted in law enforcement agencies at the federal, state and local level. Local law enforcement officers need to understand the jurisdiction of other agencies in order to work effectively. Each police department should have policies describing the crimes handled by other agencies and when they should be notified of criminal activity. Cooperation between all agencies is imperative. While the law may give one agency jurisdiction, information gathered by others is frequently essential to solving the crime. Poorly coordinated activities involving multiple agencies—whether acting together or separately—can result in injuries to law enforcement personnel and innocent people. The end result may be that the suspect flees the scene and ultimately escapes without punishment.

The FBI is the best known federal law enforcement agency. It has jurisdiction over all federal felonies that are not specifically assigned by law to other federal agencies. DEA investigates the pharmaceutical industry's handling of controlled substances as well as illicit manufacture and smuggling of drugs. ATF oversees regulation of the alcoholic beverage industry and investigates violations of federal firearm laws. It also handles cases involving bombings and thefts of explosives. One of Secret Service's functions is to provide protection for the president, vice-president and other designated officials. It investigates counterfeiting of government documents and has recently been assigned bank fraud involving electronic transfers, credit cards, and ATM cards.

Numerous state-level law enforcement agencies exit. ABC regulates the sale of alcoholic beverages. It frequently has exclusive jurisdiction over licensing establishments that sell alcohol. It also does inspections of licensed premises to verify that state laws are being complied with. Patrol officers for the local police department may also do "bar checks" and conduct surveillance to make sure that stores do not sell liquor to minors. Violations of these laws may be used to suspend or revoke the license to sell alcohol. Police officers may be called to testify at administrative hearings held for this purpose.

DMV handles registration of vehicles and drivers. Testing and registration are normally handled by DMV personnel. Citations for vehicle code violations result in trials in traffic court. Convictions are usually recorded in the DMV computer. Excessive violations result in suspension or revocation of the driver's license. Refusal to take a chemical test for intoxication when stopped on suspicion of driving under the influence may also result in suspension of the driver's license. The officer who wrote the citation may be called to testify at an administrative hearing if the driver contests DMV's action.

The state Department of Justice may provide investigators to assist local law enforcement in some situations. Experts may be available to assist a police department; special services, such as a criminalistics laboratory, may be available. Criminal history information is usually maintained by the Department of Justice. The Central Child Abuse Index is also located there. Criminal statistics are compiled and sent to the FBI from this department.

Cooperative interaction between local agencies is necessary. Mutual aid agreements are frequently established so that a city can request assistance from neighboring jurisdictions in case of an emergency. The sheriff's department usually operates the county jail; it may also provide a variety of other services for cities within the county.

The coroner is responsible for determining whether a death is by criminal means. This is usually done immediately after death; there may be no suspect at the time. Pathologists or other qualified personnel are employed to do autopsies. An inquest, sometimes with a jury, may be held to hear evidence regarding the cause of death. Once the coroner has determined that the death was caused by criminal means, it is the prosecutor's duty to decide how to proceed with the criminal case.

CPS investigates child abuse. The police department will usually handle the part of the case that goes to criminal court. CPS handles the civil proceedings to remove abused children from a home, establish foster care or place the children for adoption.

Many other agencies exist with law enforcement duties. The expertise of their investigators can greatly assist local law enforcement. Every effort should be made to identify these agencies and establish good working relationships with them.

Study Questions

1. Describe the interaction between law enforcement agencies at the federal, state and local level.
2. Explain the jurisdiction of the following federal agencies and how they work with local police departments:
   a. FBI
   b. ATF
   c. DEA
   d. Secret Service
3. Name five other federal agencies with law enforcement responsibilities.
4. Differentiate between a criminal trial and an administrative hearing.

5. Describe the functions of the following agencies in your state:
   a. ABC
   b. DMV
   c. Department of Justice

6. Name five other state-level agencies in your state who have law enforcement responsibilities and explain:
   a. what laws they enforce
   b. crimes over which they have exclusive jurisdiction
   c. how they interact with your police department

7. Describe the role of the sheriff's department in your county.

8. Describe the role of the coroner:
   a. list the circumstances under which the coroner must be notified of a death under the laws of your state
   b. when are inquests held by your local coroner

9. Describe the role of Children's Protective Services in your area.
   a. what cases must be reported to CPS?
   b. how do CPS and your local police department divide responsibilities for investigation of child abuse cases?
   c. what types of cases are handled exclusively by CPS?

10. Name five other local agencies in your area who have law enforcement responsibilities and explain:
    a. what laws they enforce
    b. crimes over which they have exclusive jurisdiction
    c. how they interact with your police department

Chapter 5

The Criminal Complaint and Arraignment

Learning Objectives

After reading this chapter, the student will be able to:

- Explain the prosecutor's role in filing criminal charges.
- Illustrate how the police interact with the prosecutor during the early stages of the case.
- Explain the decision-making process for selecting the charges that will be filed against the defendant.
- List what must be included in the criminal complaint.
- Describe what occurs at the arraignment.

Key Terms

arraignment
citation
citing out
code pleading
complaint
continuance
count
defendant
double jeopardy
fact pleading
filing the complaint
joinder
jurisdiction
nolo contendere
plaintiff
plea bargain
probable cause hearing
redacting a confession
right to a speedy trial
severed
statute of limitations
tolling the statute of limitations
venue

Once the police have arrested a person, the case must be prepared for entry into the court system. The prosecutor's office usually drafts the necessary legal papers. The first court appearance on the charges is called the arraignment.

5.1 Role of Prosecutor

Prior to making an arrest, the police frequently conduct the investigation on their own unless a warrant is needed. Key decisions on how much manpower to devote to the case, how thoroughly to investigate, and when there is enough information to justify an arrest are usually made by police officers. During the investigation, the prosecutor may provide legal advice. The extent of this involvement is primarily governed by local custom and staffing levels. When the prosecutor's office has an excessive workload, there may be little interaction with the police except on major cases. Some police departments employ their own legal advisors to fill this void.

The prosecutor serves as gatekeeper to the criminal courts. Except for independent grand jury investigations, no criminal charges can be filed without the prosecutor's approval. After the arrest, most of the key decisions will be made by the prosecutor. Although local practices vary, the following decisions are usually made by the prosecutor: whether or not to file charges; what charges to file; and whether or not to enter into plea bargains. Many prosecutors consult with the police when making these decisions.

Another important role of the prosecutor is to seek the truth on who is guilty and who is not. Law enforcement officers at times become too emotionally involved in an investigation: "catching the criminal" becomes the goal even though not all the facts are known. Incentives, such as consideration of the number of arrests an officer has made when promotions are awarded, may also cloud objectivity. The prosecutor should be objective. It is important that the prosecutor review all the facts and not merely file charges against the person that the police arrested for the crime. Care must be taken not to give undue weight to factors such as the prior criminal record of the suspect and the fact that he/she was uncooperative with the police or has a very abrasive personality. Public outcries about the crime must not lead to a rush to file charges when there are too few facts to establish a suspect's guilt.

The available evidence is a primary concern in determining which charges to file. A variety of other considerations may influence the prosecutor's decision to file charges. One is whether the case can be prepared for trial in a timely manner. The Sixth Amendment **right to a speedy trial** gives the defendant the right to have the case dismissed if the period from arraignment to trial is too long. Two key factors usually influence the length of time it will take a case to go to trial: staffing level of the prosecutor's office; and court backlog. Screening of cases becomes necessary if either the prosecutor has insufficient staff or the court becomes overloaded. This screening process usually results in refusal to file weak cases and/or relatively minor charges.

Prosecutors also try to judge the attitude of the public. Filing cases the general public feels are insignificant frequently results in jury verdicts of acquittal. For example, while sex with a juvenile is against the law in most states, in many communities it is improbable that a conviction would result if charges were filed against an 18-year-old high school student for having sex with a very willing 17-year-old sweetheart. Sometimes the reverse is also true. Public outcry may result in the prosecutor filing charges even though the case is weak.

Most prosecutors are elected officials. The performance of their personnel is an election issue. Win-loss records are used to support re-election or for attack by opponents. Some decisions to prosecute are related to these considerations.

5.2 Police Interaction With Prosecutor

The prosecutor's office is normally the preliminary stop when the police want a warrant. Most jurisdictions require that the application be screened by the prosecutor before the request is taken to the judge. A prosecutor usually reviews the facts and assists with the drafting of affidavits and other necessary paperwork. If it appears that probable cause is lacking, the prosecutor will inform the police that additional information must be obtained prior to seeking the warrant.

How the police interact with the prosecutor to obtain the complaint is usually the result of two things: local custom and the types of charges. Three scenarios are common after the suspect is booked: the arresting officer takes the case to the prosecutor; detectives handle follow-up investigations and obtain complaints from the prosecutor; or a court liaison officer takes police reports to the prosecutor's office and seeks complaints. More than one of these may be used in the same police department; for example, detectives may handle felonies while a court liaison officer handles misdemeanors. Different procedures may be used if the suspect is released on a promise to appear instead of being booked.

In some cities, the police officer who makes the arrest takes the case to the prosecutor. This may be due to a team approach used by the police department. It is also commonly used when local court rules require the testimony of the arresting officer at the arraignment which is held very shortly after arrest. One advantage of this approach is that the officer discussing the case with the prosecutor has first-hand knowledge of the facts. Lengthy delays at either the prosecutor's office or the courthouse result in inefficient use of patrol officers and inadequate patrol coverage. Excessive overtime may also be incurred.

Patrol officers rarely seek criminal complaints in some cities because detectives are assigned this function. This makes good communication between patrol officers and detectives crucial. Reports must be thorough, easily understood, and made in a timely manner. Channels for transmitting the report from one officer to the other must be clearly established. The detectives may conduct an additional investigation and/or ask the patrol officer for more information. In either case, the detective who goes to the prosecutor's office for the complaint must have access to all the facts in the case. One advantage of this approach is that the detectives develop expertise in seeking complaints and may establish rapport with the prosecutors they see frequently. A disadvantage is that the detective may not be able to answer questions about the case as well as the person who was present at the scene of the crime.

Court liaison officers are used to take numerous cases to the prosecutor at once. This approach is used more often with misdemeanor cases than with felonies. The liaison officer is usually not involved in investigating cases. He/she frequently takes the crime reports to the prosecutor, waits for a decision, and transmits requests for additional information to the appropriate police officer. Additional duties may include taking subpoenas to the police department and maintaining records so that concerned officers know when cases have been dismissed or settled by a plea bargain. The chief advantage of the court liaison officer approach is that it efficiently uses police personnel and reduces the number of officers waiting at the prosecutor's office and courthouse. A disadvantage is that the person dealing with the prosecutor can rarely provide information not included in the written reports.

Many offenders receive citations. A **citation** lists the charges the person was arrested for; the offender is released if he/she signs a promise to appear in court. Identification showing a local address is usually required. The court date is normally listed on the form given to the offender. The release may occur either before or after booking, depending on local practice and the severity of the offense. Failure to appear in court as directed on the citation is a separate offense for which an arrest warrant may be issued. This process, referred to as "**citing out**," is most commonly used for traffic violators. A growing number of other criminal offenses, including felonies, are being handled this way in some states. For traffic violations and some misdemeanors, the citation is designed so that it takes the place of a complaint. In non-traffic cases, it is more common for a copy of the police report to accompany the citation when the case is given to the prosecutor. The advantage of this system is that it cuts down on the paperwork and time expended by both the police department and the prosecutor. A disadvantage is that the court may receive inadequate information on the case.

VIOLATION

TICKET NO.	DATE	TIME CHECKED	TIME ISSUED
AA000000001	17-OCT-92	1:16 AM	2:16 AM

	STATE/PROV.	NUMBER	YEAR
LIC	AZ	789SRS	
	MAKE	STYLE	COLOR
VEH	CADI	2D	PNK

VIOLATION

FINE: $50.00

Handicapped Space

LOCATION	ZONE
Location: ALLENTOWN	

Reference: STATE

For More Information Call Danny Michel
1-800-453-5195, ext. 265

NEXT TIME PLEASE BE
MORE COURTEOUS.

FINE INCREASES IF NOT PAID BY

OFFICER: 11111

VIOLATION

In some cases, the offender is not arrested at the scene, or is arrested but released prior to filing the criminal complaint. Arresting the suspect as soon as possible may be deemed important if the charges are serious or the offender is believed to be likely to flee the jurisdiction. In less serious cases, such as traffic accidents, the police department may seek the complaint without trying to arrest the suspect. When the complaint is filed, the court may issue an arrest warrant for the police to serve. Sometimes the court will mail a notice to appear directly to the suspect and no attempt will be made to make an arrest before the court date.

5.3 Decision to Charge

Criminal charges may be filed whenever there is *prima facie* evidence that the suspect committed the crime. In practice, this means there must be admissible evidence to establish probable cause that the crime was committed by the defendant. The prosecutor will go over the crime reports and try to determine what evidence can be used to establish each element of the case. While the complaint can withstand legal challenges as long as a *prima facie* case has been established, the prosecutor usually views the case with the goal of establishing guilt beyond a reasonable doubt at trial. Sometimes the complaint will be filed but the police will be directed to complete the investigation before trial.

Complaint

The complaint is a legal document which states the charges against the defendant. It is the first document filed with the court in cases where no arrest warrant or indictment was previously obtained. An arrest warrant contains similar information, therefore some states do not require a complaint if one has already been obtained. Other states require that the police obtain an arrest warrant simultaneously with seeking the complaint if a warrantless arrest was made.

The complaint can be amended to add or delete charges or make technical corrections, such as inserting the defendant's true name. Other documents, such as the indictment or information, may replace the complaint later in the case. The complaint must give sufficient facts to establish three things: the offense occurred within the jurisdiction of the court; the statute of limitations has not run; and what crimes the defendant is charged with.

Jurisdiction

Most states give a local court (municipal court, justice court, city court, etc.) jurisdiction to handle the initial proceedings for both misdemeanors and felonies. Jurisdiction is usually based on geography: the crime must have occurred within the boundaries of the court district. In some other situations, such as when the arrest was made on a warrant from another locale, the defendant may be arraigned in the court district in which the arrest was made even though the crime occurred elsewhere.

Venue

Venue literally means neighborhood. The legal definition is the county in which the crime occurred. There is frequently more than one court district in a large county. A court district may contain more than one city; this is common in areas where population growth resulted in cities incorporating after the court district was formed. The officers responsible for seeking complaints must be aware of these boundaries so the case will be filed in the court district with both jurisdiction and venue to hear the case. Maps with the boundaries clearly marked should be available for officers who deal with more than one court district. Filing the case in the wrong court district results in dismissal of the charges and refiling them in the correct court. Refiling is not allowed if the statute of limitations expired during the delay.

Police departments in metropolitan areas and counties with large geographical areas have one additional concern when filing the complaint. These larger districts may have more than one courthouse where criminal cases are handled. Assignment of a case to a particular courthouse is usually based on the location where the crime occurred. Once again, clearly marked maps are needed. As long as the court district is correct, cases filed in the wrong courthouse are usually transferred to the appropriate one rather than being dismissed.

Statute of Limitations

A statute of limitations establishes the maximum length of time during which a complaint can be filed against an individual. The statutory period normally starts to run on the day the crime was committed. The statute of limitations is established by state law. Two main reasons for having statutes of limitations are: it is unfair to have a criminal prosecution hanging over a person indefinitely; and permitting the prosecution to unduly delay a case interferes with the defense's ability to locate witnesses and produce relevant evidence.

Statutes of limitations exist for both criminal and civil matters. Most states have at least three different statutes of limitations in criminal cases: misdemeanors; felonies; and cases that can be filed at any time. Misdemeanors have the shortest statute of limitations, typically one to three years. Felonies have statutes that are longer, with three to six years being common. Some states set the statute of limitations in proportion to the maximum sentence for the crime. There is usually a group of crimes for which no statute of limitation applies. Murder is universally in this group. State laws vary, but embezzlement of public funds and malfeasance in elected office frequently have no statute of limitations. Each law enforcement officer should know the various statutes of limitations for crimes he/she will be required to investigate.

The statute of limitations may be stopped (referred to as "tolled") if the suspect leaves the state in order to avoid prosecution. Intentionally evading the police may also toll the statute. The result of **tolling the statute of limitations** is that the statute of limitations becomes longer. For example, if the suspect left the state for six months in order to avoid arrest on a crime with a three year statute of limitations, the charges could be filed up to three years and six months from the day the crime was committed.

The trend is to have longer statutes of limitations in cases involving sexual abuse of children. The statute may extend until the child becomes an adult. Recent cases in which victims have repressed memory of a crime are raising new issues. In a few states, the statute of limitations is tolled until the victim's memory of the event is restored.

How Many Charges to File

There are usually no limits on the number of charges that can be in a complaint as long as the court has jurisdiction, the statute of limitations has not run, and the offenses are related. Each charge is referred to as a **count**. The counts in the complaint do not have to match the charges for which the suspect was arrested. Crimes occurring in two different court districts cannot be combined in the same complaint.

Suspects are frequently arrested for more than one crime. Part of the charging decision involves determining how many charges to file and for what. Local custom also enters into the way charges are filed. In some cities, the prosecutor files all possible crimes. This is done even though convictions cannot be obtained on all of them due to **double jeopardy**. For example, separate counts would be listed in the complaint for robbery and theft even though the theft was a required part of the robbery; if the jury convicts on both, the theft (lesser included offense) would be dismissed by the judge because double jeopardy prohibits multiple punishments for the same criminal act.

Other courts may require that only the most serious count be listed in the complaint and the jury be instructed on all lesser included offenses. Using the above example, a robbery charge would be filed but the jury would be instructed that it can convict on either robbery or theft (the lesser included offense). If the jury misunderstands the instructions and convicts on both, the judge would dismiss the less serious offense.

Many offenses can be charged in various degrees; for example, first- and second-degree murder; simple and aggravated assault. The one with the shortest sentence is treated the same as a lesser included offense. Depending on local custom, the complaint will list either the most serious charge or all possible degrees of the crime. Charges cannot be refiled on a degree of the crime on which the jury acquitted the defendant, although a lesser degree may be filed if the jury considered that offense and could not reach a verdict on it. For example, if the jury acquits the defendant on first degree murder but is "hung" on second degree murder, the prosecutor can refile the second-degree murder charge. The same rule applies if the jury unanimously rejects the death penalty in a murder case but cannot reach a decision on what degree of murder was committed: the prosecution cannot seek the death penalty at a subsequent trial.

Complaints frequently contain allegations that the defendant committed several crimes. Most courts require a logical connection between the crimes listed in one complaint. This connection is usually established in one of two ways: the crimes were similar; or the crimes occurred in one transaction. Numerous burglaries believed to have been committed by the defendant within the court district can be charged in the same complaint. The fact the crime is the same (burglary) and the defendant is alleged to have committed all of them is a sufficient connection. Crimes committed during a "crime spree" are considered to be in the same transaction and are usually charged in the same complaint. Some states make it mandatory that crimes from one transaction be filed in the same complaint; failure to do so bars filing the remaining charges at a later time. Most court rules permit filing multiple counts even though some of the crimes are misdemeanors and the others felonies. Under these circumstances, the case would be processed through the court which handles felonies.

Defendants who are alleged to have committed a crime together are normally tried together. Combining the cases against two defendants is known as **joinder**. If the defendants were initially charged in one complaint but asked for and received separate trials, it is said the cases were **severed**. When one complaint is used to specify charges against more than one defendant, there must be separate counts so that each defendant knows exactly what crimes he/she is charged with. For example, Count I would charge John Jones with robbery; Count II would charge Bill Smith with the same robbery. Having one trial is more efficient, especially where the same evidence will be used against more than one defendant.

Occasionally, joining the cases for one trial is not possible because evidence that can be used against one defendant is not admissible against the other. A good example of this is a confession made by Defendant Jones that implicates Defendant Smith. The confession is admissible against Jones as long as *Miranda* was complied with. Smith, on the other hand, has a Sixth Amendment right to confront and cross-examine Jones. If Jones exercises the Fifth Amendment right not to testify, Smith's Sixth Amendment rights will be violated. One solution is separate trials. Another is to "sanitize" the confession (called **redacting the confession**) to eliminate references to Smith; this may not work if the references to Smith are so intertwined with the statements about Jones that the "sanitized" version does not make sense. A novel solution was utilized in the highly publicized Menendez case: the judge ordered separate juries for each defendant. If evidence was to be admitted against only one defendant, only the jury for that defendant was allowed in the courtroom while that evidence was introduced.

Another problem with joint trials arises if charges against one defendant do not apply to the other defendant. For example, several burglaries could normally be listed in one complaint, but this may not be permissible unless both defendants are alleged to have participated in every burglary charged. The legal question is whether one defendant would be prejudiced by evidence admitted against the other defendant. Trial judges use their discretion when deciding whether to sever the trials.

Encouraging **plea bargaining** is another reason for filing numerous charges. Negotiations between the prosecutor and defense attorneys usually precede a plea bargain. As with most negotiations, each side enters the process demanding more than he/she is willing to settle for. By filing additional charges, the prosecutor sets the stage for offering to drop some counts in exchange for a guilty plea. The same can be said for filing a more serious crime, such as felonious assault, and accepting a plea to misdemeanor assault. The prosecutor is usually aware of the judge's sentencing practices. If concurrent sentences are likely, the prosecutor may be able to drop several of the charges and still have the defendant receive the same sentence as if convictions were entered on all charges. The need to drop or lower charges while negotiating a guilty plea frequently leads to over-charging in the complaint in order to obtain what the prosecutor believes is an appropriate sentence for the defendant's criminal behavior. Plea bargaining is discussed in more detail in Section 7.2.

Many other factors enter into the decision to file charges. The prosecutor will review the reports and look for inadmissible evidence. The police are allowed to make decisions in the field on hearsay and other kinds of evidence that may not be admissible at trial. Evidence may have been obtained in violations of search and seizure rules, or a confession obtained without properly giving *Miranda* warnings.

The likelihood of obtaining a conviction is also important. A weak case may not merit the time it takes to prepare it for trial. Further investigation may be requested if it appears this would help correct problems in the case. Credibility of the witnesses is a crucial consideration. No matter how obvious it is to the police that the crime occurred, the case may be doomed if victims and/or witnesses lack credibility on the witness stand. The prosecutor will consider such things as: prior criminal histories of potential witnesses; ability of victim to identify defendant; level of certainty of victim and/or witnesses when reporting the crime; and inconsistent statements made by the victim and/or witnesses.

Unfortunately, many young children make poor witnesses because they are frequently unable to clearly distinguish between their imaginary world and reality. Children also complicate a case because they become confused easily during cross-examination. The number of times the child victim has been interviewed by police, Children's Protective Services, doctors and therapists adds to the problem because each interview makes it easier for the defense to allege that ideas were planted in the child's mind. For these reasons, many cases involving sexual abuse of young children are not filed.

5.4 Drafting and Filing the Complaint

The complaint is the legal document which states the charges against the suspect. It formally initiates the legal proceedings. Several items must be included in the complaint: name of the court; names of the plaintiff and defendant; and for each charge there must be the date it was committed, the location, and a description of the charge. Information must be available to establish each of these when the case is taken to the prosecutor for filing. Failure to include any of these items gives the defense the right to have the complaint dismissed. The prosecutor's staff will usually draft and type the complaint.

The formal name of the court is given in the heading of the complaint. It usually gives both the name of the state and the court. If the court has multiple branches, the one where the case was filed must be indicated. This information is usually in a centered caption near the top of the first page. The **plaintiff** is the person who files a lawsuit. In criminal cases, the plaintiff is the government. Depending on local custom, the complaint will be worded: People of the State of . . ., State of . . ., Commonwealth of . . ., etc. The **defendant** is defined as a person against whom a lawsuit is filed or an indictment has been returned. A criminal suspect is referred to in the complaint and subsequent legal papers as the defendant; he/she technically becomes a defendant when the complaint is filed with the court clerk.

Where possible, the full name of the defendant will be listed; complaints against a defendant with an alias frequently list all known aliases. If the defendant's name is not known or there is reason to

IN THE MUNICIPAL COURT OF THE STATE OF CALIFORNIA
LOS ANGELES MUNICIPAL COURT DISTRICT, HOLLYWOOD BRANCH

People of the State of California Plaintiff, vs. John E. Doe Defendant.	CRIMINAL COMPLAINT No. 123 456

believe that the name given is an alias, the case may be filed listing the defendant as John Doe or Jane Doe. An amended complaint may be filed later to correct the name. If there are multiple suspects, the full name of each will be listed. Defendants whose true names are known will be listed before those with only aliases or no known names. The case will frequently be called by the last name of the defendant in the case (first defendant, if there are multiple defendants): *People v. Jones, State v. Jones,* or *Commonwealth v. Jones*.

The date the crime occurred must be listed for each charge in order to show that the statute of limitations has not expired. For example, "on or about the third day of January 1995." This gives sufficient information to satisfy the statute of limitations. At the same time, it provides room for minor errors in that date — the complaint would still be valid if the crime occurred on January 2, 1995. More than a few day's discrepancy between the date listed and the one established at trial gives the defendant the right to have the charge dismissed for lack of notice as required by due process. The charges must be dismissed if the date established was after the statute of limitations had run even though due process was not violated.

A court's jurisdiction is geographical; therefore, the complaint must establish that the crime occurred within the boundaries of the court district. Listing the address is an easy way to satisfy this requirement. Other methods will be used in rural areas. Officers working in such areas must be aware of what information the prosecutor will need.

Each count must give sufficient information so the defendant knows what crime is charged. There are two ways to specify this information: fact pleading and code pleading. A combination of state law and local custom determines which method of pleading is used.

Fact pleading requires that a brief statement of the facts be given. Every element of the crimes must be shown by the facts stated. An example of fact pleading would be:

> COUNT I: JOHN JONES is hereby charged with burglary in the first degree in violation of Penal Code Section 460(a) because on or about June 12, 1995, he broke a window and entered a residence located at 1234 W. Main Street, Anytown, CA with the intent to steal a stereo.

Note that this count gives the name of the defendant, location and date of the crime. It then gives enough facts to establish first degree burglary: breaking; entering; dwelling; intent. Fact pleading is more difficult to draft because it must be worded to closely match the facts of each case. Due to the greater detail that must be given, it is easier for the defendant to find errors inadvertently made by the prosecutor.

Code pleading uses the language of the penal code to give notice of the charge. An example of code pleading for the above burglary would be:

> COUNT I: JOHN JONES is hereby charged with a felony to wit, Burglary in the First Degree, in violation of Section 460(a) of the California Penal Code in that on or about June 12, 1995, he entered a dwelling at 1234 W. Main St., Anytown, CA, with the intent to commit a felony or petty theft therein.

Although the above examples have only minor variations in wording, in complicated cases the differences between code pleading and fact pleading may be substantial. Code pleading enables the prosecutor to insert certain details, such as date, location, and offense charged, into a computerized word processor which uses standardized wording. There are fewer chances for careless errors resulting in dismissal of the charges. The defendant may request more information, usually by asking for a Bill of Particulars, if needed.

The prosecutor usually is required to sign and date the complaint. It is then taken to the court clerk's office where it is stamped "Filed" and the date it is filed is indicated. This delivery of the forms to the clerk is called **filing the complaint.**

5.5 Arraignment

The arraignment is a court hearing at which the defendant is informed of the charges against him/her. It must occur without unnecessary delay if the defendant is in custody. State laws take two approaches: state that the defendant must be taken before a judge without undue delay; or give a time period in which this must be accomplished, for example, within 48 hours.

Procedures at Arraignment

In most states the following occur at arraignment: the defendant is formally notified of the charges; appropriate inquiries are made to verify that the defendant's right to counsel is protected; the defendant enters a plea; and the next court date is set. Bail may be set if it has not already been established. The judge handling arraignments frequently hears a large number of cases each day. Detailed inquiries into the facts are not usually made during this court hearing.

The defendant has the right to be present at the arraignment although he/she can waive this right. Transporting inmates to court is time-consuming and presents a risk that inmates will escape. It is also expensive if the jail is not located near the courthouse. One solution to this problem is to have a courtroom located in the jail facility. A judge is assigned to this courtroom and prosecutors and defense attorneys are present. The inmate is present at the arraignment but does not go outside the jail.

Another alternative is conducting arraignments by two-way closed-circuit television. Television equipment is installed at the courthouse and a studio is constructed at a convenient location, usually inside the jail. The defendant and defense attorney will view the court proceedings from the studio. Simultaneously, the judge will view what is occurring at the studio. Audio communications will be maintained in both directions. Depending on local custom, the prosecutor will be located either at the studio or courtroom. The judge will conduct the arraignment in much the same manner as if the defendant were present in the courtroom. Documents can be FAXed back and forth as necessary.

A copy of the complaint serves as notice of the charges that have been filed. In some courts, the defendant receives a copy of the complaint and it is read aloud during the arraignment. It is more common, particularly if the defendant is represented by an attorney, to give the defendant a copy of the complaint and dispense with reading it aloud. Either procedure satisfies the due process requirement of notice of the charges. If the complaint is amended at a later time, the defendant will have to be given a copy and may need to be arraigned on the amended complaint.

The United States Supreme Court has interpreted the Sixth Amendment right to counsel to mean that a defendant in a criminal case has the right to have counsel from arraignment through first appeal. Any actions that might alter the outcome of the case during this time period cannot be done without an attorney present or waiver of that right by the defendant. Entering a plea is such an event. Therefore, the judge must verify that the defendant is represented by an attorney, or waives that right, prior to proceeding with the arraignment.

If the defendant attends the arraignment without an attorney, the judge must inquire into the reason for this. Arraignments may be postponed if the defendant wishes to hire an attorney but has not been able to do so. A defendant who wishes to act as his/her own attorney may do so as long as the decision is made voluntarily with knowledge that there is a right to an attorney. If the defendant wants an attorney, but cannot afford to hire one, the government must provide one in all cases in which the defendant is sentenced to time in jail or prison. The judge must find the answer to three questions in order to determine if an attorney must be appointed: does the defendant want an attorney? can the defendant afford to hire an attorney to handle the present case? and does the prosecution intend to seek a sentence that will include incarceration? If there is an affirmative answer to each of these questions a defense attorney must be appointed. A public defender is usually present at most arraignment courts to consult with indigent defendants so they can be arraigned without lengthy delays.

A plea is normally entered at the arraignment. Most cases require either "guilty" or "not guilty." ***"Nolo contendere"*** may be used in some cases; the effect is the same as a guilty plea in criminal cases but it does not admit guilt for the purpose of later civil cases. If the defense wishes to raise the insanity issue, pleas of "not guilty" ***and*** "not guilty by reason of insanity" are required. The defense may wish to wait to enter the "not guilty by reason of insanity" plea until after a psychiatrist has had an opportunity to examine the defendant. State law usually establishes how long the defense can delay this decision; some courts grant a **continuance** so the plea can be entered at an arraignment which will be held at a later date. Continuances are used to reschedule a wide variety of court hearings.

The Supreme Court requires that the defendant waive the following rights prior to entering a guilty plea: speedy trial, confront and cross-examine accusers, jury trial, and proof beyond a reasonable doubt. The record must show that the defendant voluntarily waived each of these rights. A waiver of counsel must also appear as part of the record if the defendant enters a guilty plea when not represented by an attorney. State law and local customs vary on procedures for accepting guilty pleas at arraignments. Many courts have preprinted forms listing all the required warnings. The judge will read the list and the defendant must respond to each. Even when there is a guilty plea the imposition of sentence may be delayed until a later date to allow time for the preparation of a Probation and Sentencing Report. Some courts will not accept a guilty plea to a felony unless the defendant has consulted with an attorney.

The arraignment is the best time to set the next court date because all necessary parties — judge, defendant, prosecutor and defense attorney — are present and can object if there is a conflict. For felonies, the next court date frequently is the preliminary hearing. Trial dates may be set in misdemeanor cases. Dates for other issues to be decided may also be established.

PROBABLE CAUSE HEARING

The Supreme Court, in *Gernstein v. Pugh* 420 U.S. 103, 43 L.Ed. 2d 541, 95 S.Ct. 854 (1975), states that a defendant who is held in custody pending trial has the right to a probable cause hearing. A judge reviews the facts of the case at this hearing to determine if there is probable cause to support the charges. Failure to establish probable cause for at least one charge results in the release of the defendant from custody; charges do not have to be dismissed.

A probable cause hearing is required only if requested by a defendant who is in custody. No probable cause hearing is necessary if a judge has already reviewed the facts when issuing an arrest warrant. The defendant does not have the right to be present and is not entitled to have an attorney present when the judge makes the determination of probable cause. Sworn statements may be used rather than calling witnesses to the hearing.

Several approaches have been used for the probable cause hearing. One is to make the procedure for filing a criminal complaint equivalent to that for obtaining an arrest warrant: a judge must review sworn affidavits and determine that there is probable cause. Another approach is to attach sworn statements to the complaint and have the judge review them at the arraignment. Waiting for the defendant to request the hearing also meets constitutional standards but is more disruptive of the court system. Officers must be familiar with how the probable cause hearing is handled in their area and be prepared to present the necessary information in an appropriate format.

SUMMARY

Once the arrest is made, many of the important decisions regarding the case will be made by the prosecutor. Prior to filing a criminal complaint, the prosecutor will review the case to determine what charges can be supported by the facts the police have obtained. Other factors that will be considered when determining what charges to file include: workload of prosecutor's office; congestion of court calendar; credibility of potential witnesses; possible inadmissibility of evidence at trial; and likelihood of obtaining a conviction.

The process for obtaining the complaint varies with local laws and customs. Either the arresting officer, a detective or court liaison officer will take the case to the prosecutor. In addition to verifying that the facts support the charges, the prosecutor will check the statute of limitations and make sure that the offense occurred within the geographical boundaries of the court district. Local practice will govern whether all possible offenses are filed or whether the highest charge is filed with lesser included offenses being included in the jury instructions. Multiple counts can usually be included in one complaint if there is a connection between the crimes. Sometimes the prosecutor will file multiple counts with the hope of inducing the defendant to plead guilty to at least one. A complaint may list more than one defendant if both participated in the same crimes.

The complaint must contain sufficient facts to establish the court's jurisdiction. At a minimum, this includes the name of the court, defendant's name (if known), date the crime occurred, location, and what code section was allegedly violated. Some states give little more information than this and rely on other documents, such as the police report, to give detailed information. Fact pleading, which requires the complaint to give more information about how the offense was committed, is used in other states.

The complaint is taken to the court clerk's office and filed. After this point, the suspect is referred to as the defendant. The arraignment is held to officially notify the defendant of the charges. Several things are usually accomplished at the arraignment: the defendant receives a copy of the complaint and is thereby given notice of the charges; when the defendant is not represented by an attorney, the judge determines if a public defender should be appointed; a plea is entered; bail is set; and the next court date is set.

A probable cause hearing is necessary in warrantless arrest cases if a defendant who is in custody requests one. At this hearing, a judge reviews affidavits containing the facts and determines whether there is probable cause to support the charges. Neither the defendant nor defense attorney needs to be present at this hearing. If probable cause is not established, the defendant must be released from custody but the charges do not have to be dismissed. Some states design the arraignment so that it includes a probable cause hearing.

Study Questions

1. Describe the role of the prosecutor as the gatekeeper of the criminal court system.

2. How does the police department in the city where you live interact with the prosecutor's office for:
   a. filing felony charges?
   b. filing misdemeanor charges?

3. How are traffic tickets written by your local police department filed with the court? If your city uses the "cite out" method for non-traffic offenses, describe how the citations are processed by the police and prosecutor at the filing stage of the case.

4. Select a case in which charges were filed that received extensive coverage in your local news media:
   a. What was the suspect arrested for?
   b. What charges did the prosecutor file?
   c. What do you think influenced the prosecutor to file these charges?
   d. What additional charges could have been filed?

5. Obtain a copy of a criminal complaint for a crime which occurred in your city:
   a. How are the plaintiff and defendant identified?
   b. Identify facts that establish the court's jurisdiction and facts that show the statute of limitations has not run.
   c. Does your court use code pleading or fact pleading?
   d. Did the prosecutor file both the greater and lesser included offenses?
   e. If there were multiple defendants committing the same crime, will they be tried jointly or were their cases severed?

6. Draft a complaint for a case you selected out of a recent newspaper account of a crime.

7. Check with your local court and determine:
   a. name of the court where arraignments are held for crimes committed in the city where you live.
   b. address where arraignments are held.
   c. Are arraignments held in the courthouse, a special courtroom in jail, or some other facility?
   d. When are arraignments held?

8. How soon after arrest must the arraignment be held in your state?

9. Go to court and watch an arraignment court in action. Explain:
   a. how defendants are notified of charges
   b. the process for determining if the public defender will represent the defendant
   c. entry of pleas in felony and misdemeanor cases
   d. what future court hearings are scheduled at the arraignment
   e. average time to arraign a case on the day you observed court
10. Describe how probable cause hearings are handled in your local court.

Chapter 6

Indictments and Preliminary Hearings

Learning Objectives

After reading this chapter, the student will be able to:

- Explain the defendant's right to be represented by an attorney from arraignment through preliminary hearing and grand jury proceedings.
- List the factors considered when the prosecutor decides between using a preliminary hearing or taking the case to the grand jury.
- Identify the rights of the press and public to be present at preliminary hearings.
- Describe what occurs at a preliminary hearing.
- Explain the function of the grand jury in criminal cases.
- Describe the process used by the grand jury when an indictment is sought.
- Explain what occurs at the arraignment that occurs after the preliminary hearing or indictment.

KEY TERMS

access of press to preliminary hearing
  First Amendment
  Sixth Amendment
arraignment on indictment or information
chain of custody (chain of possession)
  contemporaneous objection rule
dismissed with prejudice
grand jury
  number of grand jurors
  number of votes to indict
held to answer
indictment
information
leading questions
no bill
preliminary hearing
right to counsel
  free counsel for poor
  under *Miranda*
  under Sixth Amendment
serve a *subpoena*
subpoena
true bill

6.1 DEFENDANT'S RIGHT TO COUNSEL

The defendant's right to counsel begins at the arraignment on the criminal complaint and applies to all court proceedings thereafter. A defendant may waive this right as long as this is done voluntarily after being informed of the right to counsel. The Supreme Court has interpreted the Sixth Amendment to mean that defendants who cannot afford to hire an attorney have the right to have one appointed to represent them at government expense from arraignment until the first appeal is completed. This right to free counsel is limited to cases in which the defendant is sentenced to serve time in jail or prison.

In addition to court appearances, the right to counsel applies to all questioning by government agents regarding the charges. This covers police officers as well as informants whom the police use to obtain information from the defendant. All questioning that occurs after the arraignment must comply with this rule *whether or not* the defendant is in custody at the time. The defendant may agree to talk to the officers, but such statements may be taken only after obtaining a waiver of the right to counsel. *Miranda* warnings may be used to obtain a valid waiver.

The case is more complicated if the defendant invoked the right to counsel after being given *Miranda* warnings at an interrogation session after being arrested. Under these circumstances, the right to counsel can only be waived *with an attorney present*. This right to counsel, which is part of *Miranda*, is broader than the Sixth Amendment right to counsel: it applies to subsequent custodial interrogation even if the questions relate to different crimes. The police are expected to establish a system so that all officers know that *Miranda* has been invoked; it is not a defense that an officer did not know about the defendant's invocation of *Miranda*. Fortunately, *Miranda* only applies to custodial interrogation: if the defendant has been released from custody this rule no longer applies.

These rulings regarding the right to counsel during interrogation are summarized in Table 6.1.

6.2 Choice of Preliminary Hearing or Indictment

Felony charges must be reviewed by an independent source before the case can proceed to trial. This evaluation is done by either a judge at a preliminary hearing or the grand jury. The prosecutor's decision to file misdemeanor charges is ordinarily not subject to this type of review. Both law and local customs affect the decision to take the case to the grand jury or proceed by preliminary hearing.

The Fifth Amendment begins:

> "No person shall be held to answer for a capital, or otherwise infamous crime, unless on a presentment or indictment of a Grand Jury, except in cases arising in the land or naval forces, or in the Militia, when in actual service in time of War or public danger; . . ."

The Supreme Court held that this right to have a case taken before a grand jury only applies to criminal charges filed by the federal government. States are free to pass laws providing for preliminary hearings instead of mandating grand jury proceedings.

Some states have laws that require every felony case to be presented to a grand jury. Even among these states there are variations

Comparison of *Miranda* and Sixth Amendment Right to Counsel

Questioning before arraignment

Suspect *not* in custody	• *Miranda* not required • Suspect can have an attorney present if he/she pays for it
Suspect in custody Suspect must be given *Miranda* warnings if:	
1. Suspect asks for attorney	• Questioning can continue *only with* if attorney present when waiver made • Waiver valid *only if* attorney present when waiver made • Applies to questions about any crime by any police officer
2. Suspect does not ask for an attorney	• Questioning can continue if suspect waives *Miranda* rights • Do not need an attorney present when suspect waives rights

Questioning after arraignment

Suspect in custody	• *Miranda* applies; see above
Suspect *not* in custody	• *Miranda* does not apply • Sixth Amendment right to counsel applies • Must have waiver of right to counsel • Only applies to questioning about crimes suspect has been arraigned on • *Miranda* warnings can be used to obtain waiver

Table 6.1

in procedures. For example, some require that the grand jury indict on at least one charge but permit prosecution on other crimes listed in the complaint even though the grand jury did not hear evidence on these counts; others require counts to be dismissed if the grand jury does not return an indictment on them.

The more common procedure is to allow the prosecutor to decide whether to take the case to the grand jury or hold a preliminary hearing. A variety of factors will influence this decision. One is privacy of the proceedings. Preliminary hearings must be open to the press and the public unless there is a specific showing of trauma to a witness. Grand jury proceedings are held behind closed doors. Two types of cases are frequently taken to the grand jury because of this confidentiality: crimes in which the suspect has not been apprehended and there is reason to fear flight to avoid prosecution if the suspect learns charges are being sought; and situations where public review of the evidence would cause irreparable harm to the suspect's reputation even though the charges are rejected. Major drug smuggling rings are examples of the former situation; a child molestation case exemplifies the latter. Charges against local elected officials are frequently handled by the grand jury.

Speed is another consideration. Depending on local practice, a case may be processed by the grand jury much faster than in the court proceeding required for the preliminary hearing. Grand jury proceedings are usually faster because there is no cross-examination nor is there an opportunity for the defense to call witnesses. Some states permit indictment if only one charge is established but require proof of each charge at a preliminary hearing. Where this is true, the grand jury is much faster.

A few states permit a defendant to request a preliminary hearing even though the grand jury has heard the case. This is done to compensate for the fact that grand jury proceedings do not allow the defendant the right to present a defense. Having both a preliminary hearing and taking the case before the grand jury slows the proceedings and creates extra work for the prosecutor; therefore, the grand jury is seldom used in these states.

The main differences between grand jury proceedings and preliminary hearings are presented in Table 6.2. Procedural differences that have not been discussed in this section will be covered in Section 6.7.

Comparison of Grand Jury Proceedings and Preliminary Hearing

Grand Jury Proceedings	Preliminary Hearing
Held in private—press and public not allowed	Held in open court — press and public have right to be present
Decision to indict made by group of citizens	Decision to allow case to go to trial made by judge
Defendant does *not* have right to be present	Defendant has right to be present
Defendant can be required to testify but may invoke Fifth Amendment to specific questions	Defendant has right to refuse to testify
Defense attorney *not* present when defendant testifies or at any other time	Defense attorney present during entire proceeding
No cross examination of witnesses	All witnesses are subject to cross examination
Defense *not* allowed to present evidence	Defense may present evidence
Some states require indictment on only one charge in complaint	Usually must establish every felony in complaint
Exclusionary rule does *not* apply	Exclusionary rule applies
Prosecution has no duty to present evidence that may exonerate defendant	Defense has right to discovery for any evidence prosecutor has that would exonerate defendant
Can be held prior to arrest without notice to the suspect	Can only be held after suspect arrested and arraigned

Table 6.2

6.3 Rights of Public and Press to Be Present

The First Amendment and Sixth Amendment both apply to criminal proceedings. Freedom of the press, a First Amendment right, is used to justify media access to court proceedings. The Sixth Amendment specifically guarantees the defendant's right to a "public trial" in criminal cases. Another Sixth Amendment right, an impartial jury, can be impaired by prejudicial press coverage.

The Supreme Court has used the historical function of the grand jury as a basis for permitting some practices that otherwise conflict with modern procedures. Media access to the grand jury is one of these. Since its inception in English common law, the grand jury has heard evidence in secret. Only in relatively recent times has the defense even had access to transcripts of what occurred. There is no duty to inform the press that an indictment is being sought. The media has access to what occurred in a grand jury proceeding in three ways: reporters may wait outside and observe witnesses who are leaving; in some jurisdiction they may ask witnesses about their testimony; and if transcripts are unsealed, the press may report on what is contained in them.

Preliminary hearings have been treated much like trials as far the First and Sixth Amendments are concerned. The basic rule is that they must be held in open court. Even though the Sixth Amendment refers to the defendant's right to a public trial, a law permitting the defendant to have the press excluded was declared unconstitutional. The media may report on anything that occurs in open court.

A limited restriction on holding preliminary hearings in open court applies if it is established that testifying in public would cause severe psychological damage to a child witness. Even in these types of cases, the Supreme Court has required a case-by-case showing of potential injury to the child: broad rules that close the proceedings whenever a victim of child molestation testifies have been held unconstitutional.

Within these guidelines, the judge may close the courtroom in some instances. Witnesses, except the defendant, may be excluded except when testifying. This is done to prevent witnesses from altering their testimony because of what has already been said. The judge can clear the courtroom of unruly and/or boisterous people. Even the defendant may be excluded for disruptive behavior.

Occasionally, legal arguments pertaining to the admissibility of evidence can be heard without the press or public present. A good example is a defense motion to suppress the defendant's confession because *Miranda* warnings were not given correctly. The judge may close the courtroom while the issue is being discussed if press coverage about the inadmissible confession is likely to result in extremely prejudicial publicity. The key to the judge's decision is whether there is a strong likelihood that the publicity will so inflame public opinion that it will interfere with the defendant's right to have impartial jurors. Once the evidentiary ruling has been made, the courtroom must again be opened to the public and media.

6.4 Preliminary Hearing

Most states hold the preliminary hearing in the same level court where arraignments occurred (municipal court, justice court, city court, etc.). It will be in the court district for the location where the crime occurred. Typically this means the arraignment and preliminary hearing will be held in the same courthouse; if the defendant was arrested on a warrant while in another city, this may not be true.

The timing for the preliminary hearing is set by state law. Ten days to two weeks is usually the maximum time allowed between arraignment and preliminary hearing when the defendant is in custody. A longer delay may be allowed if the defendant is not in custody. The statutory deadline must be carefully considered when scheduling the preliminary hearing, but the defense can waive this limit by requesting a later date.

A judge or magistrate will preside over the preliminary hearing. The court administrator will estimate the number of judicial days each month that must be devoted to preliminary hearings. This will take into consideration the average number of cases and the usual length of preliminary hearings. In busy court districts, several judges may do nothing but handle preliminary hearings. They may remain in this assignment for six months, one year or more. Some districts have all judges assigned to criminal cases hold preliminary hearings on one or two days a week rather than making it a permanent assignment. Courts with a lower volume of preliminary hearings usually have one judge who hears preliminary hearings on specific days of the week.

The date for the preliminary hearing is usually set at the arraignment. After the arraignment, the prosecutor reviews the case and decides which witnesses to call and what, if any, physical evidence to introduce. Witnesses are usually subpoenaed to appear at the preliminary hearing. A **subpoena** is a court document ordering a person to appear to testify at a specified date and time. Failure to appear can be charged as contempt of court. While victims and witnesses may say they will cooperate, subpoenaing them gives the court the power to compel their testimony if they change their minds. Many prosecutors even subpoena police officers; this is done more as a formal reminder of the court date than as a threat of contempt of court. The prosecutor's office prepares the subpoenas, sometimes after consultation with the officers to determine which witnesses will be needed. It may not be necessary to use all potential witnesses at the preliminary hearing because the burden of proof is lower than it will be at trial.

Police officers usually **serve the subpoena** on the witness. Serving a subpoena means delivering it to the person; state law may require that this be done in person or may allow it to be left with any adult at the residence. The officers are also responsible for checking necessary items out of the evidence locker and bringing them to court at the appropriate time. Subpoenas and requirements for serving them are discussed in more detail in Chapter 8.

Court personnel present for the preliminary hearing usually include: judge, bailiff, clerk, and in many jurisdictions a stenographic reporter. The defendant will be present and usually sits at the counsel table with his/her attorney. The prosecutor will be at the other counsel table. Frequently, the officer in charge of the investigation will sit beside the prosecutor. If the defendant is in custody, a bailiff or custodial officer will be responsible for transporting him/her to and from the courtroom and preventing escape. There is no jury; occasionally the jury box will be used for seating witnesses waiting to testify. Spectators are permitted in the courtroom, but frequently there are few except for immediate family of the defendant. The media are also permitted; local court rules regulate where they will be seated and what camera equipment may be used while court is in session. In high profile cases, the court may limit the number of reporters that can attend at one time and establish a system for determining which ones will be excluded.

A bailiff usually calls the court to order immediately prior to the entry of the judge from his/her chambers (the judge's office). The name of the first case will be read and the attorneys will state their names for the record. The fact that the defendant is present is usually stated orally so that it can be included in the transcript. The complaint is usually read aloud. Opening statements are not made because there is no jury. It is assumed the judge can follow the case as it is presented.

The prosecution presents evidence first because it has the burden of proof: it must establish probable cause (sometimes called a *prima facie* case) that the defendant committed each felony listed in the complaint. All evidence must be presented through testimony of sworn witnesses. The prosecutor does this by calling witnesses and asking questions. An item of physical evidence is admitted into evidence only after a sworn witness identifies it. The rules of evidence used at trial normally apply to preliminary hearings although some states have modified the hearsay rule, best evidence rule and occasionally other rules, to expedite preliminary hearings.

Part of the prosecutor's preparation includes deciding which witnesses to call, in what order to call them, and what questions to ask. Sometimes the prosecutor comes to court with a written list of questions; other prosecutors use notes but phrase the questions more extemporaneously. The case can never be totally scripted in advance because witnesses sometimes give unexpected answers or have memory lapses. Every prosecutor has to be ready to ask appropriate questions in these circumstances; sometimes this will require quick action to subpoena another witness.

The prosecutor usually calls each witness by stating his/her name aloud. The witness comes forward, is seated in the witness stand, and takes the oath to tell the truth. The clerk may ask the witness to spell his/her full name so the record will be accurate. The witness may be required to give a home address and occupation. Questioning usually begins with background information necessary to set the scene. Facts are established to place the witness at the necessary location where relevant observations were made. This is usually done with pointed questions such as, "Where were you at 9:30 p.m. on July 5, 1995?" The questions that follow are usually specific, asking for as complete detail as possible. Wording is important: leading questions cannot be asked at this stage. **Leading questions** are questions that imply the correct answer. For example, "You saw a gun in the defendant's hand, didn't you?" They are reserved for cross-examinations and a few other special situations. Other restrictions on the types of questions that are impermissible include: two questions in one statement ("Did you see him hit the man and shoot the lady?"); questions calling for speculation ("Why do you think he did that?"); questions assuming facts that have not been introduced into evidence yet; repeating questions that have already been answered; and argumentative questions.

The defense attorney may object to any question asked by the prosecutor. The **contemporaneous objection rule** applies: the objection must be made at the time the question is asked. Witnesses are frequently instructed to pause briefly before answering each question to permit objections to be made. If an objection is made, the judge will ask the grounds for the objection. Some legal rule, usually a rule of evidence such as the Hearsay Rule, will be given. The person who asked the question is then allowed to give a reason the question should be allowed. After hearing both sides, the judge will make a ruling: objection sustained, which means the witness should not answer the question in its present form; or objection overruled, which means the witness should answer. If the objection is obviously correct, the judge may grant it without permitting discussion from the other side. Many times a skillful attorney can reword a question in a manner that avoids the technicality which caused the objection to be sustained; if so, the evidence will still be introduced. For example, the following dialog might occur in a drunk driving case:

PROSECUTOR: Where were you at 9:30 p.m. on July 5, 1995?

WITNESS: I was on duty as an ambulance attendant. We were called to the scene of a traffic accident at First and Flower.

PROSECUTOR: Did you see the defendant at that location?

WITNESS: Yes.

PROSECUTOR: Did he appear to be intoxicated?

DEFENSE: Objection, your honor.

JUDGE: On what grounds?

DEFENSE: Calls for an opinion by the witness.

PROSECUTOR: Your honor, I am asking for what the witness observed.

JUDGE: Objection sustained.

PROSECUTOR: How close did you get to the defendant?

WITNESS: About three feet.

PROSECUTOR: Did you notice any odors?

WITNESS: Yes.

PROSECUTOR: What odors did you notice?

WITNESS: Alcohol.

PROSECUTOR: Was the defendant able to walk?

WITNESS: He staggered and then fell down.

PROSECUTOR: Did you observe the defendant's eyes?

WITNESS: Yes. They were watery and bloodshot.

PROSECUTOR: Did you hear the defendant speak?

WITNESS: Yes. His speech was slurred.

By careful questioning, the prosecutor established that the witness smelled alcohol, saw the defendant stagger, observed the defendant had watery bloodshot eyes and slurred speech: taken together, the statements allowed the jury to conclude the defendant was drunk even though the witness was not allowed to give an opinion on the issue.

Testimony must establish that physical evidence is relevant to the case, identify the item as the one seized during the investigation of the case, and account for what has happened to the item since it was seized. This is called the **chain of custody** or **chain of possession**. The purpose is to make sure that the item has not been tampered with. The defense can object if any of these facts have not been established by testimony.

PROSECUTOR: Officer Smith, was a weapon recovered at the scene?

OFFICER SMITH: Yes.

PROSECUTOR: What weapon was recovered?

OFFICER SMITH: A knife.

PROSECUTOR: Where did you find the knife?

DEFENSE ATTORNEY: Objection, your honor, assumes facts not in evidence.

JUDGE: Objection sustained.

PROSECUTOR: Who found the knife?

OFFICER SMITH: I did.

PROSECUTION: Where did you find the knife?

OFFICER SMITH: It was in the suspect's pocket.

PROSECUTOR: Please describe that knife.

OFFICER SMITH: It was a switchblade knife with a six inch blade and a white bone handle.

PROSECUTOR: What did you do with the knife after you located it?

OFFICER SMITH: I marked my initials on the base of the handle, attached an evidence tag with pertinent information, and put it in a brown 9" x 12" envelope on which I wrote the case number. I then sealed it and wrote my name over the seal.

PROSECUTOR: What did you do with the envelope?

OFFICER SMITH: I placed it in the evidence locker at the police station.

PROSECUTION: Is this the envelope.

OFFICER SMITH: Yes. It has my signature on the unbroken seal.

PROSECUTOR: Please open the envelope. Can you identify the knife in the envelope as the one you found at the crime scene on the night of July 5, 1995?

OFFICER SMITH: Yes. If you look right here at the base of the handle you will see my initials, ABS.

PROSECUTOR: Your honor, please admit the knife into evidence as People's Exhibit Number 1.

JUDGE: Defense counsel, do you have any objections?

DEFENSE ATTORNEY: No, your honor.

JUDGE: The knife is admitted as People's Exhibit Number 1.

Sometimes, it may require more than one witness to establish all of these facts. For example, if a patrol officer found a gun at the crime scene and the gun was sent to a ballistic laboratory for comparison with bullets taken from the victim, testimony of both the patrol officer and the person conducting the tests would be needed.

When the prosecution has presented all of its evidence, it will rest its case. A motion to dismiss the charges is typically made by the defense attorney at this point based on an argument that the prosecution has failed to establish all the elements of the crime or that there is not enough credible evidence to establish probable cause to believe that the defendant committed the crime(s). If the judge denies the motion, the defense then has the opportunity to present evidence. Witnesses may be called and items of physical evidence introduced. Many times, however, the defense does not present any evidence at the preliminary hearing. This is a tactical decision, usually made when it appears certain that the judge will rule that there is ample evidence to hold the defendant for trial. Rather than disclose the defense's case to the prosecution this early in the case, the defense uses cross-examination of the prosecution's witnesses as its main tool at the preliminary hearing.

After the defense completes its case, the judge will make a ruling on whether or not there has been sufficient evidence presented to warrant taking the case to trial. The judge usually makes an oral declaration before the parties leave the courtroom. If the judge finds the evidence is sufficient the defendant will be **held to answer** on the charges. The judge must also sign a declaration, the working of which is usually established by state law. For example:

> It appearing to me that the offense in the within complaint mentioned has been committed, and that there is sufficient cause to believe that the within named Jane Smith is guilty, I order that she be held to answer to the same.

If there were multiple charges, a separate ruling and declaration will be needed for each count. Charges for which the judge did not find probable cause will be dismissed. Some counts may be dismissed while the defendant is held to answer on others.

The judge must also sign a declaration if the defendant is not held to answer. For example:

> There being no sufficient cause to believe the within named Jane Smith guilty of the offense within mentioned, I order that the complaint be dismissed and that she shall be discharged.

Dismissal of a charge at this stage does not give the defendant double jeopardy protection against the charges being refiled. State law may allow the judge to indicate whether charges can be refiled: charges that are **dismissed with prejudice** cannot be refiled; other charges can be refiled if the prosecution believes it can establish the case at another preliminary hearing. If the prosecution was unable to establish the case due to unavoidable circumstances, such as sudden illness of a key witness, the judge will usually allow the case to be refiled. Any refiling of the charges must be within the statute of limitations.

6.5 Filing the Information

If the judge holds the defendant to answer on the charge(s), the prosecution must complete additional paperwork. An information must be drafted. The **information** is a formal document which states the charges against the defendant and contains acknowledgement that the judge found probable cause to proceed on the charges. The format and content requirements are very similar to that of the complaint: the name of the court must be included; geographical jurisdiction established; facts must show the statute of limitations has not run; and the specific charges stated.

In many jurisdictions, the prosecutor has the discretion to drop charges at this point by not including them in the information even though the judge held the defendant to answer. This decision may be based on the strength of the testimony of key witnesses at the preliminary hearing, inability to locate potential witnesses, or other factors that make the prosecutor believe proceeding on a charge is not merited at this point. Since misdemeanor charges do not have to be presented to the judge at the preliminary hearing, the prosecutor can usually add misdemeanor charges to the information that were not previously considered.

6.6 Obtaining an Indictment

An **indictment** is returned by a grand jury after investigating a case brought to it by a prosecutor. An indictment is a formal charging document which will be filed with the court. If the grand jury investigates the case on its own accord, a document called a presentment will be prepared. In some states, the presentment merely asks the prosecutor to investigate the case, possibly including bringing the case back to the grand jury at a later time for an indictment; in other states, it is filed with the court and serves to initiate criminal charges against the defendant.

Historically, the grand jury protected citizens from malicious prosecution by the government: felony charges could be filed against a person only if the grand jury held that they were warranted. Apparently the grand jury also served as a trial jury during its earliest history, but this function is not considered part of our common law. The role of the grand jury in protecting citizens from government resulted in rules which made grand jury proceedings secret. The secrecy was to protect the grand jurors, not the persons being investigated for criminal conduct. Most jurisdictions still regard grand jury proceedings as secret, some to the extent that even after indictment the defendant does not have the right to receive a copy of the minutes of the grand jury or a transcript of testimony presented. Some states even prohibit individuals who appear before the grand jury as witnesses to disclose what they were asked or testified about.

The Supreme Court has held that the Fifth Amendment right to a grand jury only applies to federal felonies. The states have been free to enact their own laws regulating grand juries. This section will present general rules on grand jury proceedings, but each student should investigate his/her state's laws on the issues because there is substantial variation across the nation.

Grand juries are normally appointed by the court of general jurisdiction of the county and must represent the demographics of the population. A grand jury usually serves for a term. This will coincide with the court's term, if the court divides its time this way. Many states provide that the grand jury serves for one year or eighteen months. Some states permit more than one grand jury to be empaneled at the same time. The grand jury has jurisdiction to hear cases where the crime was committed within the court's jurisdiction. If a hearing is being held on a case when the term expires, the grand jury is usually empowered to continue until the case is complete.

The method of selecting grand jurors must not discriminate on the basis of race, gender, religion, or political affiliation. A defendant can challenge the indictment if the selection process is discriminatory even though he/she is not a member of a group discriminated against. The challenge is to the selection process, not the composition of a single grand jury. For example, a white male could challenge the grand jury if Hispanics were systematically excluded from grand juries for the last ten years, but not based on the fact that there were no Hispanics on the grand jury that indicted him.

Grand jurors do not have to be selected in the same manner as trial juries. Some states use a sponsor system, whereby judges or other officials provide names for a list of individuals to serve on the grand jury. Names are drawn from this list to make the grand jury. A person is usually disqualified for grand jury duty if he/she is not a citizen, cannot speak English, or is currently serving as a trial juror. Economic hardship caused by missing work for extensive service on the grand jury is usually grounds for exemption. There is usually no process whereby a defendant can remove individual grand jurors for personal prejudice or by peremptory challenge.

At common law, a grand jury consisted of 23 people and a positive vote of 12 was required to indict. Many states still use these numbers. Those that do not typically require a vote of one more than half of the grand jurors in order to indict. The combination of the majority vote and the lengthy term served by grand jurors has led to rules that permit indictment even though not all members were present to hear the evidence: a majority of the grand jurors must have heard all of the evidence and statutory minimum must vote to indict. For example, if only 20 of the 23 grand jurors heard the evidence of Jane Smith's guilt, the indictment would still be valid as long as 12 members who heard all the evidence voted for the indictment.

All states empower grand juries to hear felony cases brought to them by the prosecutor. Unlike trial jurors, grand jurors are usually allowed to consider facts in their personal knowledge when making decisions. Some states authorize grand juries to initiate criminal investigations on their own and return indictments. Government corruption is frequently an area the grand jury is authorized to investigate without the prosecutor's cooperation. Some states provide investigators and legal counsel to assist the grand jury; others prohibit these forms of assistance.

Grand juries frequently are also required to make a variety of reports on government functions. They may tour all custodial facilities and report on their conditions. Some states go so far as asking the grand jury to make recommendations for improving the efficiency of local government.

The judge may charge the grand jury with investigating a specific crime but in most cases the prosecutor presents the case to the grand jury. An experienced prosecutor will have prepared the case by making a list of potential witnesses and questions to be asked. Relevant physical evidence will be ready for presentation. Taking testimony by the grand jury is usually less formal than in court. Most of the rules of evidence do not apply but confidential and privileged communications cannot be obtained. Grand jurors are usually allowed to ask questions and request that additional witnesses be subpoenaed. The exclusionary rule does not apply: the grand jury can base its decision on evidence seized in violation of the Fourth Amendment. A person who has been summoned does not have to be told what crime is being investigated or who is suspected of criminal wrongdoing. Refusal of a subpoenaed witness to testify, except when invoking the self-incrimination clause of the Fifth Amendment, is grounds for holding the witness in contempt of court and can result in incarceration for the remainder of the grand jury's term.

The defendant's rights are vastly different before a grand jury than when a preliminary hearing is held. See Table 6.2. The defendant does not have to be told that he/she is the focus of a grand jury investigation. Neither does the defendant have the right to cross-examine witnesses nor present evidence to exonerate him/herself. Unsolicited attempts to communicate such information to the grand jury are considered contempt of court, and in some states can also be charged as misdemeanors. If the grand jury decides to call the defendant to testify, most states do not give him/her the right to refuse to testify but, the Fifth Amendment can be invoked as grounds to refuse to answer specific questions. A common practice is to allow the defense attorney to wait in the hallway and consult with the defendant when the defendant so requests. This works to the disadvantage of the defendant who does not know his/her rights well enough to anticipate when legal advice is needed prior to answering a question.

The length of time a grand jury devotes to one case varies enormously. Sometimes the prosecutor can present a fairly simple case in less than an hour. Complicated cases take longer. Sometimes a grand jury may hear evidence for several months. Unlike a trial jury, which ordinarily meets daily or at least four days a week, a grand jury may devote only one day a week, or sporadic meetings, to the investigation.

A vote will be taken after all the evidence has been heard. Some states use the prima facie case standard for grand jury proceedings.

Others ask the grand jurors to consider whether all the evidence before them, if unexplained or uncontradicted, would warrant a conviction. State law specifies how many grand jurors must agree in order to indict: it is usually a simple majority or slightly more. If the requisite number of grand jurors vote to indict, the indictment will be endorsed a **"true bill"** and must be signed by the foreman. A variety of terms is used to endorse an indictment if there are insufficient votes to indict: ignoramus (Latin for "we are ignorant" of the facts); **"no bill,"** and "not a true bill." Most states make the failure of a grand jury to indict a bar to seeking an indictment on the charges against the same suspect in the future.

The indictment serves as an arrest warrant for the defendant if he/she was not in custody at the time of the indictment. Sometimes law enforcement is poised to act as soon as the indictment is returned in order to prevent the suspects from fleeing the state to avoid prosecution. In some cases, the defense attorney will make arrangements for the suspect to appear for arraignment on the indictment without being arrested.

6.7 Arraignment on Indictment or Information

An arraignment is held on the information, presentment or indictment. The rights afforded the defendant at the arraignment on the complaint apply: the defendant has the right to be present and represented by an attorney; the charges will be read or a copy of the formal pleading entered into the record and given to the defendant; a plea will be entered; future court dates will be set; and a bail hearing will be incorporated into the proceedings if necessary.

This arraignment has legal significance for several reasons. In states with a two-tier court system for felonies and misdemeanors, the original arraignment is usually held in the lower court but the arraignment on the indictment or information will be at the higher court. This second arraignment is necessary to establish the jurisdiction of the higher court. The charges filed originally may be different from those that will be brought to trial. Providing the defense with a copy of the indictment or information fulfills the due process notice requirement. Some cases are presented to the grand jury before the defendant is arrested so there has been no previous arraignment. Due process mandates the arraignment on the indictment under these circumstances.

Summary

The defendant has the right to be represented by an attorney at all proceedings from the arraignment through the first appeal. Law enforcement officers are not allowed to question the defendant after arraignment without a waiver of this right to counsel.

All felonies tried under federal law must be taken to the grand jury. State legislatures have the option of authorizing proceeding by preliminary hearing or indictment. The need of secrecy prior to arresting the suspect, as well as the amount of time required for a preliminary hearing versus an indictment, are considerations for the prosecutor when deciding which avenue to pursue.

The defendant has the right to a public hearing. Even if the defendant wishes to waive this right, the press have the right to attend preliminary hearings. The judge may close the preliminary hearing during the testimony of a child victim if testifying before the public would cause severe emotional trauma. Grand jury proceedings are held in secret and the press has no constitutional right to attend. Some states also prohibit grand jury witnesses from discussing their testimony with the press.

The preliminary hearing proceeds much like a trial except that there is no jury and usually no opening or closing statements. A judge hears the case. The prosecution has the burden of proving that there is probable cause to take the case to trial. Witnesses will be called, questioned and cross-examined much like at trial. Some rules of evidence may be modified to expedite the preliminary hearing. The defense has the right to present evidence, including testimony of the defendant. At the end of the preliminary hearing, the judge will determine if sufficient evidence has been presented on the charges. If so, the defendant will be held to answer. The prosecutor will draft an information stating the charges.

Grand juries have traditionally been considered a protection against government harassment. Their proceedings are held in secret to protect the grand jurors from outside pressures. Today, the prosecutor prepares most cases for the grand jury although the right of jurors to conduct independent investigations still exists. Many of the constitutional rights afforded the defendant at the preliminary hearing and trial do not apply to grand jury proceedings. Statutes establish how many grand jurors must vote for the indictment. If sufficient votes are obtained, the indictment is endorsed a "true bill." Warrants will be issued if no one is in custody on the charges and arrests made where possible.

The defendant must be arraigned on the indictment or information. This establishes jurisdiction of the court which will try the case. It also complies with due process notice requirements by informing the defendant of the charges against him/her and when the trial is scheduled.

Study Questions

1. Explain the defendant's right to counsel after indictment:
   a. if defendant is in custody and previously invoked *Miranda* right to counsel
   b. if defendant is in custody and has NOT previously invoked *Miranda* right to counsel
   c. if defendant is not in custody
2. Explain when it is mandatory to take a criminal case to a grand jury:
   a. charges filed in federal court
   b. charges filed in state where you live
3. List 10 ways grand jury proceedings differ from a preliminary hearing.
4. How soon after arraignment must a preliminary hearing be held in your state:
   a. if the defendant remains in jail?
   b. if the defendant has been released from jail?
5. At a preliminary hearing:
   a. who has the burden of proof?
   b. what level of proof is required?

c. who has the right to subpoena witnesses?
d. who has the right to present evidence?

6. Determine the following facts about preliminary hearings for crimes committed in the town where you live:
   a. location where preliminary hearings are held
   b. days of the week when preliminary hearings are held
   c. how judges are assigned to preliminary hearings
   d. average court time needed for a preliminary hearing
7. What does the law in your state require for service of a subpoena?
   a. how is the subpoena initiated?
   b. who may serve the subpoena?
   c. are there restrictions on when the subpoena may be served?
   d. are there restrictions on how long a subpoena is valid?
   e. when can subpoenas be served out of state?
8. How is the grand jury selected in your county?
   a. how are names selected for grand jury service?
   b. how many members are there on a grand jury?
   c. how many members must vote in favor of bringing charges against the suspect in order to indict?
   d. how long do members of the grand jury serve?
   e. how often does the grand jury meet?
   f. can more than one grand jury be empaneled at the same time?
9. What are the local rules regarding grand jury proceedings?
   a. can a suspect refuse to testify?
   b. does the suspect have the right to have an attorney present?
   c. are witnesses before the grand jury sworn to secrecy?
   d. what level of proof is required to indict?
   e. how many grand jurors must vote in favor of indictment?
   f. is the suspect entitled to a transcript of the grand jury proceedings after he/she has been indicted?
   g. is the press entitled to see a copy of the transcript of the grand jury proceedings after the suspects have been arrested?
10. What are the local practices for arraignment on the information or indictment?
    a. in what court are the arraignments held?
    b. when are they held?
    c. are there time limits on how long after the preliminary hearing or indictment the arraignment must be held?

Chapter 7

Pretrial Court Proceedings

Learning Objectives

After reading this chapter, the student will be able to:

- Explain the process used to determine if a defendant will be released from custody before trial.
- Describe the plea bargaining process.
- Explain the use of pretrial diversion in criminal cases.
- Explain at least four types of legal challenges that can be made to a complaint, indictment or information.
- Explain the pretrial proceedings to obtain rulings on the admissibility of evidence.
- Describe the discovery process in criminal cases.
- Explain the purpose of pretrial conferences in criminal cases.

Key Terms

bail
bail bond
cash bail
charge bargaining
challenge to the pleadings
discovery
diversion
double jeopardy
electronic monitoring
failure to state a cause of action
geographical jurisdiction
house arrest
insufficiency of evidence
lack of jurisdiction
non-cash bail
own recognizance release
plea bargaining
points and authorities
pretrial conference
question of fact
speedy trial
  Sixth Amendment
  state law
statute of limitations
subject matter jurisdiction
suppression hearing
suppression motion

7.1 Pretrial Release

Defendants in capital cases are nearly always kept in custody from the time of their arrest until trial. The death penalty is considered to be sufficient motivation to cause these inmates to flee the jurisdiction if allowed to leave the jail. Most other defendants are eligible for release prior to trial. Traditionally, the decision to release has focused on the likelihood that the person will appear in court as scheduled; many jurisdictions now consider other factors, such as likelihood the person will commit additional crimes, or threaten potential prosecution witnesses if released from custody. The most common device used to assure that the defendant will appear for trial is to require the posting of bail or a bond. Releasing inmates on their own recognizance (commonly referred to as OR) has become common during the last thirty years. Electronic monitoring is now being used to verify that the defendant has not violated the conditions of release.

BAIL

Bail can be defined as setting an inmate free when security has been posted for his/her appearance at a specific location on the date indicated. It is commonly used before trial and, under some circumstances, defendants are released on bail while appealing a conviction. The amount of the bail is set high enough so that a person will appear for trial in order to have the bail returned. Bail is set higher in felony cases because a defendant facing a prison sentence is more likely to flee to avoid conviction and sentencing. Since the consequences of a misdemeanor conviction are less serious, a lower bail is considered adequate to obtain the defendant's attendance at trial.

At one time, bail was routinely set at the arraignment. If the defendant wanted an earlier release, the defense attorney filed a habeas corpus petition requesting a bail-setting hearing. This process was both time consuming for the courts and expensive for defendants. Today many courts have bail schedules: a list stating the bail for specific offenses. At the time of booking, the person who has been arrested is told the amount of bail. Arrangements for posting bail can be made without waiting for a court appearance.

Sometimes the amount stated in the bail schedule is not appropriate for the case. Two opposite reasons result in deviation from normal bail: a poor defendant who cannot afford the normal bail but is likely to appear at trial; and a rich defendant who is not likely to be deterred from fleeing by the normal bail for the offense. In either of these cases, a bail hearing may be held to review the personal situations of the defendant and determine what is reasonable bail under the circumstances. Excessive bail is considered a violation of the Eighth Amendment.

Traffic court is the most common example of posting bail. Many states permit the person who receives a traffic ticket to post bail in the amount of the fine for the offense. If the person does not appear for trial, a conviction is entered and bail forfeited. In practice, many people believe they are paying the fine and do not even think of it as bail.

Bail can be posted in several forms. **Cash bail** is deposited with the court clerk or at another designated location such as the jail or police station. Either cash, money order or cashier's check is required. The entire amount of the bail is usually returned if the defendant appears in court as ordered. Cash bail is not costly for the defendant who keeps

Pretrial Release on $10,000 Bail

Type of Release	Cost to defendant who appears in court as scheduled	
Bail		
Cash	Deposit:	$10,000 with court
	Refund:	$10,000
	Net Cost:	0
Non-cash	Deposit:	$20,000* worth of deeds, stock certificates, etc., with court
	Refund:	All items deposited
	Net Cost:	0
Bail Bond	Pay:	$1,000** to bail bond company
	Refund:	0
	Net cost:	$1,000
Personal bond	Deposit:	1,000** with court
	Refund:	$900
	Net cost:	$100
OR release	Deposit:	0. Must show ties to community indicating likelihood defendant will appear for trial
	Refund:	Not applicable
	Net cost:	0

* estimate based on posting twice cash bail
** based on estimate of 10%
Actual amounts vary

Table 7.1

the scheduled court date because the entire amount is returned: all that is lost is interest that would have been earned on the money used for bail.

Many defendants can not afford to post cash bail. A **bail bond** may be posted instead. This bond functions like an insurance policy: the person needing bail pays a premium, usually ranging from 10% to 25% of the bail depending on the risk to the bonding company; in return, the bonding company gives the court its guarantee that the person will appear for trial. If the person does not go to court as scheduled, the bond company must pay the court the full amount of the bail. On the other hand, if the defendant appears as scheduled, the bond company keeps the premium and owes the court nothing. Bond companies employ investigators to locate people who do not appear as scheduled. Court rules frequently permit the bond company a period of time, such as 10 days, in which to bring the defendant to court rather than paying the full amount of the bail. The bond company frequently has the option of returning a person to jail before the court date if it believes there is likelihood he/she will leave the jurisdiction.

Some jurisdictions use an intermediate device, referred to here as personal bond, when the defendant cannot afford cash bail but appears likely to keep the court date. The defendant posts an amount equivalent to what would be paid to a bail bond company. A processing fee may be charged, perhaps 10% of the amount posted, but the remainder of the money is returned to the defendant when all court dates have been kept. This provides a less expensive way for low income people to post bail.

Non-cash bond may also be posted. Deeds to real estate can be used for this purpose. State law usually specifies the ratio of property value to bail. For example, a person may have to post deeds to property appraised at twice the dollar amount of bail. The reason for requiring more than face value is that the price received at forced sales is usually below market value. Only equity in property can be used as bond; the amount of outstanding mortgages will be deducted when determining if sufficient property has been posted. A lien is usually filed against the property so that the amount of the bail can be recovered if the property is sold.

Own Recognizance Release

An inmate may be released on his/her promise to appear in court as scheduled. This is referred to as an own recognizance release or being released OR. OR releases are usually given to inmates who are believed to be very likely to attend trial. The inmate is usually asked to complete a questionnaire and the facts given are verified. Factors usually considered favorable for OR release include: currently employed; stable job record; live in community for some time; family in the community; relatively short possible sentence; few prior arrests or convictions. There may be points assigned to each of the factors involved and an inmate who has a specified number of points will be released OR. As with bail, a person who has been released OR may be returned to jail if there is evidence of plans to flee the jurisdiction rather than stand trial or another crime has been committed.

Electronic Monitoring

A variety of electronic devices are currently being used to monitor activities of defendants released pending trial as well as to supervise those on probation and parole. Pretrial monitoring can be done as a condition of either being released on bail or OR. Two basic types of devices are in use: an electronic device that must be inserted in a special receiver attached to a telephone; and one that sends a radio signal that can be used to determine where the transmitting device is located. Both procedures rely on having tamper-proof equipment that is worn by the defendant, usually as a bracelet or leg band, that the defendant cannot remove. Many jurisdictions require the person being released to pay the cost of the monitoring equipment; some also permit the court to assess the cost of supervision.

House arrest is used to describe cases where the defendant is released but ordered to stay at home, or some other location, and wear electronic monitoring equipment. Frequently the defendant wears an electronic bracelet that must be inserted into a device attached to a telephone in order to verify where the wearer is. The person is directed to activate the monitor at specific times and verify his/her presence whenever the probation officer calls. By calling at unpredictable times, the probation officer attempts to maintain surveillance over the defendant's activities. Other identifying techniques, such as asking for specific personal data, may be requested to insure the defendant has not transferred the device to another person.

More mobile tracking devices are used for defendants who are not required to stay at one location. By transmitting a honing signal, it is possible to determine where the device is currently located. This gives the probation officer the ability to monitor the defendant's movements without voice or visual contact. The defendant is deterred from committing additional crimes because he/she knows his/her movements can be traced to the crime scene.

7.2 Plea Bargaining

The prosecutor and defense attorney frequently reach an agreement on the charges the defendant will plead guilty to. Bargaining done before the arraignment is technically called **charge bargaining**. The same type of negotiations done later in the case is called **plea bargaining**. Both are frequently called plea bargaining; that practice will be followed in this book. Plea bargaining may occur at any time from arrest until the jury returns a verdict. The key questions usually are: on which charges will the defendant enter guilty pleas; and what sentence will be imposed. State law and local practice may set limits on plea bargaining. In some states, the judge retains the power to sentence and therefore the plea bargain cannot guarantee a maximum sentence. The defendant can usually withdraw the plea if the judge will not honor the conditions the prosecutor agreed to when making it.

An experienced prosecutor can usually make a reasonable estimate of the case's chances of success and the sentence the judge is likely to give. Based on this estimation, a plea bargain may be offered to the defendant. In other cases, the defense attorney approaches the prosecutor and initiates the bargaining process. Lengthy negotiations may be involved before the deal is completed. A variety of inducements are used: drop one or more of the charges; do not use enhancements that would increase the sentence, such as use of a weapon or prior felony conviction; recommend shorter sentence; or dismiss charges in this case if the defendant will assist the prosecution on other cases. The Supreme Court has upheld the prosecutor's right to file additional charges if the defendant refuses to plead guilty provided there is a factual basis for each new charge. Refusal to admit guilt can also be considered as an aggravating factor when sentencing the defendant.

There is no trial when all of the charges are settled by plea bargaining. The agreement will be formalized before a judge. This is frequently done in the arraignment court. The proceedings include the defendant's waiver of the rights associated with a trial as well as the entry of the guilty plea. The judge usually asks the defendant to respond to the following items: plea is entered voluntarily and without coercion; defendant is represented by an attorney or has voluntarily waived the right to counsel; defendant waives trial rights including public trial, confrontation of witnesses against him, present defense, and having jury of peers decide case. The judge may sentence the defendant at the same hearing where the plea is accepted or a probation and sentencing report may be requested and the sentencing hearing scheduled for a later date.

Many ask if plea bargaining is fair. Does it give the victim justice? Is it fair to society? At its best, plea bargaining reaches a conclusion that is fair in that the defendant receives a sentence similar to other defendants with similar charges. To the extent that plea bargaining has driven down the "cost" of crime for all defendants, this result is not fair to society. Some victims are well served by plea bargaining because it reduces the number of court sessions they must attend and the trauma of testifying and facing grueling cross-examination. This is particularly so if they believe the defendant receives a "fair" sentence. Other victims are outraged by the plea bargaining process because it reduces their case to a commodity to be bartered away by the attorneys. The greatest anger is voiced when a very lenient punishment is the result of the process.

A less often asked question is whether plea bargaining is fair to defendants. Some defendants benefit greatly by plea bargains that substantially reduce the sentence they receive. Some unscrupulous defense attorneys who take cases for a flat fee see plea bargaining as a way to increase their incomes and avoid time-consuming trials. These attorneys pressure their clients to enter a plea that may not be much of a bargain. A few innocent defendants, frequently at the prompting of their attorneys, weigh the cost in time, money and emotional energy of a trial to vindicate their reputation plus the uncertainty of a jury verdict against probation or a short sentence and plead guilty. These defendants may claim plea bargaining is not fair.

Plea bargaining as practiced in many courts has little to do with the above concerns. Judges with too many cases to handle are inclined to make "moving the calendar" a high priority. Prosecutors who face having cases dismissed because the statutory time between arraignment and trial is about to expire frequently decide a plea bargain, however favorable to the defense, is better than no conviction at all. Experienced defense attorneys understand the pressures on the system and utilize these problems as leverage to achieve the best possible result for their clients. Habitual criminals also know how the process works and take advantage of its weaknesses.

7.3 DIVERSION

Some cases can be best handled outside the criminal justice system. Diversion is the process of sending these cases to sources outside the court system. Diverted cases typically involve first offenders with misdemeanor charges when there appears to be a high potential for rehabilitation through counseling. The main problem may be alcoholism or drug abuse, lack of parenting skills in child abuse cases, and poor anger control and communication skills between spouses. Many states have established programs to divert these cases. Each is governed by specific state laws, but general patterns will be discussed here.

Defendants are usually screened prior to entering the program; only those who have not been diverted into the program previously and have no serious criminal record are usually accepted. The screening criteria is usually stated in the state statute. The probation department or other court officers verify eligibility. In addition to meeting the entry criteria, the defendant must consent to be in the program. Conditions of diversion usually include attending counseling sessions for six months to two years, committing no new crimes similar to the one which triggered diversion, and refraining from other specified conduct. Many states require the defendant to pay for the cost of counseling and any other services used.

Some programs divert the defendant before the charges are filed. The prosecutor will keep the complaint so it can be filed if the offender does not satisfactorily complete the program. When pre-filing diversion is used, the case can only be held until the statute of limitations has expired. The defendant who successfully completes the program has no record because the case was never filed in court.

A more typical pattern is to file the criminal charges and then have the defendant agree to diversion. The judge obtains the defendant's waiver of speedy trial, agreement to attend counseling for a specific period, and acknowledgment that charges can be prosecuted if the defendant does not perform satisfactorily during the diversion program. A court hearing is usually required to obtain a ruling that the defendant has failed diversion so prosecution may be reinstituted. Charges are dismissed against defendants who satisfactorily complete the program and their arrest records are expunged.

There are several problems with diversion. One is the level of supervision provided. Counselors frequently feel that their therapeutic role is compromised by reporting violations to the court. A probation officer or other person assigned by the court is needed to ensure that the counseling sessions are attended and determine if the defendant has been arrested, and if so, for what charges.

Finding appropriate counseling programs can be another problem. Most combine formal instruction with a group therapy format. They need to be focused on specific problems. Defendants from child abuse cases need to go to parenting classes; permitting them to attend counseling for drunk drivers is inappropriate. Some defendants, however, may have more than one problem and need to be involved in multiple counseling programs: for example, an alcoholic parent who abuses his/her children may need a program for alcoholics as well as one to teach parenting skills.

Prosecuting the case after the defendant fails diversion may also be a problem. If the defendant was on diversion for a lengthy period of time, it may be difficult to locate witnesses needed for the trial. Even when located, some may not want to testify. While the case can be prosecuted whenever the defendant fails diversion, many cases ultimately are dismissed because of uncooperative or missing witnesses. This is particularly true in spousal abuse cases. Even when the case is tried immediately, many victims do not want to testify. Where the victim has tried to start a new life, facing the abuser again after one to two years and going over the old incidents is often traumatic. Another problem is that some victims continue their relationship with their abusers and are fearful of testifying.

7.4 Challenges to Pleadings

There are a variety of technical challenges that defense attorneys make prior to trial. Many are based entirely on the content of the complaint, indictment or information. The challenge can be to the entire document or to only one of the counts. A formal motion is usually made to the court and a hearing held. This procedure is called a challenge to the pleadings. State court rules frequently mandate that the defense make these motions before trial. Failure to make a timely motion waives the right to raise the issue later. If the motion is made at the appropriate time but the judge denies it erroneously, the issue can be raised again on appeal or through some other procedure.

Challenges to Pleadings

Challenge	Defense must show
Double jeopardy	Official court records indicating prior conviction or acquittal on same offense or greater/lesser included offense
Lack of subject matter jurisdiction	State law that this court does not have the authority to handle the charges in the case
Lack of geographical jurisdiction	Official map of court district and testimony showing crime occurred outside boundaries
Statute of limitations	Time between date crime occurred and date of filing case in court exceeds statute of limitations for crime charged
Speedy trial	
Sixth Amendment	Defendant's right to fair trial was violated. Need combination of: lengthy delay, defendant asserted right to speedy trial, no valid reason for delays, and prejudice to defendant caused by delays
State law	Time between filing charges and first day of trial, excluding continuances requested by defendant, exceeds time limit specified in state law

Table 7.2

Double Jeopardy

The Fifth Amendment protection against double jeopardy applies in state court. A defendant cannot be convicted for an offense after being acquitted on it. A conviction on a lesser included offense is void if the defendant has already been convicted on a crime which includes the lesser offense. The opposite is also true: the defendant who has been convicted of the lesser offense cannot be convicted for the greater one. To be considered a lesser included offense, all elements of the lesser offense must be included in the definition of the more serious one. For example, theft is a lesser included offense in robbery.

Many times the judge will not know that there has been a prior prosecution for the crime. Procedurally, it is up to the defense to bring double jeopardy to the court's attention. This is usually done with a motion to dismiss the case on grounds of double jeopardy. A certified copy of the prior conviction must be presented to the judge in order to establish double jeopardy. Even with this in hand, dismissal of the charge may not be required if the prosecution successfully demonstrates that the two offenses are not the same: for example, what the defense claims is a lesser included offense may not qualify. If the prosecution is able to demonstrate that the two prosecutions are by separate sovereigns (for example, state and federal governments) double jeopardy does not apply.

Either a conviction or acquittal on the charge must have occurred to qualify for pretrial dismissal based on double jeopardy. It is not a defense that the complaint lists a crime and its lesser included offense. Neither does it apply to pretrial dismissal of charges filed previously, for example, the judge's ruling that there was insufficient evidence to hold the defendant to answer at the end of the preliminary hearing. If the jury finds the defendant guilty of crimes to which double jeopardy applies, the judge should dismiss the lesser one at the time of sentencing or the appellate court will make a similar ruling.

Lack of Jurisdiction

A challenge based on lack of jurisdiction raises the issue of whether the court is authorized to hear the case. It can be based on lack of either subject matter or geographical jurisdiction. In a two-tier court system, it is possible to allege that the court does not have jurisdiction over certain offenses; for example, a lower level court may not have jurisdiction to proceed on felony charges after the preliminary hearing or a higher level court may not have jurisdiction to hold a trial on misdemeanors unless at least one felony is charged in the same complaint. These technical challenges to **subject matter jurisdiction** are based on intricacies of state law. Legal maneuvers, such as suppression hearings, that caused some of the charges to be dismissed may affect the subject matter jurisdiction of the court on the remaining charges.

The court also lacks jurisdiction if the offense occurred outside the geographical boundaries of the court district, or in the case of large districts, outside the boundaries of the particular subdivision of the district that the court hearing the cases services. Challenges to **geographical jurisdiction** are more mechanical: the exact location where the crime occurred must be established and the boundaries of the court district must be proven. Proof of the court's geographical jurisdiction is established by introducing the official map. Testimony of eye witnesses may be required to establish where the offense occurred. For example, if the defense can show that the offense occurred 30 feet outside the judicial district's boundary, the court would not have geographical jurisdiction to try the case. The analysis may be complicated by the fact that some crimes, such as kidnapping, can occur in more than one court district.

Statute of Limitations

Much like challenges based on geographical jurisdiction, the statute of limitations is a combination of very specific rules and the facts. State law establishes a **statute of limitations**, the maximum length of time during which a prosecution can be begun, for most crimes. Capital offenses and a few other crimes usually have no statute of limitations. For all other cases, it is a matter of checking the code for the applicable period. Many states consider the statute of limitations satisfied as long as an arrest warrant is issued within the limitation period. In such cases, the code specifies how long the warrant is valid; an arrest after the expiration date has a similar effect as one after the statute of limitations has run.

The factual question is determining whether the time period from the day the crime occurred until the date the complaint was filed exceeds the statute of limitations. For example, the defense could successfully challenge a misdemeanor battery charge with a statute of limitations of one year if the complaint alleges the offense occurred on August 1, 1993, and the complaint was stamped "Filed" on August 3, 1994. At the pretrial stage, the date given in the pleadings is considered correct. If at trial it appears that the crime was committed on an earlier date, the challenge can be renewed. The defendant is entitled to the statute of limitations in effect on the date the crime was committed; changes by the legislature that go into effect at a later date cannot be used to defeat a motion raising this issue.

Lack of Speedy Trial

The Sixth Amendment gives defendants the right to a speedy trial. This refers to the period from arrest to the first day of trial. The Supreme Court has identified four factors that must be considered in evaluating this issue: length of delay; reasons for the delay; defendant's assertion of the right to a speedy trial; and prejudice to the defendant. No one factor is determinative. The defendant must show that the combination of these factors resulted in the denial of a fair trial. The longer the delay, however, the less evidence there needs to be of actual prejudice.

Defendants cannot ignore the issue during lengthy delays and then claim their right to a speedy trial has been violated: timely objections must be made. A defendant who requests a continuance waives the right to claim a denial of speedy trial for the time consumed by the continuance; lengthy delays by the prosecution after the defense has requested the trial begin can be considered. Pretrial appeals taken in good faith by the prosecution cannot be used as grounds for claiming denial of speedy trial. An example of a successful challenge based on denial of speedy trial would be a case that did not go to trial for four years because the prosecution repeatedly asked for continuance on the grounds it was not ready while the defense was demanding that the trial begin; during this lengthy delay, the defendant's key witness died.

Most states have statutes which establish timelines for bringing the case to trial. It is usually easier for the defense to win motions based on these statutes than on the Sixth Amendment because the codes normally state specific time periods, such as 120 days. Demonstrating violation of such rules is easier than showing prejudice to the case: the judge counts the calendar days from the last relevant proceeding, such as the judge's holding the defendant to answer at the end of the preliminary hearing, to the first day of trial.

Other

"Failure to state a cause of action" is a challenge to the pleadings. It claims that the information given on one or more counts does not adequately describe a crime. The judge must review the wording of the complaint and determine if every element of the crime charged is included in the pleading. Motions based on careless drafting, typographical errors or omitting words when typing the documents are successful. Challenges on this ground are more common in fact-pleading states because the documents must show facts for each element of the crime. In code-pleading jurisdictions, a cause of action can be stated by merely referencing the code section. The judge will usually allow the prosecution to correct the error and refile the charges if the statute of limitations has not run.

A variety of other technical challenges can be made depending on local court rules. Failure to have the correct signatures on the documents is one. The fact that the code section being charged has been repealed or ruled unconstitutional is another. Defense attorneys keep abreast of local rules so they can make any challenge that is feasible.

7.5 Challenges to Evidence

Pretrial procedures can be used to restrict what evidence will be admitted at trial. In criminal cases, the defense makes most of the suppression motions. A hearing will be held during which each side will have the opportunity to present its side of the issue. If the defense's suppression motion is successful, a motion may follow to dismiss the charges for insufficient evidence. The outcome of the case depends on how much credible evidence remains after inadmissible evidence is suppressed.

Suppression Motion

Most states permit the defense to ask for a hearing on the issue of admissibility of evidence before the trial starts. Trial time is saved by settling these issues before trial. Knowing what evidence cannot be used at trial makes trial preparation more efficient for both sides. The pretrial hearing on whether evidence will be admissible is called a **suppression hearing** because one party is asking the court to suppress evidence. Some states permit an appeal of the admissibility ruling before trial. This gives the prosecution the opportunity to appeal it might not otherwise have: if the case went to trial and the defendant was acquitted, double jeopardy would prevent the prosecution from appealing an incorrectly granted suppression motion.

The normal procedure used to schedule the hearing is to file a request, called a **suppression motion**, with the court. This written

Challenges to the Evidence

Challenge	Evidence Considered	Legal Issue
Warrant not valid No probable cause	Facts in affidavits submitted to judge when warrant issued	Do all facts in affidavit, taken together, establish probable cause?
False information in affidavit	Hear testimony to establish what facts were known to be false or included with reckless disregard of truth	Excluded known falsehoods and lies included with reckless disregard of truth: do facts that remain show probable cause?
Search and seizure violation	Transcripts of preliminary hearing and grand jury plus sworn testimony at suppression hearing	Determine what law applies to search that was conducted; then determine if facts show that search violated that law
Confession obtained in violation of *Miranda*	Transcripts of preliminary hearing and grand jury plus sworn testimony at suppression hearing	Determine if *Miranda* warnings were required; if so, were warnings given correctly and did defendant make a knowing, intelligent and voluntary waiver?

Table 7.3

document states what evidence the moving party believes should be suppressed and is accompanied by "points and authorities." **"Points and authorities"** is a legal document, prepared by the attorney, requesting the court to take action; it cites statutes, case law, and legal arguments supporting the request. A court date is obtained for the hearing and a copy of the motion, points and authorities, and notice of time and place for the hearing are served on the opposing side. The opposition then has time, frequently a minimum of ten days, to prepare points and authorities to support its view of the law. Both sides may present relevant testimony and oral arguments at the hearing.

Suppression Motion Challenging Validity of Warrant

Both arrest warrants and search warrants are issued by judges based on the affidavits accompanying the warrant application and any other sworn testimony given before the judge at that time. Therefore, the validity of the warrant is evaluated based on the affidavits and transcripts of the sworn testimony. No other evidence can be introduced to support probable cause. Facts the police were aware of but did not include in the affidavits are irrelevant because the judge did not consider them when making the determination that probable cause existed. For this reason, no witnesses testify at a hearing which decides if the warrant was based on probable cause.

If an arrest warrant is being challenged, the issue is whether the facts in the affidavit, and any other sworn testimony the judge heard, are sufficient to cause a reasonable person to believe it is more probable than not that the person named in the warrant committed the crimes indicated. The judge is allowed to make reasonable inferences from the facts stated. To win the suppression motion, the defense must establish that the facts are so weak that it was erroneous to conclude that probable cause existed. Two types of attacks are typical: the facts, even if believed, do not establish every element of the crime; and the facts are from sources, such as unreliable informants, that lack credibility. Both of these are questions of fact: the judge must weigh the facts and inferences reasonably drawn from them and make a decision. The same process is used to challenge search warrants: the affidavits must show that there was probable cause to believe that evidence which may legally be seized was at the location where the search was to be conducted and that the information came from credible sources.

Another avenue for attacking a warrant is to allege that the facts presented to the judge are untrue. The Supreme Court has ruled that falsehoods the police knowingly included in the affidavits, and statements included in reckless disregard of the truth, cannot be used to support probable cause. False information given to the police, which they had no reason to suspect was untrue, can be used to establish probable cause. The procedure at the suppression hearing starts with taking testimony on the question of whether the officers knew, or should have known, that they were including falsehoods in the affidavit. The officers may be called by the defense. Sources named in the affidavit may be called to testify that they did not provide the information stated or that the officers never questioned them. The judge must be convinced that the officers intentionally included lies, or included information they should have known was not true without check the validity of the source.

Once the judge is convinced the officers violated this constitutional standard, the affidavit must be reconsidered. All facts included by officers who knew they were false or recklessly disregarded the question of truthfulness of the source, must be deleted from the affidavit. The judge reviews the revised affidavit to determine if probable cause can be established based on the remaining facts. If there is still probable cause, the warrant is considered valid: appropriate actions taken pursuant to the warrant are constitutional. If probable cause cannot be established based on the remaining facts, the warrant is not valid; therefore, actions taken in reliance on it are unconstitutional. The prosecution is not allowed to bring in additional facts to support the warrant. It can, however, show that the actions were valid under an exception to the warrant requirement. For example, even though it is determined that the warrant was not valid, the arrest would be legal if it was made under circumstances that did not mandate the use of an arrest warrant.

Suppression Motion for Police Actions Taken Without a Warrant

The suppression motion must give an outline of what facts the party hopes to establish by testimony at the hearing, use of transcripts of the preliminary hearing, and testimony given before the grand jury. The points and authorities will be based on what the attorney believes will be shown. Opposing counsel has a right to know what to prepare for and draft "points and authorities." Sometimes the testimony at the suppression hearing does not accomplish what was anticipated; in these cases, oral arguments will attempt to explain what law applies to the facts given. If necessary, the court may grant a continuance so both sides can prepare additional arguments.

Most suppression motions focus on either search and seizure violations or confessions. The focus is on the procedures used, not the item to be introduced into evidence. For example, the issue may be whether *Miranda* warnings were given properly; the defendant's confession is not admitted at the hearing because the contents of the confession are not relevant at this stage of the proceedings; if the defendant claims a car was searched unconstitutionally, the court addresses the issue of how the Fourth Amendment rules apply to the search, not whether drugs or stolen credit cards were found in the car.

Both sides have the right to call witnesses at a suppression hearing and cross-examine those testifying for the other side. Testimony of police officers is frequently needed to establish details about the event in question. Due to the intricacies of the laws in this area, both direct and cross-examination are usually very detailed and focus on minute details and the sequence in which events occurred. Many states make the defendant's testimony at the suppression hearing inadmissible at trial. This is done to allow the defendant to exercise Fourth Amendment rights without waiving the Fifth Amendment.

Sometimes, testimony introduced at the preliminary hearing or before the grand jury reveals that evidence was obtained illegally. Examples include: testimony may not establish probable cause for the arrest; testimony may indicate that an item of evidence was seized without legal justification; the officers may have testified to obtaining a confession without giving *Miranda* warnings. These statements were made under oath and usually are recorded in a verbatim transcript. The defense need only cite the transcript as grounds for requesting suppression of the item involved.

The prosecutor usually combines two tactics when defending against a suppression motion: presenting points and authorities to show that the item was legally obtained; and arguing that the facts do not merit suppression of the evidence. There are hundreds of cases dealing with search and seizure, many of which will not be relevant to the case. The defense points and authorities cite those believed to justify suppression of the evidence. The prosecutor will look for cases that hold differently. The variations of facts that are present during police activity result in each case being unique. Arguments will be made using analogies to convince the judge which case should be applied to the facts in the present case.

Most search and seizure rules are based on reasonable police conduct. Once the correct rule of law is determined, the judge must address the **question of fact**: an individualized determination must be made on how the law applies to the events that occurred in this case. The defense attorney presented the evidence in the light most favorable to the defendant, therefore the prosecutor needs to convince the judge that what the police did in the case was reasonable. Many times the transcripts do not provide enough information to make this decision. Testimony of police officers and other witnesses who were present when the search was performed may be used at the suppression hearing to fill these gaps.

Motion to Dismiss for Insufficient Evidence

If the defense is successful in suppressing evidence, it will frequently make a motion to dismiss the charges based on insufficient evidence. Success with this tactic depends on how important the evidence was that the judge ruled should be suppressed. If key items of evidence, such as the murder weapon and the defendant's confession, were suppressed it is likely that the charge will be dismissed. On the other hand, if there is ample evidence left after something was suppressed, the motion to dismiss will be denied. In cases with multiple counts, it is possible to dismiss one or more counts but allow the prosecution of others to continue.

Other Challenges to the Evidence

A variety of other reasons exist for suppressing evidence. One is that the testimony relates to privileged conversations. Some courts will consider this issue before trial if the questioned statements are key parts of the case. The hearing would relate to two distinct legal issues: did the conversation occur under circumstances covered by the evidentiary privilege; and, if so, do any exceptions to the privilege apply to the facts. Testimony regarding the circumstances under which the conversation occurred, but not the content of the conversation, is presented at the hearing.

Another challenge might be to the use of scientific evidence. One of the requirements for expert testimony is that there be an established body of knowledge in the field. Newly developed scientific tests may not meet this test. As long as the test is considered experimental, the courts will not permit testimony about the test results. For example, DNA testing (genetic fingerprinting) has been used to establish that body fluids recovered at the crime scene are from the defendant. For many years, the courts have been confronted with the issue of whether there is sufficient scientific recognition of DNA testing. Some courts permit challenges to the test on this basis before trial if the evidence will be crucial to the case. The secondary issue of procedural errors by the technician are considered at trial.

7.6 Discovery

Discovery is the pretrial process of learning what evidence the other side has. Long ago, and in some mystery movies today, one side wins the case by producing a surprise witness. Modern court procedures require the pretrial disclosure of much of the evidence in the case. Formal discovery motions can be made in court. Frequently, local practice is to give some items, such as the police reports, without waiting for a motion in court because the court automatically grants such requests. Discovery enables both sides to prepare for trial and also encourages settlement of the case without going to trial. Both of these results facilitate more efficient operation of the court system.

Discovery operates somewhat differently in criminal cases than in civil cases. This is primarily due to the defendant's Fifth Amendment privilege against self-incrimination. This privilege has been interpreted to mean that the defendant does not have to reveal information that would assist the prosecution in establishing the elements of the crime.

Discovery Requests by Defense

The Supreme Court ruled that due process requires the prosecution to disclose any information it has that would exonerate the defendant. Information requested by the defense under this rule is frequently called *Brady* material because the case that established this right was *Brady v. Maryland* 373 U.S. 83 (1962). Later cases clarified the extent of the prosecution's duty to disclose information: evidence that either obviously tends to show the defendant is not guilty (such as a confession by someone else) or appears to be helpful to the defense (such as the statement of a person who claims to have seen the defendant at a different location at the time the crime occurred) should be given to the defense even though the attorney did not ask for it; items that, on their face, do not appear to show the defendant's innocence only have to be revealed if the defense makes a discovery motion to obtain them. Intentional failure to reveal evidence the court deems valuable to the defense is grounds for reversing a conviction. All evidence known to the police department is considered to be in the prosecutor's file for the purpose of this rule: sanctions, including dismissing the case, can be applied based on the fact the police had the information even though the prosecutor did not know it existed.

Most states have rules which require either side to provide the other with a list of witnesses before trial begins. During trial, an attorney is allowed to choose not to call a person whose name appears on the list. Intentional failure to include a person on the witness list in order to gain unfair advantage over the other side can be grounds for refusing to allow the person whose name was left off to take the witness stand.

Prior statements made by a witness are important tools for cross-examination. They may be crucial for impeaching the credibility of the witness. Timing of the release of these statements varies from state to state. Some statements, such as testimony at the preliminary hearing, are public record. Police reports are usually subject to discovery, therefore statements included in them are available to the defense. Testimony made before the grand jury is released before trial in some states but remains sealed in others. Federal courts, and those of some states, require that a witness's statement be given to the opposing side, but permit disclosure to be delayed until the time when the person takes the witness stand.

Lists of physical evidence are usually part of the discovery process. The defense has the right to examine evidence before trial and have its own experts perform relevant tests. There is no duty, however, for police departments to preserve evidence for the sole purpose of enabling the defense to do these tests. The Supreme Court ruled, for example, that breathalyzers used in DUI cases do not have to be modified to save a breath sample for independent testing. Some states also permit discovery of reports by experts who will be called to testify. Normally, the factual content of the report is given to the other side (such as the blood found at the scene was human type B blood), but conclusions made for the benefit of the attorney (such as a recommendation that the defense not enter a plea of not guilty by reason of insanity because the defendant had no prior history of mental illness) are considered privileged and not subject to discovery. Reports by experts who examined the evidence but will not be called to testify are not usually subject to discovery, although some states permit discovery of the names of all experts employed by the other side.

Names of police informants used in the case may be requested by the defense. Many states make such information privileged. The Supreme Court has ruled that it must be disclosed pretrial only if it is crucial to the defense. A showing that the informant was the only eyewitness to the crime would meet this requirement. Names of people who provide information to the police are not discoverable if the police conducted an investigation and observed the key events in the case themselves.

Discovery Requests by Prosecution

Discovery by the prosecution must not interfere with the defendant's Fifth Amendment rights. Some states have gone to the extent of prohibiting all discovery by the prosecution for this reason. Such an approach is not constitutionally mandated. For example, the Supreme Court ruled that requiring the defendant to file a list of witnesses and to give notice that an alibi defense would be used does not violate the privilege against self-incrimination. Statements made by the defendant, however, cannot be obtained. State laws and local court rules vary a great deal on what other items the defense is permitted to withhold.

7.7 Pretrial Conferences

Settlement conferences are used in civil cases to help the parties reach an agreement on the issues of liability and how much compensation is justified. Plea bargaining serves the purpose of settlement conferences in most criminal cases. Judges are usually prohibited from being involved in negotiating a guilty plea.

Pretrial conferences are used to make the trial more efficient. They normally consider administrative matters rather than issues relating to the defendant's guilt or innocence. The number and timing of pretrial conferences varies based on local practice as well as the type of case involved. Many simple misdemeanor cases do not have any pretrial conferences. Complex felony cases in which lengthy trials are anticipated may require several conferences. Pretrial conferences are usually held within 30 days of the anticipated trial date; a final one may occur on the day the trial is scheduled to begin.

Prosecutors and defense attorneys meet with the judge at the pretrial conference to discuss such issues as: expected length of the trial; equipment that may be needed by expert witnesses; the need for interpreters for the defendant and/or witnesses; and any other special needs for the case. The discussions are frequently informal and may occur in the judge's chambers rather than in the courtroom. Verbatim stenographic notes are usually made only if disagreement on an issue might lead to an appeal.

Details concerning selecting the jury will be discussed. The number of potential jurors that need to be available for *voir dire* will be estimated. A decision will be made on how many alternate jurors to seat. Whether the jury should be sequestered (kept in a hotel rather than allowed to go home each night) will be decided. Transportation for the jury must be arranged if either side is requesting that the jury view the crime scene.

Some courts use questionnaires to obtain information from prospective jurors in controversial cases. Pretrial conferences will be used to determine what will be included in these questionnaires. Questions may focus on potential prejudice due to pretrial publicity. In death penalty cases both direct and indirect questions attempt to determine if jurors have objections to capital punishment that will interfere with their ability to apply the law in the case.

In high publicity cases, a pretrial conference may be used to decide how to handle the press: how many reporters will be allowed in the courtroom and, if space restrictions make it necessary, what methods will be used to decide which reporters will be allowed to attend. If the court policy is to permit the press to bring audio and/or video equipment into court, decisions will be made on how much equipment will be permitted and where it can be located.

SUMMARY

Defendants in non-capital cases are usually eligible for release on bail. The bail is set high enough to motivate the defendant to return for the trial rather than forfeit bail. Cash can be posted as bail and so can non-cash items such as deeds to land, stock certificates and other valuable items. A bail bond company will post bond for a fee. Defendants in misdemeanor cases who are not considered likely to flee before trial may be released on their own recognizance without posting bail.

Plea bargaining can occur at any time between arrest and trial. The prosecutor considers the strength of the case and the likely sentence. Some charges may be dismissed in order to induce the defendant to plead guilty. Additional charges may be filed if the defendant refuses to enter a guilty plea if there is probable cause to support each charge.

Some misdemeanor cases are diverted from the court system. Typically these cases involve alcohol abuse, spousal abuse and child abuse. The defendant must attend counseling; upon successful completion of the program, the charges are dismissed and the defendant has no criminal record for the charge.

The defense may challenge the legal sufficiency of the pleadings before the trial begins. Motions may be filed based on double jeopardy, the court's lack of either geographical or subject matter jurisdiction, expiration of the statute of limitations, or a violation of the right to a speedy trial. Depending on the error, success by the defense will result in dismissal of the charges with or without prejudice. The prosecution can refile charges dismissed without prejudice if the statute of limitations has not run.

Some evidentiary issues, particularly those related to unconstitutionally obtained evidence, can be settled before trial. Among the issues the defense can raise by making a suppression motion are: warrant not supported by probable cause; affidavit in support of warrant contained false information; police violated Fourth Amendment in obtaining evidence; and *Miranda* warnings not properly given before obtaining a confession. If evidence is suppressed, the defense will likely make a motion to dismiss for insufficient evidence. The success of this motion depends on what evidence remains in the case that is admissible.

The modern trend is to permit either side to discover what evidence the other has before trial. Opinions of lawyers and experts do not have to be released. Lists of witnesses to be called to testify may be required. Statements made by witnesses who testify usually must be given to the opposing side no later than the time when cross-examination begins. Physical evidence in the other side's possession may be examined by opposing experts. The Fifth Amendment privilege permits the defendant to refuse to disclose his/her own statements.

Plea bargaining in criminal cases generally replaces settlement conferences. Pretrial conferences may be held to settle issues related to the trial such as: jury selection; arranging for interpreters; preparing for the press; and other unique needs of the case. These conferences are usually held during the last month before trial.

Study Questions

1. Define bail, and explain how it operates in your local jail:
   a. Is a bail schedule used? If so, what is the bail on:
      1) misdemeanor battery
      2) robbery
      3) sale of cocaine
   b. Where is bail posted?
   c. Does your court permit posting a personal bond instead of paying for a bail bond?
   d. What are the procedures for posting:
      1) cash bail?
      2) non-cash bail?
      3) bail bond?
2. Define own recognizance release.
   a. For what crimes may an inmate in your local jail be released OR?
   b. How does an inmate initiate a request to be released OR?
   c. Who processes requests for OR releases?
   d. What factors are used in making the decision to release an inmate OR?

3. Is electronic monitoring used for pretrial release in your area? If so:
   a. What type of equipment is used?
   b. How does a defendant qualify for electronic monitoring?
   c. What fees must the defendant pay?

4. What is plea bargaining? Explain how it operates in your local court.
   a. Do state laws restrict plea bargaining?
   b. Does the prosecutor's office have policies that restrict plea bargaining?
   c. Approximately what percentage of cases is settled by a plea bargain?

5. Do laws in your state provide for pretrial diversion? If so:
   a. What types of cases may be diverted?
   b. What are the conditions of diversion?
   c. How long does diversion last?

6. Explain how the defendant can raise each of the following issues in pretrial:
   a. double jeopardy
   b. court's lack of jurisdiction
      1) subject matter jurisdiction
      2) geographical jurisdiction
   c. statute of limitations has expired
   d. violation of right to speedy trial
      1) under the Sixth Amendment
      2) under state law

7. Explain the process used to obtain a pretrial ruling on the admissibility of evidence.
   a. What is a suppression motion?
   b. What are "points and authorities?"
   c. What occurs at a suppression hearing?
   d. What issues do your state's laws permit to be raised at pretrial suppression hearings?
   e. Does your state allow pretrial appeal of the ruling on a suppression motion?

8. Explain how a defendant in a case filed in your local court can make a pretrial challenge to the legality of police conduct.
   a. How can the probable cause supporting a search warrant be attacked?
   b. How can the defense attack the warrant based on false information contained in the affidavits?
   c. How can the defense have evidence excluded from trial based on the fact it was seized in violation of the Fourth Amendment?
   d. What process can the defense use to have the defendant's confession suppressed on grounds that *Miranda* was not correctly followed?

9. How is discovery conducted in criminal cases under the laws of your state:
   a. What items does the prosecutor routinely give the defense attorney without the defense making a formal motion for discovery?
   b. How does the court handle discovery motions:
      1) what judge hears them?
      2) when are they heard?
   c. What must the defense disclose to the prosecution?
   d. Does your local court require:
      1) filing list of anticipated witnesses? If so, when is it filed?
      2) defense to file notice that alibi defense will be used? If so, when is it filed?
      3) giving opposing side statements made by witnesses who testify at trial? If so, when are they given?

10. Check with the clerk of your local court:
    a. What types of pretrial conferences, if any, are held in misdemeanor cases?
    b. What types of pretrial conferences, if any, are held in felony cases? If they are held:
       1) How long before trial are they scheduled?
       2) Who normally presides over them?
       3) What issues are addressed?

CHAPTER 8

PREPARATION OF CASE FOR TRIAL

LEARNING OBJECTIVES

After reading this chapter, the student will be able to:

- Identify what steps must be taken to prepare physical evidence for trial.
- Describe what must be done to subpoena witnesses for trial.
- Explain what can be done to refresh the memory of a witness before trial.
- Give examples of what can be introduced into evidence if a witness cannot recall events related to the crime.
- Explain five things than can be done to attack the credibility of a witness at trial.
- Describe how the prosecutor evaluates strengths and weaknesses of a case.
- Interpret how the prosecutor anticipates defense strategy.
- Describe the trial brief.

Key Terms

case management system
chain of custody
chain of possession
impeachment
- inability to perceive events
  - physical limitations of witness
  - physical layout of crime scene
- inconsistent statements
- motive, bias or prejudice
- prior convictions
- prior inconsistent statements
- reputation for dishonesty

"on call" subpoena
past recollection recorded
present memory refreshed
proof of service
rehabilitation
serving a subpoena
subpoena
subpoena duces tecum
trial brief

8.1 Assembling the Physical Evidence

As the trial date approaches, the police officer in charge of the case must assemble the items that will be needed in court. This includes evidence recovered at the crime scene, such as weapons, ammunition, demand notes, bloodstained clothing, etc. Other items, such as diagrams and pictures of the crime scene and photographs taken through a comparison microscope in the ballistics laboratory, may also be needed. A list should be made identifying each item that will be needed. It is better to include items that may not be introduced at trial than have a judge refuse to admit evidence because the prosecutor did not have it ready when needed.

Each police department should use a **case management system** to keep records on all aspects of the case: reports that have been filed; status of court case; physical evidence; and potential witnesses. By using one system throughout the department, it will be possible for officers to assist one another and, if necessary, prepare the evidence and subpoenas even though the officer initially handling the case is unavailable.

It is particularly important to know the location of physical evidence so that each item can be retrieved quickly and facts needed as a foundation for its admissibility can be easily established. File cards can be used for this purpose but computerized systems make it easier to keep track of the case and update information. A computerized system can cross-reference all entries and update common items, such as court dates, whenever new information is added. It can also alert the person in charge of evidence storage that items will be needed for court or can be released to the owners. The case management system might include the following screen for each piece of evidence in the case:

Case Management System

Physical Evidence Information

Police Department File Number: Court File Number:

Defendant's Name:
Names of other defendants:
File numbers of related cases:

Next scheduled court date:

Evidence locker tag number:

Description:
Who found this item:
Where was it found:
Witnesses needed to establish chain of possession:

	Witness	Date	Reason for possession
1.			
2.			
3.			

Current location of item:
Tests performed on this item:
Results of tests:
Use of this item at trial:
Weaknesses of this item:

Remarks:

Knowing how each item fits into the case is important. Of equal legal significance is the list of everyone who has had access to the item.

The side introducing the item must lay the foundation and establish the **chain of possession** (also called the **chain of custody**) before an item can be introduced into evidence. The foundation establishes the relevance of the evidence to the case. For example, the gun was taken from the defendant at the crime scene. Establishing that the gun looks like one a witness claims the person who committed the crime had is not enough.

The chain of possession establishes what has been done with an item of evidence since it was taken into police custody. The purpose of this requirement is to verify that the item has not been tampered with and is in the same condition it was when found. Testimony will be needed from every person who had possession of the item from the time it was taken into police custody until it is introduced into evidence at trial. This includes evidence technicians and personnel from the criminalistics laboratory. Information on transporting items to and from the evidence locker must be included.

Questions will be asked to establish: description of the item (man's blue plaid shirt, size medium); identifying marks on the item (officer's initials — JS — written on underside of the collar); the condition of the item when found (covered with dirt and caked with dark red dried material); how it was packaged (air dried and placed in a brown 8 inch by 12 inch envelope, Case No. 94-5678 written in upper left corner of the envelope, envelope sealed and Officer J. Smith's signature placed across seal); what was done with it (taken to criminalistics laboratory by Officer J. Smith for test to determine if human blood was present, and if so what blood type); what was done with it after processing was complete (returned to envelope it came in, envelope sealed with tape, and AB Cowan — signature of laboratory technician — written across seal and envelope taken to evidence locker by AB Cowan); and what was done with it after it was checked into the evidence locker (Officer J. Smith checked envelope out of evidence locker, brought it to court, and kept it in his possession until he opened it while testifying). If the test altered the appearance of the item, it will be necessary to inform the jury what was done so they will understand why the item does not match the description of the one recovered at the crime scene.

A similar process is involved if fingerprint comparisons were made. The person who dusted for prints at the crime scene will be needed to testify about lifting the prints. A latent print expert must testify about the match that was (or was not) made. It will be necessary to have latent prints and fingerprint cards available for introduction at trial. The prosecutor may want enlargements to show to the jury. It may also be necessary to call the officer who rolled the prints used for the comparison. The case management system can be used to keep track of where latent prints and fingerprints cards can be found and whose testimony will be needed to introduce them.

This same case management system can be used for diagrams, photographs, and other items that were made to assist at the trial. The person in charge of assembling the evidence should check local court rules on any size restrictions for such items. For example, some courts require that all photographs be 8 inches by 10 inches; others permit enlargements of any size. No chain of custody is needed for most of these items but other details will be necessary. Diagrams prepared in advance for use at trial normally must be made to scale. The scale should be indicated on the diagram. Testimony must be given regarding all facts used as a basis for the diagram. Information about photographs is usually given through testimony of the photographer: when and where pictures were taken; lighting; enlargement factor (frequently satisfied by reference to an item, such as a ruler, placed in the picture for this purpose); and factors, such as angle used to shoot picture, that might cause visual distortion. In controversial cases, the negative may be needed to establish that the picture has not been tampered with.

8.2 Subpoenaing Witnesses

Keeping track of witnesses is also the responsibility of the officer in charge of the case. Information on all potential witnesses should be kept in the case management system. Addresses should be kept current. The prosecutor will need to know both the potential strengths of the witness, such as being six feet away from the victim at the time the crime was committed, as well as possible weaknesses, such as having memory loss due to recent severe head trauma. Information on witnesses who do not appear to be useful for the prosecution should also be kept in the system: if they are called by the defense, the prosecutor will need to know as much as possible about them in order to cast doubt on their credibility. A screen from the case management system for witnesses might look as follows:

Case Management System
Witness Information

Police Department File Number: Court File Number:

Defendant's name:
Names of other defendants:
File numbers of related cases:

Next scheduled court appearance:

Name of witness:
Home address:
Business address:
Daytime telephone:
Evening telephone:
What this witness can testify about:
Physical evidence this witness can identify:
Strengths of witness:

Weaknesses of witness:

Subpoena issued for: Date: Time:
Served: Yes No
Proof of Service filed: Yes No
Witness on call: Yes No

If witness on call:
Telephone number to contact witness:
How long will it take witness to come to court?

Remarks:

Police officers whose testimony may be needed at trial should be included in the case management system as witnesses. It is best to include all officers involved with the case, not just the ones who wrote reports. Vacations, retirements, and illnesses may make it necessary to call officers whose testimony was not originally anticipated. Names of officers from other law enforcement agencies, firefighters and emergency medical personnel who were at the scene or otherwise involved should be included. This list will be more accurate if made at the time the investigation is begun and routinely updated.

Occasionally there will be a material witness who is uncooperative and believed to be likely to flee the jurisdiction. Many states give the judge discretion to require such witnesses to post a bond or written undertaking as security under these circumstances. The amount of the security is left to the discretion of the judge. A person who refuses to post the required security or appears ready to flee the jurisdiction rather than testify usually can be taken into custody and held in jail until called to testify. Immediate review of these cases is provided in order to prevent abuse of judicial discretion.

Victims and eyewitnesses normally receive little, if any, compensation for testifying. State law may give the court discretion to pay them; if so, they normally receive about the same compensation as jurors. Expert witnesses are normally paid for their services by the side calling them. Those that work for indigent defendants in criminal cases are usually paid by the government. Witness fees frequently must be posted in advance when government employees are subpoenaed by private attorneys to testify as expert witnesses or regarding events not involved in criminal trials.

Obtaining Subpoenas

Once the trial date is set, the prosecutor and officer handling the case usually meet and decide which witnesses need to be subpoenaed to testify at trial. Subpoenas must be typed, signed and served on each witness. A **subpoena** is a court order directing a person to appear at a specific date and time at the location stated in the subpoena; a person who fails to appear when subpoenaed can be held in contempt of court. If documents are to be brought to court, a ***subpoena duces tecum*** is required. When a witness is to testify and bring documents, both types of subpoenas should be issued. The court clerk and judge have the authority to issue subpoenas; in criminal cases, the district attorney and public defender are usually authorized to sign subpoenas. Private defense attorneys obtain blank subpoenas from the court clerk and complete them in the same manner as public defenders.

Subpoenas are usually preprinted forms identifying the document as a subpoena in a criminal case and stating the name of the judicial district and address of the court as well as other relevant information such as the penalty for failing to appear. Blanks are provided for the following information to be inserted: name of the case; case number; whether prosecution or defense is subpoenaing the witness; date, time and courtroom where witness is to appear; documents to be produced in court; and the signature of the person issuing the subpoena. A copy of the completed subpoena is filed with the court.

Many subpoenas list the time and date the trial is scheduled to begin as the time the witness must appear. This can be very inconvenient for witnesses who must wait at the courthouse during a lengthy trial. Giving the witness an **"on call" subpoena** means that the witness does not have to wait in the courthouse as long as it is possible to call the witness and have him/her appear when needed. This is done only

SUPERIOR COURT OF THE STATE OF CALIFORNIA FOR THE COUNTY OF ORANGE

☐ Courthouse – 700 Civic Center Drive West   Santa Ana, California 92701
☐ Courthouse – 1275 N. Berkeley Avenue   Fullerton, California 92632
☐ Courthouse – 8141 13th Street   Westminster, California 92683

THE PEOPLE OF THE STATE OF CALIFORNIA, Plaintiff
vs.
Defendant(s)

Case No.

SUBPOENA – CRIMINAL

THE PEOPLE OF THE STATE OF CALIFORNIA

TO:

YOU ARE COMMANDED to appear in the above entitled court to testify as a witness in a criminal action prosecuted by the People of the State of California against the above named defendant(s) at the following time and place:

Date: ______________________
Time: ______________________
Department: ______________________

AND YOU ARE REQUIRED, also, to bring with you the following:

MICHAEL R. CAPIZZI, DISTRICT ATTORNEY
COUNTY OF ORANGE, STATE OF CALIFORNIA

Given under my hand this date: ______________________ Telephone: (714) 834-3600

Disobedience to this subpoena may be punishable as contempt of court. (Penal Code Sec. 1331)

You may be entitled to witness fees, mileage, or both, in the discretion of the court. After your appearance contact Victim-Witness Office in the courthouse.

CERTIFICATE OF SERVICE

I hereby certify that on ______________________, 19___, I served the within subpoena on the person(s) named hereafter by personally delivering a true copy thereof to said witness(s). (1)__________ (2)__________ (3)__________ (4)__________

Not Served (name and reason): ______________________

I declare under penalty of perjury that the foregoing is true and correct.

Executed at ______________________, California, on ______________________, 19___.

By: ______________________

VICTIM NOTIFICATION OF DEFENDANTS RELEASE
"If the Defendant in a case is sentenced to State Prison, the victim or next of kin of the victim may request notification prior to the release of the Defendant from State Prison, by writing the Director, Department of Corrections, 630 K Street, Sacramento, CA 95814. As defined, a victim is any person sustaining physical or financial injury to person or property." (C.P.C. 11155)

F 0232-425.7 (R1/90)

Typical Criminal Subpoena

if the prosecutor is sure the witness can be depended on to come quickly when called. Failure of an "on call" witness to be present when it is time to take the witness stand can result in sanctions, including refusal to allow that witness to testify later, against the side that subpoenaed the witness. This may ultimately lead to failure to sustain the burden of proof.

The normal rule is that a person served with a subpoena must appear in court as directed. Many states have placed distance limitations on this; for example, a witness cannot be compelled to attend court more than 150 miles from home or place of business unless there is a special showing that the witness has material evidence in the case. A judge's signature, rather than that of the prosecutor or defense attorney, is typically required to certify that there has been a preliminary showing that the witness' testimony meets this requirement.

The Uniform Act to Secure the Attendance of Witnesses from without the State in Criminal Cases is a compact signed by most states. As the name indicates, it is used to subpoena witnesses who are outside the state. It can be used to subpoena witnesses before the grand jury or for criminal trials. A judge in a court where the person is to testify must determine that the person is a necessary and material witness and sign a certificate indicating how many days the person is needed and the time and place where the witness must appear. The state requesting the witness must agree to protect the witness from arrest and service of civil or criminal process while he/she is in the state. This protection also applies to travel through other states while going to and from court. The certificate is presented to a judge in the county where the person being subpoenaed resides. This judge will hold a hearing to review the determination that the witness has material testimony; undue hardship to the witness will also be considered. If the request is granted by the local court, the witness must be given travel expenses and per diem fees prior to going out-of-state. Uncooperative witnesses may be taken into custody and transported to the out-of-state court.

Serving the Subpoena

Most states permit anyone over 18 who is not a party to the case to serve subpoenas, but it is more common to have peace officers serve them in criminal cases. Delivering the subpoena in person qualifies as serving the subpoena. Some states provide for mail service, but if this is done it is usually valid only if the person receiving it cooperates and returns a document acknowledging service. The person who serves the subpoena must complete a form entitled **"Proof of Service"** which gives: name of the document; name of case and case number; date, time and location where subpoena was served; and signature of the server. The law frequently specifies alternate procedures when a police officer must be subpoenaed regarding events that occurred in the line of duty. Delivering two copies of the subpoena to the police department is usually adequate; the department becomes responsible for forwarding one copy to the officer.

8.3 Assessing the Ability of Witnesses to Recall Relevant Events

No one is expected to have perfect recall. A witness in court is asked to testify regarding his/her recollection of facts relevant to the case. This current recollection is important; how the person's memory was refreshed is not. Officers may help the witness recall key events: this is called present memory refreshed. Memorizing facts for the purpose of repeating them on the witness stand is prohibited. Prior to calling a witness to testify at trial the prosecutor will need to know if there are any recall problems. Under some circumstances, the hearsay exception for past recollection recorded can be used if the witness cannot recall enough details.

Present Memory Refreshed

Witnesses are allowed to use any device available, with the exception of hypnosis, to refresh their memories. Attorneys at trial may ask what was used to refresh the witness' memory, but the important thing will be what was recalled. A wide variety of things helps people remember events. If a person intentionally memorized facts in sequence or by use of a mnemonic device, recall may operate in the same manner; if so, recall of the first fact usually triggers memory of the second. Memory is also triggered by sights, sounds or meeting people associated with the main event; for example, hearing a song on the radio may cause a person to remember what he/she was doing when that song was popular.

Written documents may be used to refresh memory. These can be anything from a formal report to notes written on a scrap of paper. Two things are important: that whatever was written down was accurate and that it served to refresh memory. Police officers frequently refer to their field notebooks both before trial and while on the witness stand. An experienced prosecutor will ask appropriate questions when this is done: what are you looking at? does it contain notes regarding this case? when did you make those notes? has looking at those notes refreshed your memory? can you now testify from memory of the event or are you merely repeating what your notes say?

Witnesses need to be told that they have the right to refresh their memories but that cross-examination may focus on what they did to help recall the event. The judge will usually permit the opposing side to see notes or other documents used to refresh memory. If, during cross-examination, it can be shown that the witness' testimony was nearly verbatim from the notes, the attorney can cast doubt on the witness' memory. This is damaging to the witness' credibility, particularly if testimony has been given claiming an exceptionally good memory.

Past Recollection Recorded

The past recollection recorded exception to the hearsay rule is used when a witness has unsuccessfully attempted to refresh his/her memory but there is a written report stating the facts. In most states, the requirements for using this rule include all of the following:

1. Statement made in report would have been admissible if witness made it while testifying from memory.
2. Witness has insufficient present recollection to testify fully and accurately.
3. Statement is contained in a writing which:
   a. was made at time when the facts were fresh in memory of person making the report
   b. was made by the witness personally or by another person at his/her direction for the purpose of recording the witness' statement
   c. witness testifies that written document is a true and accurate statement of the facts

d. the written document is authenticated as an accurate record of the statement.

Portions of the report will be inadmissible if they were not based on firsthand observations of the witness unless some other evidence rule applies. For example, statements of an eyewitness to the crime telling of a conversation overheard between two other people would be inadmissible hearsay.

The report will be used at trial if testimony establishes that it is covered by past recollection recorded. Local practices vary, but it is common to have the report read into evidence by the court clerk, the attorney introducing it or the witness who made the report. Some courts permit a copy of the report to be introduced as an exhibit; others feel that this places undue weight on the report. Most states allow the report to be introduced by the opposing side if done to show inaccuracies or otherwise raise doubts about the report.

The attorney seeking to have the written document admitted will ask the witness pertinent questions to establish the required facts. The most contradictory fact that must be established is that the witness does not remember the facts but he/she knows that the report is accurate. This is usually done by testimony that the report was reviewed immediately after it was completed and all errors corrected. Officers are trained to sign reports only after the corrections have been made. When this is the normal practice, an officer can testify that the signature indicates that the report was accurate. The prosecutor's line of questioning in a case seeking to admit the police report as past recollection recorded might be:

PROSECUTOR: Did you make a written report about what you observed at the crime scene?

OFFICER: Yes.

PROSECUTOR: Did you write the report or dictate it to a secretary?

OFFICER: I typed it into my computer.

PROSECUTOR: When?

OFFICER: Before I went off duty that day.

PROSECUTOR: Were the facts fresh in your memory at that time?

OFFICER: Yes. It was only two hours after I saw the fight.

PROSECUTOR: Did you use any notes to help you make the report?

OFFICER: Yes. The notes I made in my field notebook while talking to witnesses.

PROSECUTOR: Did you review the report after it was printed out?

OFFICER: Yes. I always do.

PROSECUTOR: Is this a copy of that report?

OFFICER: Yes.

PROSECUTOR: Is it accurate?

OFFICER: Yes.

PROSECUTOR: How do you know the report is accurate?

OFFICER: I was trained to read my reports carefully, make needed changes, and never sign one until it is totally correct. I have made this a habit. I never sign a report that is not accurate.

PROSECUTOR: Is this your signature on the report.

OFFICER: Yes.

PROSECUTOR: Do you believe that this report is accurate?

OFFICER: Yes. My signature is on this report so I know I reviewed it and determined that it was accurate.

The report can be read into evidence based on this dialogue between the prosecutor and the officer and proof of authenticity. It may be necessary to call someone from the police Records Bureau to testify that the document referred to is a true copy of the report filed by the officer on the day of the crime. This authenticates the report. Some courts allow the officer to identify his/her handwriting in order to authenticate the report; others accept a certified copy of the report without calling a witness to authenticate it.

Opposing counsel will be allowed to cross-examine the person whose report is being admitted into evidence. The cross-examination may attempt to show that there is sufficient current memory to require the officer to testify rather than use the report. The legal test is that the witness has insufficient present recollection to testify fully and accurately. This is a question of fact. It does not require total memory lapse: the judge will use his/her discretion based on the facts introduced at trial to determine whether there is sufficient memory to permit the person to testify. The fact that the report contains more details than the witness can now recall is not sufficient grounds to introduce the report.

Another approach taken on cross-examination is to point to inaccurate facts (such as listing the wrong color for the vehicle involved or giving the wrong time or date) and other errors (grammatical, spelling, etc.) in the report. This challenges the officer's statement that the report was proofread and determined to be correct. The content of the report remains in evidence but the attorney is trying to raise doubt in jurors' minds about its accuracy and the ability of the officer to correctly record facts.

8.4 Evaluating Strengths and Weaknesses of Case

Prior to trial, the prosecutor must develop strategy for handling the case. This requires assessment of the strengths and weaknesses of each witness and every piece of physical evidence. The officer in charge of the case should be prepared to discuss this realistically with the prosecutor. Providing over-optimistic analysis can be very damaging because the prosecutor will be unprepared for serious challenges by the defense. If a witness cannot be located, or if a witness is hostile and may not testify as anticipated, the prosecutor must try to find alternate means of presenting the desired evidence to the jury.

Physical Evidence

An objective review of each item of physical evidence is necessary. The case management system should contain information needed to establish the chain of possession. Evaluation at this point needs to focus on the strengths and weaknesses of each item. Strengths would include: positive identification as the weapon used in the crime; eyewitness who can connect item to crime; conclusive laboratory tests establish point in question. Weaknesses might be: eyewitness description of item does not match physical evidence; item recovered damaged and no tests could be performed to establish that this was item used in crime; inconclusive laboratory tests; fingerprints recovered at scene were smeared and no match could be made. The prosecutor needs to be prepared for any challenge the defense attorney might make.

WITNESSES

Information in the case management system should describe what each witness can testify about. The strengths and weaknesses of each potential witness should be reviewed. Prosecutors consider witnesses strong if they believe the witness has important information and can testify in a manner that will impress the jury that he/she is telling the truth. Weak witnesses may possess important information but there are factors that may lead the jury to disbelieve the witness. Factors considered when deciding if the witness is strong or weak include: was the witness in a position to clearly observe the events? is the witness able to communicate well? does the witness have behavioral traits, such as nervousness and failing to make eye contact, that may cause the jury to doubt the testimony? and can the witness' credibility be attacked? If there are numerous witnesses available, it may be possible to establish guilt beyond a reasonable doubt without calling the weaker ones. In cases with few witnesses, the prosecutor may have to call all of them.

Each witness will be subject to impeachment during cross-examination. **Impeachment** is the process of showing that the witness lacks credibility. It is an attempt to imply that the witness is not telling the whole truth; rarely will a witness outright admit to lies. While the attorney may use voice inflections, gestures and dramatic pauses to make this point during cross-examination, the argument that the witness should not be believed comes during closing statements. The testimony on direct examination remains part of the evidence even if the witness is impeached: the witness is not barred from testifying. Jurors are told it is their duty to decide who to believe.

There are a variety of methods for impeaching a witness. Some of the most common include: witness was unable to observe what he/she testified about; inconsistent statements; motive, bias or prejudice for distorting the truth; prior convictions; and reputation for dishonesty. The prosecutor needs to be aware of any potential problems. Facts that can be used to rehabilitate the witness should also be in the file. **Rehabilitation** is the process of showing that the witness should be believed in spite of the opposing side's efforts to cast doubt on the testimony. For example, if the defense establishes that the eyewitness is very near-sighted, the prosecution can introduce testimony that on the night in question the witness was wearing glasses and was able to see 20/20.

Attacks on the witness' ability to make the observation testified to fall into two categories: inability to observe due to the observer's physical limitations; and inability to observe because physical barriers made the observation impossible. Facts such as poor eyesight and bad hearing are in the first group. Rehabilitation could focus on the witness wearing corrective lenses or a hearing aid. It may also be possible to show that the victim was able to make the same observation an unimpaired person would have; for example, the parties were shouting so loudly anyone could have heard them.

The second attack on the ability to observe focuses on the physical layout of the scene at the time the observation was made. For example, the witness testified that he/she had a clear view of the intersection and observed the car enter on the red light, but a photograph taken at the location where the witness claims to have been standing shows a large tree blocking the line of vision so that the traffic light could not be seen; or someone may claim to have looked out a window and observed the shooting but an officer, standing at the same location at the same time of day, discovered that the lighting was so poor a positive identification was impossible. The key to impeachment and rehabilitation on these items is a detailed knowledge of the scene *as it was at the time in question*. Merely going to the scene a few days before trial is not enough: bushes grow and can be trimmed, walls may have been built or torn down, etc., between the day of the crime and the trial. Detailed descriptions in police reports made on the day/night of the crime are very helpful for this purpose.

Prior inconsistent statements made by the witness can be used to impeach. The statement made during direct examination is evidence in the case: the inconsistent statement is introduced to attack the credibility of the witness and is not evidence that can be used to meet the burden of proof. These statements range from totally contradictory, such as recanting a confession, to minor inconsistencies; they can be oral or written. The statement which is inconsistent with what is said on the witness stand can be made to anyone. It does not have to be recorded in a written document or on tape. One key question will be the credibility of the person who claims to have heard the prior statement: is that person honest? did he/she hear the statement clearly? was there a chance that what was said was taken out of context or misinterpreted? The jury is likely to be impressed by statements that differ on important aspects of the testimony; time spent on minor discrepancies is usually wasted and may irritate the jury.

Most courts require that the witness be given the date the inconsistent statement was made, who it was made to, the content of the statement, and then be allowed to explain. For example, if the witness testified that she saw the defendant rob the victim, defense counsel might try to impeach as follows:

> DEFENSE ATTORNEY: You have testified that you saw the defendant at the crime scene, is that correct?
>
> WITNESS: Yes.
>
> DEFENSE ATTORNEY: Describe the person you saw take the victim's purse.
>
> WITNESS: The guy looked just like the defendant — about 6' 4" tall, about 225 pounds, stringy brown hair. I'd recognize him anywhere.
>
> DEFENSE ATTORNEY: Did you make a statement to a police officer immediately after you saw the crime?
>
> WITNESS: Yes.
>
> DEFENSE ATTORNEY: Did you tell the officer everything you saw?
>
> WITNESS: Yes.
>
> DEFENSE ATTORNEY: Did you say, and I'm quoting from the police report, "I didn't get a good look at the guy because I was hiding from him, but he was skinny and couldn't have been over 6 feet tall."
>
> WITNESS: I may have said that. I don't remember. I was really scared that night — he shot my best friend.

Some judges allow the police officer who took the statement to be called to testify about what the witness said on the night in question. This is more likely to be done if the witness denies making the statement. Rehabilitation will follow, usually by showing the statement was taken out of context or was not accurately reported. Sometimes it can be shown that the witness was too emotional to make an accurate report at the time but, after calming down, recalled the events more clearly.

Exercise of the Fifth Amendment privilege against self-incrimination cannot be used to attack the defendant's credibility. The jury may not be urged to conclude that invocation of *Miranda* rights indicates guilt. No argument may be made that an innocent defendant would have taken the witness stand. A defendant who does take the witness stand, however, can be cross-examined. Any voluntary pretrial statements made by such a defendant can be used to impeach. This includes statements obtained under circumstances that would not satisfy *Miranda* as long as there was no coercion. In cases where the defendant takes the witness stand and for the first time claims to be innocent, some lower courts have permitted questioning on why no attempt was made to explain this earlier. Most states permit defense witnesses to be asked to reconcile their testimony regarding the innocence of a friend with the fact that they made no previous effort to obtain the defendant's release from custody.

A witness can be impeached if there are conscious or unconscious reasons to distort the facts. This is known as impeachment on motive, bias, or prejudice. It includes any reason a person would be less than objective. The more obvious ones are people motivated by personal dislike for the defendant or by racial prejudice against the defendant's ethnic group. The opposite would also be grounds for impeachment: someone who likes the defendant may see things in a light more favorable toward him/her; racism can cause the witness to believe that what the defendant did was right. It is this type of favorable prejudice that makes a mother a poor alibi witness: she may be unable to see the faults in her children and, some would assume, be willing to lie to protect them.

Financial motives may cause a person to testify less than objectively. Being the beneficiary of an insurance policy is one illustration. Another would be testifying on behalf of an employer: if the defendant is convicted, the witness may be fired. While it is occasionally possible to show that the witness was threatened, it is more common to merely infer that potential financial hardship has subconsciously influenced the witness. Financial rewards for testimony can also be considered. Attempts to bribe the witness would be relevant. Questions about the fee paid an expert witness are used to show that the testimony may unduly favor the side that hired the expert.

Prior convictions are used to impeach: people may infer that a convicted criminal is less than honest. Many states place limits on what convictions can be used. The most common is to permit the use of felony convictions but not those for misdemeanors. Some states require that the conviction relate to an offense that involves dishonesty or moral turpitude. Sometimes a conviction may not be admitted because it occurred too long ago. There may be a specific policy, such as a conviction is inadmissible if the defendant has been out of custody for at least ten years and has had no convictions during that time, or the judge may have discretion to exclude evidence of a conviction if the judge believes it is so old that it is not relevant.

A witness' reputation (sometimes called character) for untruthfulness is always relevant for impeachment. If this method of impeachment is used, rehabilitation can be attempted by calling witness(es) to testify about the witness' reputation for honesty. State rules vary on how reputation is established. The traditional approach is to use witnesses who can testify to the person's reputation in the community. Community, as used here, is the town or neighborhood where a person lives; many courts now accept the workplace as a community. This type of testimony focuses on what the witness has heard others say, not on the witness' own belief or observations. Some states also permit testimony about specific acts of dishonesty; others allow the reputation witness to give his/her own opinion of the person being impeached.

An example of reputation in the community would be testimony by Mary that she has talked to many people who know Sam and everyone says Sam is a liar and a thief. In states permitting the reputation witness to give personal opinion, Mary could testify that she has had business dealings with Sam and believes that Sam is a liar. If specific examples were allowed, Mary might testify that she had a conversation with Sam on September 9, 1994; during that conversation Sam told Mary that he had paid $2,000 for a stereo but wanted to sell it because he needed cash for medical bills; Mary later learned that Sam stole the stereo in question during a burglary.

8.5 Anticipating Defense Strategy

Anticipating defense strategy is almost as important as evaluating the prosecution's case. The approach is quite similar to assessing the strengths and weaknesses of the prosecution's case. All potential defense witnesses should be reviewed; methods of impeaching each must be considered. The prosecutor must plan to counter their testimony either by cross-examination or by calling other witnesses.

Physical evidence the defense is likely to introduce must be considered. Necessary arrangements should be made to have prosecution experts examine this evidence and conduct relevant tests. Credibility of defense expert(s) must be considered: do they have the necessary education, training and experience? have they conducted appropriate tests? can the equipment used for these tests be challenged? does the witness testify in favor of defendants so often than he/she can be impeached for bias? are the fees being charged so high the jury will believe the opinion has been influenced by them? The prosecutor must also consider whether the prosecution should call one or more experts to refute the opinions given by the defense expert(s). This decision will need to be made based on an evaluation of the evidence, the strength of the defense expert, and the allocation of burden of proof.

Possible legal challenges must be anticipated. Those related to the Fourth Amendment and *Miranda* may have been resolved before trial. Others, such as applicable exceptions to the hearsay rule and privileges, are usually raised at the time testimony is being given. Attorneys are expected to be able to spontaneously cite the rules, case law and statutes supporting their arguments at trial. Research may be needed on these points before trial.

A growing trend is for defense attorneys to attack the personal credibility of prosecution witnesses, particularly police officers. This usually takes one or both of the following approaches: showing prior untruthful statements and revealing statements that show bias against the defendant or a group that he is a member of on account of race, ethnicity, gender, religion, sexual preference or other factors. Catching the officer lying under oath is classic impeachment; so is the use of earlier statements that are inconsistent with testimony given at trial. Other forms of untruthfulness that can be used include "padded" overtime vouchers and expense accounts, false claims for insurance benefits, and inappropriate claims for workman's compensation benefits and disability retirements. Statements made while handling the present case are very damaging: but derogatory comments about members of the defendant's race, for example, may be admissible even though they occurred in the witness' personal conversations several years before the case began. These types of negative comments are used during cross-examination to impeach the witness. The prosecution needs to be aware of any conversations or written communications that can be used for this purpose.

8.6 Dismissing Charges

Part of the preparation of the case for trial is a serious review of the charges. Events after the arraignment may indicate that there is no longer a strong possibility that the prosecution can establish its case at trial. Two main reasons contribute to this decision: lack of admissible evidence and problems with the witnesses.

Pretrial suppression hearings frequently challenge many items of physical evidence as well as statements obtained from the defendant. As discussed in Section 7.5, the judge will determine what items the prosecution cannot use at trial. The impact of such rulings varies. Sometimes the loss of the use of one piece of evidence is so damaging to the case that it will be impossible to meet the burden of proof. Suppression of everything seized in a case charging possession of controlled substances is a good example: without the drugs and related laboratory tests there is no way to establish that the items in the defendant's possession were contraband. In other cases, the suppressed evidence may not seriously affect the case; for example, the loss of the defendant's confession many not be important if there is overwhelming physical evidence.

Even though the prosecution may have won at a hearing on the defense's motion to *dismiss for insufficient evidence*, it may still be prudent to drop the charges before trial. The prosecutor may reassess all the evidence in the case and decide that the available evidence will not be sufficient to meet the burden of proof. One reason for this is that at trial the prosecution must convince a jury beyond a reasonable doubt that the defendant is guilty but the burden at a pretrial hearing is lower. Other factors are accidental loss or destruction of evidence; and laboratory tests may not have produced the results originally anticipated.

One or more witnesses may have disappeared or died before trial. When this is a problem, records of the case should be reviewed for statements that can be admitted in court without the person taking the witness stand. The most useful hearsay exceptions for this purpose are former testimony (usually from the transcript of the preliminary hearing) and dying declaration.

Uncooperative witnesses can also foil a prosecution. This category includes victims who are afraid to testify due to possible retaliation, hostile witnesses who have personal reasons to favor the defendant, and individuals who are generally antagonistic to law enforcement and the courts. The prosecutor must weigh the alternatives. Subpoenaing the witness may ensure that the witness attends the trial, but witnesses may change their testimony to be more favorable to the defense or repeatedly claim they cannot remember. A commonly cited example is the battered wife who has reconciled with her husband before trial and now tries to avoid saying anything negative about him. Other evidence may be available, such as eyewitnesses to the crime who can testify. Some forms of hearsay are admissible even though a witness refuses to testify.

The prosecutor reviews all of the above factors when deciding when to dismiss the charges. The "bottom line" is: will the evidence be sufficient to convince the jury of the defendant's guilt? If the prosecutor believes that the physical evidence and anticipated testimony of available witnesses will not meet this standard, one or more charges will be dismissed (also called dropping the charges).

Entries in the court record of "Dismissed in the interest of justice" reflect the discretion that is inherent in the process. Factors ranging from a defendant who is suffering from a terminal disease to agreements to act as a police informant are in this category. In misdemeanor cases, it is also common to see docket entries "Dismissed because the victim did not appear in court." This is most likely to occur when the victim was the only eyewitness to the crime other than the defendant; therefore, there is no way to prove the case without the victim's testimony. Some prosecutors honor the victim's request to dismiss charges even if there is other evidence that could be used.

8.7 Trial Brief

A trial brief is a written document that outlines the evidence and legal issues in the case. Points and authorities are included if the attorney believes they are necessary. The trial brief is presented to the judge, either on the first day of trial or a few days before, by an attorney. A copy must also be given to the opposing side. A trial brief is usually optional.

An attorney in the case or a member of his/her staff prepares the trial brief. Consultation with the officer handling the case may be necessary to outline the evidence. Some trial briefs include a list of witnesses who will be called to testify and a synopsis of the testimony anticipated from each. In lengthy and/or complex cases, the trial brief is very helpful: the judge can refer to it to see the relevance of the testimony of each witness. It is beneficial if scheduling problems make it necessary to alter the normal sequence in which witnesses are called. The brief will also help the judge make rulings on the admissibility of questions and physical evidence. It serves as a guide to the trial; it is not evidence in the case.

Summary

The final case preparation for trial is usually shared by the prosecutor and officer in charge of the investigation. One or more meetings is usually necessary to decide which witnesses to subpoena and what evidence to introduce. Complete candor is necessary in order for the prosecutor to prepare the case effectively. The strengths and weaknesses of each witness and item of physical evidence need to be considered. The officer will be responsible for making sure that the evidence is in the courtroom at the appropriate time and that the subpoenas have been served.

In criminal cases, the subpoenas can usually be signed by the prosecutor, public defender or court clerk. The subpoena must indicate where and when the witness is ordered to appear and must be served on the witness. A proof of services must be filed with the court for each subpoena. Special showings regarding the importance of the testimony are usually required to subpoena a witness from a substantial distance.

There is no legal barrier to refreshing the memory of a witness prior to trial. The witness must, however, be able to testify from memory. A witness can be discredited if it is shown that the testimony was memorized. The past recollection recorded exception to the hearsay rule can be used to introduce written reports made shortly after the event if the witness cannot remember enough to testify fully about them. The witness must be able to vouch for the accuracy of the report.

Objective evaluation of the physical evidence is important. The prosecutor needs to be prepared to meet defense challenges based on improperly handled evidence, inconclusive laboratory tests, and attacks on the credibility of the witnesses. The extent of each witness' knowledge of the case must be reviewed. Behavioral characteristics that either enhance or detract from credibility must be considered.

Potential impeachment of both prosecution and defense witnesses needs to be evaluated. Credibility can be attacked based on: physical limitations of the witness interfered with the ability to perceive the events in question; layout of the location made the observation testified to impossible; prior inconsistent statements by the witness indicate untruthfulness; motive, bias or prejudice which may influence testimony; witness has prior convictions; and reputation of the witness for dishonesty.

Prosecutors need to go over every aspect of the defense's case and try to anticipate the defendant's strategy. Each possible piece of physical evidence needs to be considered. Every potential defense witness must be evaluated and methods of discrediting his/her testimony reviewed.

Each attorney may give the judge a trial brief. This document, prepared by the attorney's staff, summarizes the case and presents legal arguments. Its content is not evidence in the case, but it assists the judge in understanding why the attorney is calling each witness and asking specific questions. The trial brief is usually optional.

Study Questions

1. Explain how to establish the chain of possession for the following items:
   a. gun found at murder scene
   b. body of victim so the autopsy report will be admissible
   c. ballistic test showing gun found at murder scene fired bullet recovered from victim during autopsy
2. Check your local court rules, and explain how to subpoena the following people:
   a. police officer who took crime report
   b. pathologist from coroner's office who conducted autopsy
   c. person believed to have been with the victim at time of death—this person lives in your state but is 250 miles from the courthouse
   d. person who can refute defendant's alibi—this person is now an inmate serving time in another state

3. What can be done with witnesses who have memory problems:
   a. List three ways to refresh a witness' memory.
   b. Prepare a script for the prosecutor and defense attorney where the officer who wrote a report about the theft of a six-pack of soda from a grocery store cannot remember very many details in the case.
4. Prepare a script for the defense attorney to use when attempting to impeach Wendy, an eyewitness to a robbery, on each of the following:
   a. prior inconsistent statements—on night crime was committed Wendy gave police a description of the robber that does not match defendant
   b. inability to observe—Wendy has bad eyesight and was not wearing glasses
   c. inability to observe—Wendy claims to have been able to see everything but the officer's diagram shows there was a large bush between the victim and where Wendy was standing
   d. motive, bias, prejudice—Wendy is victim's sister; and Wendy recently broke off her romance with defendant after a bitter fight
   e. prior convictions—Wendy was convicted of petty theft three years ago
   f. reputation—a person who works with Wendy claims everyone at work knows Wendy submits false expense account claims
5. Collect newspaper clippings on a major criminal case that occurred recently in your area. Make a report:
   a. List strengths and weaknesses of each potential witness including specific facts to be used for:
      1) impeachment
      2) rehabilitation
   b. List strengths and weaknesses for each possible item of physical evidence:
      1) How will the chain of possession be established?
      2) What witness(es) are needed to introduce each item into evidence?

Chapter 9
The Trial

Learning Objectives

After reading this chapter, the student will be able to:

- Identify six rights the Sixth Amendment guarantees for defendants in criminal trials.
- Describe the process used to select a jury.
- Explain the purpose of opening and closing statements in criminal trials.
- Explain what the prosecutor does during the case in chief.
- Explain the function of the defense's case in chief.
- Explain when an attorney may reopen testimony and/or present rebuttal.
- Describe how the jury is instructed on the law.
- Identify what the jury does during deliberations.
- Explain the process for entering a jury verdict.

Key Terms

alibi witness
alternate jurors
bench trial
case in chief
change of venue
character
challenge for cause
closing statements
contemporaneous objection rule
continuance
cross-examination
cumulative evidence
direct examination
expert witness
hostile witness
hung jury
in propria persona
jury commissioner
jury instructions
jury pool
lay witness
leading question
limited admissibility
mistrial
opening statements
peremptory challenge
narrative question
objection overruled
objection sustained
poll the jury
pro per
relevant evidence
rest the case
Sixth Amendment rights
- assistance of counsel
- compulsory process
- confront witnesses
- impartial jury
- informed of nature and cause of accusation
- speedy and public trial

stipulation
sua sponte
voir dire

9.1 Defendant's Constitutional Rights

The **Sixth Amendment** protects the criminal defendant's trial rights. It states:

> In all criminal prosecutions, the accused shall enjoy the right to a speedy and public trial, by an impartial jury of the State and district wherein the crime shall have been committed, which district shall

> have been previously ascertained by law, and to be informed of the nature and cause of the accusation; to be confronted with the witnesses against him; to have compulsory process for obtaining witnesses in his favor, and to have the Assistance of Counsel for his defense.

Streamlining the federal and state court systems cannot be done at the expense of these rights.

Speedy and Public Trial

The Sixth Amendment was designed to protect against the practices that were common at the time of the revolution: leaving the defendant to languish in jail for years without trial; and secret trials where the government was able to obtain a conviction. The right to a speedy trial was discussed in Section 7.4: the delay between arrest and trial must not be so long as to be prejudicial to the defendant. Factors considered include: length of delay; reasons for the delay; defendant's assertion of the right to a speedy trial; and prejudice to the defendant. No one factor is determinative. The defendant must show that the combination of these factors resulted in the denial of a fair trial. The longer the delay, however, the less evidence there needs to be of actual prejudice.

The right to public trial is in the Sixth Amendment's list of the defendant's rights, but the Supreme Court has ruled that it does not belong solely to the defendant. The right of the public to attend trials and be informed about what occurs is also of constitutional dimension. First Amendment issues of freedom of the press are involved. The result of the confluence of these rights is that the trial must be open to the public and press except when there is an urgent need to close it temporarily. Witnesses waiting to testify, except the defendant, may be excluded because listening to other witnesses may directly or indirectly influence their testimony. Unruly people, including defendants, may be removed from the courtroom to maintain decorum. Excluding the public and press en mass requires a showing of a more urgent need. The most common situation where this is allowed involves children who have been sexually assaulted. Closing juvenile court proceedings to the public has been permitted because this protects the juvenile defendant and encourages rehabilitation.

Impartial Jury

Despite the Sixth Amendment's reference to juries, there is no constitutional right to be tried by a jury if the maximum sentence is six months or less. The rule used by the Supreme Court parallels the United States Code's definition of "petty offenses" (18 U.S.C. §1). The defendant's constitutional right to a jury trial does not mean the opposite is true: the defense cannot have a trial without a jury if the prosecutor requests a jury. Trials by a judge without a jury, called **bench trials**, occur only if neither side requests a jury.

Impartiality of the jurors is determined during their *voir dire* examination. They can be questioned regarding any preconceived opinions and prejudices which would interfere with their ability to decide the case based on the evidence introduced at trial and the law given in the jury instructions. The system for excluding jurors who may be partial to one side is discussed in Section 9.2. In high publicity cases the media's coverage of the case may make it difficult to find impartial jurors. The courts have limited authority to restrain the media in order to protect potential juror's neutrality. See Section 6.2. A **change of venue**, which means to move the trial to another location, is frequently used if the judge is convinced that the publicity has influenced so many people that finding an impartial jury is unlikely. A **continuance**, which is a postponement of the trial, may be granted so that inflamed public opinion may cool.

Traditionally, the jury consisted of 12 members who had to reach a unanimous verdict. Neither of these requirements is constitutionally mandated. The Supreme Court has approved six-member juries but held that smaller ones are not acceptable. When using a six-person jury, the verdict must be unanimous. State laws allowing convictions based on votes of 11 to 1, 10 to 2, and 9 to 3 have been accepted by the Supreme Court. This gives individual states flexibility in determining rules on juries in criminal cases. The jury used in each case must comply with the state law (i.e., a defendant cannot be convicted on a 10 to 2 vote if the state law requires unanimity).

Informed of the Nature and Cause of the Accusation

Prior to trial, the defendant must be given notice of the charges. The arraignment partially satisfies this requirement. Charges may be dropped after the arraignment for a variety of procedural reasons, as discussed in Chapter 7, or the prosecutor may decide there is insufficient evidence, due to the disappearance of witnesses or other reasons, to justify going forward on one or more of the charges. The result is that the charges to be adjudicated at trial may not be the same as those in the original complaint, the information filed after the preliminary hearing or the indictment. The defendant usually has knowledge of the charges because the defense attorney was present in court when they were made. Even so, trials begin with a reading of the charges unless the defendant requests that this not be done. This gives official notice of the charges and also informs the jury of the nature of the case.

Confronted With the Witnesses Against Him

The right to confront the witnesses takes two forms: the accuser must testify at trial and the defense has the right to cross-examine each prosecution witness. Both have exceptions. There may be circumstances that justify not calling an eyewitness. For example, the witness may have died from natural causes, accident or by criminal means. Statements made by witnesses who are unavailable to testify at trial are hearsay but the traditional exceptions to the hearsay rule are viewed as incorporated in the Sixth Amendment right to confrontation. In other words, the defendant's rights are not violated by admission of statements if there is a long-standing exception to the hearsay rule that permits the statement to be used at trial. Newer exceptions which are not based on the trustworthiness of the testimony have been viewed as violating the right to confront the accuser.

Normally, the confrontation clause is interpreted to mean that the witness must testify in court in the presence of the defendant. The Supreme Court has allowed the use of closed-circuit television as an alternative to eye-to-eye contact when there was a specific showing that normal procedures would produce damaging trauma to a sexually abused child testifying against the assailant. The Court made it clear that an individualized showing of trauma was necessary; standing rules permitting televised testimony in all molestation cases were not permitted; neither was a standing policy that allowed the prosecution to place a screen between the defendant and the victim so that the victim would not have to look at the attacker.

Our adversarial system considers cross-examination the key to determining the truth. The defendant therefore has the right to cross-examine any witness that is called by the prosecution. Unreasonable restrictions on cross-examination violate the Sixth Amendment. Judicial discretion may be used to stop cross-examination that is irrelevant, repetitious or done solely to harass the witness.

The defense attorney must be allowed to question each witness. The ability to ask questions, not the witness' ability to answer them, is the heart of this right. The defendant's rights are not violated by prosecution witnesses who have limited memory. Tactical decisions are made by the defense on how extensive cross-examination will be or whether to waive cross. For example, the Supreme Court found no violation of this right when a prosecution witness testified to identifying the defendant as the assailant but, due to a head injury, could not recall all the facts relating to the crime. Neither are the defendant's rights violated by the use of testimony from the preliminary hearing where the defense attorney chose not to cross-examine the witness.

Compulsory Process for Obtaining Witnesses

Compulsory process means the right to subpoena witnesses. It would be grossly unfair if the prosecution could use the power of the court to compel witnesses to attend trial but the defense could not. The Sixth Amendment guarantees the defendant's right to use the authority of the court to compel witnesses to attend trial and testify. There is no provision for the defense to grant immunity to a witness. The defense must comply with appropriate procedures and deadlines when using the subpoenas. It is also the defense's responsibility to locate the people to be subpoenaed. See Section 8.2 for details on how subpoenas are obtained and served.

Assistance of Counsel

The Sixth Amendment guarantees the defendant's right to have an attorney at any criminal trial. A series of cases starting with *Gideon v. Wainwright* 372 U.S. 335 (1963) interpreted this right to include appointing attorneys at government expense if the defendant cannot afford to hire private counsel. An indigent person cannot be sentenced to jail or prison as a result of a trial in which he/she was not represented by counsel or voluntarily represented him/herself. The Supreme Court does not require appointment of an attorney in cases in which only fines or probation without time in custody are imposed.

Defendants who understand their right to counsel may act as their own attorneys, called being ***in propria persona*** or ***pro per***. The only test the judge may use when deciding whether to permit a defendant to be a *pro per* is whether there is a voluntary waiver of a known right. The defendant must be informed that there is a right to free counsel and no coercion may be used. No questions may be asked regarding court procedures. *Pro per* defendants can be required to follow court rules the same as licensed attorneys. Some judges appoint an attorney to assist a *pro per*, but this is not constitutionally mandated. A defendant who is granted the right to be a *pro per* cannot appeal a conviction based on incompetent trial counsel.

One attorney representing more than one defendant raises questions of adequate representation. Frequently, the best defense is to try to blame everything on the other defendant. This is impossible if there is only one attorney. Forcing defendants to share an attorney violates their Sixth Amendment rights if it interferes with their ability to present a defense. The judge must honor a request for separate representation if there is any reason to believe there is a conflict. The Supreme Court also held that the judge may deny joint representation if the judge believes it is impossible for one attorney to handle multiple defendants even though the defendants have agreed to accept the same lawyer.

The right to counsel would be meaningless unless there is a right to a competent attorney. The constitutional standard is: the attorney's conduct was below the norm for defense attorneys in criminal cases and it is likely that this incompetence was a factor in the outcome of the case. The courts will not second-guess tactical decisions made at trial as long as they were made with knowledge of the law. Acts done due to ignorance or failure to prepare the case properly are signs of incompetence. The standard is based on the average criminal defense attorney in the area. The second prong of the test is the effect of the incompetence on the outcome of the case. Appellate judges base their decisions on the likelihood that the defendant would not have been convicted if the defense attorney had performed competently. If the prosecution's evidence was strong, errors by the defense attorney may not merit reversal of the conviction; in close cases, the defense attorney's inadequacies give the defendant the right to a new trial with a better attorney.

9.2 Jury Selection

Our justice system uses juries as the conscience of the community. To do this, the jury panel must represent a cross section of the local population. The process of selecting a jury actually begins with the summonsing of people to jury duty. A government official, frequently called the **jury commissioner**, is in charge of selecting the people who will be called. Race, gender or religious affiliation cannot be used to exclude people from participating. Voter registration records were traditionally used for this purpose. Many states now combine voter registration with other sources, such as driver's license records, to make up the initial pool.

A formula derived from past experience is used to determine how many people should be summoned for jury duty. Factors considered are: percentage of people normally excused from jury duty; number of trials anticipated; and the number of potential jurors usually questioned in order to select a jury. State law specifies who is exempt from jury duty. Minors, people who are not citizens, police officers and people who do not speak English are usually exempt; convicted felons normally are disqualified. These people can notify the jury commissioner and be excused from appearing at the courthouse. In addition to automatic exemptions, there are usually a variety of personal circumstances that may be considered. For example, teachers and college students may be able to delay jury duty until school vacations; some states permit people who are the primary caregivers for pre-school children to be excused. The summons to jury duty may include a form to be used to request exemption on these grounds.

A large group of potential jurors will be ordered to appear at the courthouse. This is usually called the **jury pool**. A waiting room is provided and some form of orientation is usually given. When a judge is ready to start jury selection, the court clerk telephones the jury commissioner's office and requests a jury panel. A group of people will be selected from the jury pool. This may done by drawing names each time a judge requests a jury panel; some jury commissioners place names on lists before the jurors arrive and send everyone on a list to the courtroom at the same time. These potential jurors go to the courtroom and are given an oath to truthfully answer questions during *voir dire*. Names are randomly selected to make a jury. ***Voir dire***, the process of asking questions to determine qualifications, follows. Local rules govern how *voir dire* is conducted. The attorneys may ask individual jurors questions, the judge may ask the questions or a combination may occur. Sometimes questions are directed at all potential jurors; at other times jurors may be queried individually.

There are two types of challenges that can be used to exclude jurors: challenge for cause and peremptory challenge. A **challenge for cause** excludes a juror because that individual is unable to objectively base a decision on the evidence presented and the law given by the judge. There is no limit on the number of potential jurors who can be challenged for cause. Either side may exercise a challenge for cause but the judge must be convinced that there is a factual basis for the challenge. Questions used during *voir dire* as a basis for a challenge for cause include: do you believe everyone the police arrest is guilty? can you base your decision in this case on the facts presented at trial and not what you already know about the case? do you understand that the prosecution must establish guilt beyond a reasonable doubt and that the defense does not have to disprove the charges?

Peremptory challenges give an attorney the right to exclude a potential juror for subjective reasons. Neither race nor gender may be used as a reason for challenging a juror, but almost any other factor can. If the opposing side suspects that challenges are being made on the basis of race or gender, an objection must be made at that time. Once this objection has been made, the judge is required to ask the attorney for the reason for the challenge and determine if there is a permissible reason behind the challenge. General questions, such as "Do you have friends that are police officers?" are used during *voir dire* to help the attorneys decide how to use peremptory challenges. Other questions frequently relate directly to the facts of the case. For example, in a drunk driving case jurors may be asked whether they believe driving while mildly intoxicated is wrong; in a domestic violence case they might be asked if they have ever had a violent argument with their significant other. The answers to these questions rarely establish grounds to exclude a juror for cause, but they help the attorneys judge the possible reaction of the juror to the evidence in the case. Body language and general demeanor are also considered. Attorneys try to exclude jurors they believe are likely to vote for the other side.

State law establishes how many peremptory challenges may be used in a case. The number is usually based on the severity of the case (misdemeanor, felony, death penalty case) and the number of defendants. For example, six peremptory challenges may be permitted in misdemeanor cases. If there is only one defendant, the prosecutor and defense attorney have the same number of challenges; the quotas may be different if there are multiple defendants.

The process of selecting the jury begins with challenging jurors for cause. An attorney will ask the judge to excuse a specific juror. Opposing counsel may argue that the request should be denied. The judge gives a ruling after hearing arguments from both sides. If a juror is excused, another name will be drawn. The new person will undergo *voir dire*. Additional challenges for cause are made and replacements drawn until enough people to make a jury are seated.

Peremptory challenges are utilized next. Local rules designate who starts; the sides then alternate. During this process, jurors are frequently addressed by number: "The Prosecution would like to thank and excuse Juror Number Three." No grounds are given for exercising the peremptory challenge. Once a juror is excused, a name must be drawn for a replacement who undergoes *voir dire* and may possibly be challenged for cause. Once the replacement juror has been seated, the other side will exercise a peremptory challenge. The process continues, going back and forth between prosecution and defense, until one side runs out of peremptory challenges or both sides accept the jury.

Extra jurors, called **alternate jurors**, are selected to hear the case and act as substitutes if one or more of the jurors becomes ill or otherwise unable to continue. They are needed because a mistrial must be declared if the number of jurors falls below the legal minimum. The judge decides on the number of alternate jurors based on the estimated length of the case and past experience with the drop-out rate of jurors. Alternate jurors are selected last. They undergo *voir dire* and are subject to challenge for cause. Separate rules usually govern the number of peremptory challenges; for example, one peremptory for every two alternate jurors.

Once jury selection is complete, the jury is sworn in. The oath given at this point requires the jurors to decide the case on the evidence presented at trial and to follow the judge's instructions. The judge may give a brief speech telling the jurors to take notes, not discuss the case until it is time for deliberations, and to avoid discussion about the case with people who are not on the jury. Administering this oath officially starts the trial. Actions after this point are covered by double jeopardy. In a bench trial, double jeopardy attaches when the first witness is sworn.

9.3 Opening Statements

Trials usually begin with the reading of the charges followed by opening statements. Opening statements are speeches made by the attorneys; they are not evidence in the case. The purpose of the opening statement is to provide an outline of the case. A good opening statement gives the jury a summary of the facts that will be presented. If there will be a large number of witnesses, the opening statement highlights how the testimony will fit together. It also points out things the jurors should watch for and explains things that may not be obvious, such as why experts will be called. Bench trials frequently do not have opening statements because it is assumed the judge will be able to understand the evidence.

Each side is entitled to make an opening statement in a jury trial. They are optional, but the prosecutor almost always makes one. The defense attorney has three choices regarding opening statements: make one immediately after the prosecutor; delay the opening statement until the defense is ready to call its own witnesses; or do not make an opening statement at all. This is a tactical decision. Many defense attorneys feel their statement has more impact if made when defense witnesses will be testifying. Waiting until this time also gives the defense attorney a chance to hear the prosecution's evidence and tailor its opening statement accordingly. Postponing the opening statement also allows the defense to conceal its strategy until after the prosecution's case in chief is concluded. Waiving the opening statement is most common in cases in which the defense decides not to call any witnesses. When an opening statement is made, the defense usually summarizes the facts and emphasizes the rule that the prosecution has the burden of proof.

9.4 PRESENTING EVIDENCE AT TRIAL

Testimony at trial must relate to something that is relevant to the case. **Relevant** means the evidence tends to prove or disprove any disputed fact in the case. In most cases it takes many pieces of evidence to establish guilt beyond a reasonable doubt. Each piece is relevant whether it relates to establishing an element of the crime, laying the foundation for admission of an item of physical evidence, or impeaching a witness. The entire case may be circumstantial; it is not necessary to have direct evidence.

WHAT IS ADMISSIBLE

Anything tending to establish an element of the crime(s) charged (or a defense) is relevant unless the point is no longer in dispute. What is relevant can only be determined from the facts of the case. For example, questions regarding the floor plan of a restaurant would be relevant if a robbery was committed there but totally irrelevant if all events related to the crime occurred somewhere else; questions regarding education may be relevant for an expert witness but irrelevant for an eyewitness to the crime.

Relevant evidence may be excluded for a variety of reasons. The Exclusionary Rule makes evidence seized in violation of the Fourth and Fifth Amendments inadmissible even though it is relevant. If both sides admit an event occurred, called a **stipulation**, facts that establish that event are no longer in dispute and testimony that would otherwise be admissible is irrelevant. Privileged information is relevant but not admissible: the strong policy favoring confidential communications between attorney-client, physician-patient, clergy-penitent, husband-wife and certain other relationships, permits the parties to refuse to reveal relevant evidence at trial.

Judicial discretion can be used to exclude relevant evidence if it is highly inflammatory, confusing or would take an excessive amount of court time compared to the probative value of the item in question. A balancing process is involved. For example, if a complicated scientific test was used that would require hours of testimony to explain to the jury, the judge would consider the importance of the test versus the time and possible confusion caused. If the test was a major factor in the prosecution's case, it might be allowed if it was extremely accurate, but if it was reliable in only 20% of the cases it would be excluded.

Some evidence is relevant for one purpose but not another. This is called **limited admissibility**. When such evidence is admitted, the jury will be told that it can consider the item for one purpose but must not use it for another. Impeachment evidence is a good example. The fact that the witness made an inconsistent statement is relevant on the issue of the truthfulness of the witness, but the prior statement is not admissible as evidence to prove an element of the crime.

Lay witnesses (eyewitnesses, crime victims and others) are allowed to testify to what they observed with their five senses: hearing, smell, taste, touch and sight. Opinions are not usually allowed. The reason for this rule is that it is the jury's function to draw conclusions from the facts in the case. Some opinions are so ingrained in everyday life that many judges will permit lay witnesses to give them; for example, he looked sick; she seemed upset; he walked like he was drunk.

Patrol officers and detectives usually testify as lay witnesses. They can relate everything they observed at the crime scene and while investigating the crime. Statements made to them by victims, eyewitnesses, suspects, and other people are admissible ***only if*** covered by an exception to the hearsay rule. Other restrictions may apply, for example, a confession by the defendant must have been obtained in compliance with *Miranda*. Common opinions, such as "he was driving too fast," are usually allowed, but statements such as "the car was going 75 miles per hour" must be established by some other form of evidence such as a radar gun.

Expert witnesses, on the other hand, are allowed to give opinions. In fact, they are called to testify specifically so the jury can hear their opinions. To introduce this type of testimony, the side calling the expert must show: the jury needs the help of an expert to understand the evidence; there is a recognized body of knowledge on the subject; and the expert has appropriate training and/or experience. *Voir dire* will be done to determine if the expert is qualified. Once the expert is on the witness stand, questions can be used to determine whether tests were conducted correctly and the equipment used was accurate.

Some officers testify as expert witnesses. Special training is required to achieve this status and is usually combined with many years of experience. Examples include latent fingerprint examiners, those who conduct ballistics tests, and officers trained to calculate speed based on skid marks at the accident scene. These officers only testify as experts when providing information relating to their specialized knowledge and skills. If they testify regarding things observed when they were not utilizing their expertise, they must testify as lay witnesses. The same is true for all expert witnesses.

Objections to a question must be made immediately after the question is asked. This is called the **contemporaneous objection rule**. The main reason for the rule is to exclude improper questions before the jury hears the answers. When an objection is made, the judge will hear arguments from both sides and then rule on the question: **objection sustained**, meaning that the question cannot be asked, and **objection overruled**, inferring the objection was meritless. The objections and arguments regarding them are normally made without leaving the courtroom. Sometimes the judge or attorneys wish to discuss the objections outside the hearing of the jury and/or witness. When this is desired, the discussion is usually done in muted voices at the sidebar, the side of the judge's bench furthest away from the jury box. The judge may tell the attorneys to "approach the bench" or refer to this as a bench conference. If lengthy debate is expected, the jury may be asked to leave the room.

Prosecution's Case in Chief

A **case in chief** is the portion of the trial during which one side has the opportunity to prove its case. During it's case in chief the prosecution must establish every element of each charge beyond a reasonable doubt. This is done by calling witnesses to testify and, when appropriate, using their testimony to introduce physical evidence of the crime. The prosecutor may ask the officer in charge of the investigation to sit at the counsel table. This makes it easier for the prosecutor to ask the officer for details needed to question witnesses. Arrangements must also be made to have each item of physical evidence in court when needed.

The process of questioning a witness begins with **direct examination**. This means that the side that called the witness asks questions. Questions should be phrased so that they are easy to understand and provide an opportunity for the witness to reveal what he/she knows. Many times questions are worded so that the answer need be only yes or no. **Narrative questions**, which ask the witness to give an unstructured response, are usually not allowed for two reasons: witnesses tend to ramble and waste court time, and the witness may bring up information that the court has ruled is inadmissible. For this reason, the witness is rarely asked a question like "Tell us about what happened on June 25, 1994." Specific questions are used to focus the testimony: Where were you at 3:00 p.m. on June 25, 1994? Did you see a person enter the building? etc.

Leading questions are usually not allowed on direct examination. A leading question is one that infers the answer. For example, "He had on a red shirt, didn't he?" Appropriate questions on direct examination to establish what the robber was wearing might be:

PROSECUTOR: Where were you at 3:00 p.m. on June 25, 1994?

MS. JONES: At the Denny's restaurant on First and Main.

PROSECUTOR: Did anyone talk to the cashier while you were there?

MS. JONES: Yes. One man did.

PROSECUTOR: Please describe that man.

MS. JONES: He was about 25 years old and probably six feet tall. I think he weighed about 200 pounds.

PROSECUTOR: What was he wearing?

MS. JONES: Red shirt and blue jeans.

PROSECUTOR: Describe the shirt.

MS. JONES: It was red plaid, sort of dirty. It had short sleeves.

PROSECUTOR: What else was he wearing?

MS. JONES: Blue jeans and dirty white tennis shoes. No socks.

Sometimes leading questions are permitted on preliminary matters in order to save time. These would relate to setting the scene as to date, time and location.

An exception to the rule prohibiting leading questions is made for hostile witnesses. A **hostile witness** is a person who is unfriendly to the side that subpoenaed him/her. In a criminal case, this is usually due to the witness' friendship with the defendant or the fact that the witness is being prosecuted for some related offense. A police officer subpoenaed by the defense would also be a hostile witness in most cases. Since the hostile witness is not willing to cooperate, leading questions are allowed in order to force answers to specific questions. Normally a motion must be made asking the judge to consider the person a hostile witness. Being declared a hostile witness does not prevent the witness from claiming the Fifth Amendment as grounds for refusing to answer questions. In the following example, the prosecution calls the defendant's brother as a hostile witness.

PROSECUTOR: Where do you work?

MR. SMITH: At the Denny's restaurant on First and Main.

PROSECUTOR: Were you working there on the afternoon of June 25, 1994?

MR. SMITH: Yes.

PROSECUTOR: Where were you at 3:05 p.m.?

MR. SMITH: I was cooking at the grill.

PROSECUTOR: Did you hear loud voices coming from the area near the cash register?

MR. SMITH: Yes.

PROSECUTOR: Describe what you heard.

MR. SMITH: Someone was yelling "Give me the money!"

PROSECUTOR: Did you recognize the person who was shouting?

MR. SMITH: Ah, well, no, I don't wanna say.

PROSECUTOR: Mr. Smith, are you related to the defendant in this case?

MR. SMITH: Yes. He is my brother.

PROSECUTOR: Your Honor, the People request that Mr. Smith be declared a hostile witness.

DEFENSE ATTORNEY: We object, your honor. The People subpoenaed this witness. They should not be allowed any special privileges.

PROSECUTOR: He was an eyewitness to the crime. We should be allowed to question him about what he saw but he is refusing to cooperate because the defendant is his brother.

JUDGE: Motion granted. Mr. Smith, you are under oath. You must answer the questions.

PROSECUTOR: Mr. Smith, did you have a clear view of the cash register?

MR. SMITH: Yes.

PROSECUTOR: Could you see the person who shouted "Give me the money"?

MR. SMITH: Yes.

PROSECUTOR: Mr. Smith, you recognized the person who said "Give me the money," didn't you?

MR. SMITH: Yes.

PROSECUTOR: Your brother said, "Give me the money," didn't he?

MR. SMITH: Uh huh.

PROSECUTOR: Please answer yes or no. Did your brother, who is the defendant in this case, say "Give me the money"?

MR. SMITH: Yes.

PROSECUTOR: And what did he have in his hand when he said "Give me the money"?

MR. SMITH: Something.

PROSECUTOR: He had a gun in his hand, didn't he?

MR. SMITH: Yes.

PROSECUTOR: Where was the gun pointed?

MR. SMITH: I didn't see nothin.

PROSECUTOR: Mr. Smith, you testified that you had a clear view of the cash register. You said he had a gun in his hand. Now you must have seen where it was pointing. Was it pointed at you?

MR. SMITH: No.

PROSECUTOR: Was it pointed at the ceiling?

MR. SMITH: No.

PROSECUTOR: It was pointed at the cashier, wasn't it?

MR. SMITH: Yes.

PROSECUTOR: Did you tell your brother where the cashier kept the extra money?

MR. SMITH: You can't ask me that! My public defender told me to take the Fifth.

Due to the fact that Mr. Smith was declared a hostile witness, the attorney conducting the direct examination was allowed to ask leading questions just like on cross-examination. This does not mean that only leading questions may be asked.

The prosecution normally is allowed to call as many witnesses as it deems necessary. The judge does have the discretion to refuse to allow a witness to testify if it appears that the testimony will merely duplicate what has been said by several other witnesses. This is called **cumulative evidence**. This would be the case where there are numerous eyewitnesses to the crime and several have already given very similar descriptions of what occurred.

The defense attorney is entitled to conduct **cross-examination** after direct examination of each witness by the prosecutor. During cross-examination, the witness will be asked for additional details that were not previously included, questioned on discrepancies in the testimony, and possibly impeached. See Section 8.4 for a detailed discussion of impeachment. Unlike direct examination, leading questions may be used during cross-examination to force the witness to answer specific questions. The defense might cross-examine Ms. Jones as follows:

DEFENSE ATTORNEY: Ms. Jones, on this diagram of the restaurant I want you to put a J to indicate where you were sitting.

MS. JONES: I was right here.

DEFENSE ATTORNEY: Please put a "C" where the cashier was.

MS. JONES: She was right here at the end of the counter.

DEFENSE ATTORNEY: How far were you from the cashier?

MS. JONES: About 20 feet, I guess.

DEFENSE ATTORNEY: Which direction were you facing when you were eating?

MS. JONES: Toward the window.

DEFENSE ATTORNEY: Were you facing the cashier?

MS. JONES: No. She was behind me.

DEFENSE ATTORNEY: So you couldn't see her?

MS. JONES: Only when I turned around.

DEFENSE ATTORNEY: What was in this square on the diagram?

MS. JONES: That was where they put the dirty dishes.

DEFENSE ATTORNEY: Was it out in the open so you could see it?

MS. JONES: No. It had a little wall around it.

DEFENSE ATTORNEY: A little wall? What kind of wall?

MS. JONES: Sort of a partition, maybe four feet high, covered with carpeting.

DEFENSE ATTORNEY: Could you see through the wall?

MS. JONES: No.

DEFENSE ATTORNEY: What did you hear the man say?

MS. JONES: "Give me all your money."

DEFENSE ATTORNEY: Are you sure?

MS. JONES: Yes.

DEFENSE ATTORNEY: Are you sure it wasn't "Give me all my money?"

MS. JONES: Yes.

DEFENSE ATTORNEY: When was the last time you had your hearing tested?

MS. JONES: A year ago.

DEFENSE ATTORNEY: Did the doctor say you had perfect hearing?

MS. JONES: No.

DEFENSE ATTORNEY: Did the doctor say you needed a hearing aid?

MS. JONES: Yes.

DEFENSE ATTORNEY: Were you wearing a hearing aid on June 25, 1994?

MS. JONES: No, but...

DEFENSE ATTORNEY: That will be all, Ms. Jones.

If the witness denies facts relevant to impeachment, the judge may permit another witness to be called to verify that the event used for impeachment occurred.

The credibility of every officer is important. Officers must avoid the temptation to alter their testimony to appear more competent, conform testimony to what other officers will say, or show compliance with the Fourth Amendment or *Miranda*. Defense attorneys zero in on any hint of dishonesty in the present case as well as prior allegation of untruthfulness. An officer's reputation as a liar or for misstating facts is targeted. A law enforcement agency's negative reputation will be brought up to insinuate that the officers who testified should not be believed.

Re-direct examination follows cross-examination. This gives the attorney that called the witness a chance to follow up on testimony given during cross-examination. Using this stage for asking questions the attorney forgot during direct is not appropriate; the judge will sustain objections by the opposing side if this is attempted. Re-direct attempts to rehabilitate a witness that was impeached. This is usually done by showing that the statements introduced on cross were taken out of context or specifically asking the witness about his/her objectivity. The prosecutor might try to rehabilitate Ms. Jones:

PROSECUTOR: Ms. Jones, you testified that there was a partition surrounding the area where they stored the dirty dishes. Was this partition between where you were sitting and the cashier?

MS. JONES: Yes.

PROSECUTOR: Could you see over the partition when you were sitting down?

MS. JONES: No.

PROSECUTOR: Were you sitting down when you first heard the man yelling?

MS. JONES: No. I had just gotten up to go to the rest room.

PROSECUTOR: From where you were standing could you see the cashier clearly?

MS. JONES: Yes.

PROSECUTOR: You testified that you have a hearing loss. Is that true?

MS. JONES: Yes.

PROSECUTOR: How severe is the loss?

MS. JONES: The doctor said is was mild to moderate.

PROSECUTOR: Did you hear what the defendant said?

MS. JONES: Yes.

PROSECUTOR: Are you sure?

MS. JONES: Yes. He was shouting, and I was only a few feet away.

If impeachment took the form of attacking the witness's reputation for honesty, another person may be called to testify to that reputation.

The prosecutor must constantly evaluate the strength of the evidence that has been presented. It is not necessary to call all possible witnesses but the defendant will be acquitted if there was not enough evidence to meet the burden of proof. At some point, either after all potential witnesses have been called or when it appears that the charges have been established beyond a reasonable doubt, the prosecutor will **rest the case**. This means that a decision has been made not to call additional witnesses. This is usually done by stating "The prosecution rests" when it is time to call the next witness.

Defense's Case in Chief

There is no requirement that the defense prove anything: the prosecution has the burden of proof. If the prosecution's case was not overwhelming and cross-examination went well, the defense may decide not to call any witnesses. This is a tactical decision. The attorney must consider the alternatives and know the relevant law; as long as this has been done, the appellate courts will not reverse on incompetent counsel even though no evidence was introduced. The defense attorney does not have to inform the court of his/her decision to present a case until after the prosecution rests.

If the defense decides to present a case in chief, it will start after the prosecution rests. An opening statement may be made if one has not already been given. Witnesses with relevant testimony may be called. The defendant may testify. As with the prosecution's case in chief, there is no set limit on the number of witnesses who may be called or the length of time allotted. During its case in chief, the defense will attempt to do two things: present its side of the story and discredit the prosecution's version of the facts. The defense attorney will conduct direct examination of the witnesses and the prosecutor will be entitled to conduct cross-examination.

Alibi witnesses may be called to testify that a person was at a different location at the time in question. In effect, when the defendant calls an alibi witness he/she is claiming to be a victim of mistaken identification. Suppose the defendant's girlfriend was called to establish an alibi:

DEFENSE ATTORNEY: Ms. Green, please tell us where you live.

MS. GREEN: At 4321 Elm Street.

DEFENSE ATTORNEY: Is that near First and Main?

MS. GREEN: Oh, no. That's on the other side of town.

DEFENSE ATTORNEY: Where were you at 3:00 on June 25, 1994?

MS. GREEN: I was home watching TV.

DEFENSE ATTORNEY: What were you watching?

MS. GREEN: The Yankees play the BoSox.

DEFENSE ATTORNEY: Were you home alone?

MS. GREEN: No, my boyfriend was there, too.

DEFENSE ATTORNEY: Was anyone else there?

MS. GREEN: No. It was just us two — the way we like it.

DEFENSE ATTORNEY: What is your boyfriend's name?

MS. GREEN: Matt Smith.

DEFENSE ATTORNEY: Is Matt Smith in the courtroom today?

MS. GREEN: Yes. That's him sitting beside you.

Alibi witnesses are vulnerable to impeachment for bias because they are usually friends of the defendant. More impartial witnesses, such as the receptionist in a doctor's office, are more likely to convince the jury.

The defense may put the defendant's **character** in issue. This means the defendant argues to the jury that he/she is a person of good character and, therefore, would not have committed the crime. Specific character traits may be introduced if they are relevant; for example, the defendant may claim to be mild mannered in order to show that he/she would only use force in self-defense. Character is introduced by calling witnesses who testify about reputation. For example, defendant Matt Smith in our hypothetical robbery case might call Larry Wright as a character witness:

DEFENSE ATTORNEY: Mr. Wright, where do you live?

MR. WRIGHT: 5678 Lime Street.

DEFENSE ATTORNEY: Is Matt Smith, the defendant in this case, your neighbor?

MR. WRIGHT: Yes.

DEFENSE ATTORNEY: How long have you lived there?

MR. WRIGHT: Five years.

DEFENSE ATTORNEY: Do you know how long Matt Smith has lived there?

MR. WRIGHT: He rented the house next door to me about a year after I moved in.

DEFENSE ATTORNEY: Are you familiar with Matt Smith's reputation in the neighborhood?

MR. WRIGHT: Yes.

DEFENSE ATTORNEY: How did you learn about his reputation?

MR. WRIGHT: I have a large rose garden in my front yard. I work on it a lot, and when I do, I frequently talk to the neighbors. I know just about everybody that lives around there.

DEFENSE ATTORNEY: What do those neighbors say about Matt Smith?

MR. WRIGHT: They like him, think he is a nice guy.

DEFENSE ATTORNEY: Specifically, do they think he is honest?

MR. WRIGHT: Yes. I've heard a lot of them say they think Matt is honest.

DEFENSE ATTORNEY: Does he have a reputation for being a thief?

MR. WRIGHT: Oh, no. There's another neighbor everyone thinks is a thief. A couple people mentioned that Matt returned things they accidentally left at his house.

The prosecution is not allowed to attack the defendant's character during its case in chief. If the defense raises the issue, the prosecution may attack his/her character either by cross-examining the defense's witnesses or by calling witnesses who have different views of the defendant's reputation.

The defense attorney must try to judge the cumulative impact of the testimony on the jury. When it appears the desired effect has been achieved or the defense has run out of witnesses, the defense rests. This is done by stating "The Defense rests" when it is time to call the next witness.

Reopening and Rebuttal

Reopening the case is used to present evidence in response to facts introduced by the other side. Rebuttal attempts to refute what specific witnesses said. Witnesses who have already testified may be recalled to the stand or new witnesses may be called. If the defense presented alibi or character witnesses, the prosecutor will have an opportunity to call witnesses to refute their testimony. For example, the prosecutor may wish to impeach Ms. Green, Matt Smith's alibi witness, by calling Mr. Adams as a rebuttal witness:

PROSECUTOR: Mr. Adams, where are you employed.

MR. ADAMS: Handyman Hardware.

PROSECUTOR: What is your job?

MR. ADAMS: I am manager on the afternoon shift.

PROSECUTOR: Do you post a schedule of when employees are scheduled to work?

MR. ADAMS: Yes. We post one every Friday for the next week.

PROSECUTOR: Is this the schedule for Handyman Hardware for the week of June 20 to 27, 1994?

[Prosecutor shows sheet of paper to defense attorney and then hands it to Mr. Adams.]

MR. ADAMS: Yes, that was our schedule.

PROSECUTOR: Did Barbara Ann Green work at Handyman Hardware during the month of June 1994?

MR. ADAMS: Yes.

PROSECUTOR: What shift was she scheduled to work on June 25, 1994?

MR. ADAMS: 3:00 p.m. to 6:00 p.m.

PROSECUTOR: Are you responsible for keeping the time cards for employees who work on your shift?

MR. ADAMS: Yes.

PROSECUTOR: Did Ms. Green come to work as scheduled?

MR. ADAMS: Yes.

PROSECUTOR: Did you see her there?

MR. ADAMS: Yes, I did. I talked to her in my office when she picked up her paycheck about 5:00 p.m.

PROSECUTOR: Was she at Handyman Hardware at 3:00 on June 25, 1994?

MR. ADAMS: Yes.

PROSECUTION: How can you be sure?

MR. ADAMS: Here is her time card. She clocked in at 2:58 p.m. and out at 6:00.

PROSECUTOR: Is it possible that someone else, maybe another employee, punched Ms. Green's time card?

MR. ADAMS: I don't think so. We're very strict about not letting employees clock in for each other.

If the prosecution reopens the case or presents rebuttal witnesses, the defense will be entitled to attack the new testimony by cross-examination and calling additional witnesses if necessary.

9.5 CLOSING ARGUMENTS

Closing statements are speeches the attorneys make to the jury at the end of the case. They are not evidence but merely attempts to persuade the jury to interpret the facts in the light most favorable to the side making the statement. They are tailor-made to fit the facts of the case. There are usually at least three speeches: a summation by the prosecutor; a summation by each defendant's attorney; and then a closing argument by the prosecutor. The prosecution goes first because it has the burden of proof. For this same reason, it is allowed to make a closing argument, a rebuttal speech, after the defense. No time limitations are placed on closing statements.

The closing statement must parallel the trial testimony. The factual summary presented in the closing statement may be different from the one given in the opening statement if the evidence produced at trial was not exactly what the attorney expected. The more important function of the closing statement is to persuade the jury how to interpret the facts. Attorneys argue how inferences drawn from the facts can be used to establish elements of the crime or defense. Attempts will be made to persuade the jurors to believe witnesses favorable to the attorney's side and to discount what other witnesses said. Any impeachment evidence that was introduced will be stressed by the attorney that elicited the testimony; opposing counsel will try to show the witness was completely rehabilitated. An attorney may not, however, argue that the jury should believe a witness because the attorney does, or that witnesses were called because the attorney could personally vouch for their truthfulness.

Prosecutors frequently inform the jury what the elements of the crime are and refer to specific testimony which supports each element. In complicated cases, it may take testimony from several witnesses to establish one point. They may give excerpts from the anticipated jury instructions and tell the jury what testimony may be used to establish the crime. Defense attorneys usually argue that the prosecution has failed to establish the elements of the crime and that the witnesses who testified are not worthy of belief. They normally make a major point of the burden of proof being beyond a reasonable doubt and stress that this is a very high standard.

The Fifth Amendment privilege not to incriminate oneself poses unique problems during closing argument. The Supreme Court held that there can be no reference to the defendant's invocation of this right. The prosecutor cannot ask the jury to infer that the defendant is guilty because he/she did not testify. Some defense attorneys feel that more is necessary: the jury should be told that they may not draw any negative inference from the defendant's failure to testify. Others feel that the judge merely draws the jurors' attention to the fact and may trigger suspicion. If the defense requests a jury instruction on this point, the judge must give it. The opposite is also true: the judge may not give such an instruction if the defense objects.

9.6 Jury Instructions

Jury instructions are statements made by the judge to inform the jurors of the law that must be applied to the facts of the case. Near the end of the defense's case in chief, the judge will meet with the attorneys to discuss jury instructions. The meeting is frequently held in the judge's chambers and is not open to the public. The court reporter is present to record any disagreements that might later be part of the appeal.

In some states, there is an official book of jury instructions, frequently with each instruction given a number for easy reference. For example, Part 9 of *California Jury Instructions Criminal* contains instructions relating to crimes against the person. Instruction 9.01 gives the definition of simple assault; 9.03 relates to unlawful shootings and contains instructions for Discharging a Firearm at Unoccupied Motor Vehicle (Instruction 9.03.1) and Grossly Negligent Discharge of Firearm (Instruction 9.03.2). The content of the instructions usually comes from quotations in leading cases on the issue or directly from relevant statutes. Some instructions are in a "fill-in-the-blanks" format so facts from the case can be inserted. Attorneys and/or the judge may draft instructions if the case has unique issues that are not covered by published instructions. States without official jury instructions rely on the judge to draft the statements. Wording is discussed in the conference called to select jury instructions.

Attorneys usually come to the conference with a list of jury instructions that they want the judge to give. This may be merely a list of numbers, such as Instruction 9.01, 10.2, etc., if the state has official instructions. The attorneys may draft instructions in advance and ask the judge to read them to the jury. The prosecutor frequently has a standard list for the burden of proof, how to assess credibility of the witness, and other routine issues.

All proposed instructions are discussed at the conference and the judge will make rulings on which ones to give. There may be mutual agreement on many of the instructions. Failure to request an instruction normally waives the right to appeal because the jury instructions on that issue were inadequate; so does failure to object to the judge's decision to give an instruction requested by the other side. The judge has the duty ***sua sponte*** to give some instructions. This means the judge has a duty to do it even though neither attorney requested it. For example, if no one specifically asked for an instruction defining proof beyond a reasonable doubt, the judge still has a duty to make sure the jury is instructed on this topic. Failure to include these types of instructions is grounds for reversal on appeal even though the attorney forgot to raise the issue at the time.

Jury instructions are normally read to the jury after the closing arguments. In states with officially approved instructions, this may literally be a reading of the instructions. Judges in other states may work the information into a speech admonishing the jury about its duty to decide the case. Some states that use standardized jury instructions provide printed copies for the jurors.

9.7 Jury Deliberations

The judge instructs the jury on their duties: select a foreman; deliberate on the evidence; consider opinions of other jurors; and vote on verdicts. The verdict forms will be explained. Then the jury is sent to the jury room to deliberate. Prior to voting on the case, they should review the testimony and exhibits. All jurors should enter into a discussion of the evidence and their varying interpretations of what was said and inferences that arise from the testimony. Witnesses may not be called to clarify their testimony, but if there are serious differences of opinion about what a witness said the jury may ask to have the court reporter read the verbatim transcript aloud to them.

Jurors may ask the judge to clarify the jury instructions. Prior to responding to this request, the judge usually holds a conference with

Sample California Jury Instructions Criminal

Instruction 2.81 OPINION TESTIMONY OF LAY WITNESS

In determining the weight to be given to an opinion expressed by any witness who did not testify as an expert witness, you should consider [his][her] credibility, the extent of [his][her] opportunity to perceive the matters upon which [his][her] opinion is based and the reasons, if any, given for it. You are not required to accept such an opinion but should give it the weight, if any, to which you find it entitled.

Instruction 8.24 MURDER BY TORTURE

Murder which is perpetrated by torture is murder of the first degree.

The essential elements of murder by torture are:

1. One person murdered another person, and
2. The perpetrator committed the murder with a willful, deliberate, and premeditated intent to inflict extreme and prolonged pain upon a living human being for the purpose of revenge,extortion, persuasion or for any sadistic purpose.
3. The acts or actions taken by the perpetrator to inflict extreme and prolonged pain were a cause of the victim's death.

The crime of murder by torture does not require any proof that the perpetrator intended to kill his victim, or any proof that the victim was aware of pain or suffering.

The word "willful" as used in this instruction means intentional.

The word "deliberate" means formed or arrived at or determined upon as a result of careful thought and weighing of considerations for and against the proposed course of action.

The word "premeditated" means considered beforehand.

Table 9.1

the attorneys in the case to discuss what new instructions, if any, should be given. In states that do not give the jury written instructions, the jury may also ask to have instructions repeated.

After the evidence has been thoroughly discussed, the jurors vote on the verdicts. Individual verdict forms are usually provided to facilitate the voting process. Each form states one charge and the possible verdicts, usually guilty and not guilty. For example, in a robbery case where petty theft is a lesser included offense, there would be two verdict forms: one for robbery and one for petty theft. When there are lesser included offenses, the jury is usually instructed that they should vote on the greater offense first and take a vote on the lesser one only if they do not convict on the greater charge.

Juries reach a verdict when the vote is sufficient to convict or acquit under the law of the state (federal law for federal courts). As previously mentioned, many states require an unanimous verdict but some accept 11-1, 10-2, or 9-3 votes. When the verdict cannot be reached the jury usually sends a note to the judge announcing this fact. The judge has the discretion to encourage the jury to try again to reach a verdict rather than dismiss the jury at this point.

The last resort with a jury that cannot agree on a verdict is to declare a mistrial. The result is a trial with no legally binding conclusion. The trial did not occur as far as double jeopardy is concerned.

9.8 Entry of Verdict

Verdicts are not official until they are read in open court. This must occur with the judge, prosecutor, defendant, defense attorney, and all jurors present. The judge usually formally asks the foreman "Have you reached a verdict?" Upon an affirmative reply, the foreman reads the verdict or the verdict forms are handed to the court clerk who reads them aloud. After the verdicts have been read, either side has the right to **poll the jury**. This means that each juror is asked if he/she agrees with the verdict. When the jury is polled, the verdict is not final until each juror has affirmed that he/she agrees with the verdict. Once the poll is complete, the judge tells the clerk to enter the verdict in the minutes. Jurors are dismissed by the judge after the verdicts are accepted. Death penalty and insanity cases are an exception to this because there is a second phase of the trial which is heard by the same jury.

If a conviction was entered, the defense attorney usually makes a motion for a new trial. This is frequently only a formality, but a judge may grant it if he/she believes serious mistakes, whether involving admissibility of evidence or unreasonable decisions by the jurors, will result in reversal on appeal.

Sentencing may occur immediately after the entry of the verdicts. Most felony cases, and some misdemeanors, require a probation and sentencing report to guide the judge in imposing sentence. Some courts order the report before the verdict is entered but many wait until after the conviction has occurred. This requires a delay before the sentencing hearing can be held. Local practice and the backlog of cases will determine how long this delay will be; six weeks is not uncommon. The judge will hear arguments and make a ruling on whether the defendant will be free on bail, or released OR or remain in custody until this hearing.

9.9 Mistrials

Mistrial is the term used to describe any trial that ends without a verdict. The two main reasons for a mistrial are prejudicial misconduct during the trial and a jury that cannot agree on the verdict. The judge hears arguments from both sides before declaring a mistrial. Double jeopardy does not bar refiling charges after a mistrial because there has been neither a conviction nor an acquittal. State law may prohibit refiling the case if there was serious misconduct by the prosecutor; a limit may also be set on the number of times a case can be refiled.

Many errors occur in trials, but few result in mistrials based on prejudicial misconduct. The most common problems related to introduction of testimony on a topic that the judge has already ruled should not be presented to the jury. Such rulings are usually made at suppression hearings. Even so, a mistrial is only justified if the statements are likely to adversely influence the jury's verdict. Most errors are not this serious. Comments by the attorneys while questioning witnesses or making opening and/or closing statements may also be so inflammatory that the judge considers the only available recourse to be starting over with a new jury.

The defendant is entitled to a mistrial if there are insufficient jurors remaining to decide the case. Alternate jurors are empaneled to avoid this possibility but occasionally so many jurors become ill or must be excused for other reasons that there are not enough alternates remaining. A new trial is usually held when this occurs.

A **"hung jury"** means the required number of jurors deliberated on the facts of the case but were unable to reach a verdict. If there are multiple charges there can be a "hung jury" on some charges and verdicts on others. When an impasse occurs during deliberations, the jury foreman notifies the judge that they have not been able to reach a verdict on specific count(s) but usually does not reveal the final vote. The judge holds a conference with the attorneys in the case to decide what admonitions should be given to the jury. The judge usually calls the jurors back into the courtroom and asks if there is any possibility that further deliberation may change anyone's opinion. If there is any indication that progress is possible, the judge will instruct the jurors to continue deliberations. Many times additional jury instructions are given about the deliberation process. Jurors can be urged to consider each other's viewpoints but cannot be told that the opinions of other jurors should be weighted as evidence in the case. The judge has discretion to send the jury back to continue deliberation more than once. At some point, the judge will decide that a deadlock has occurred and declare a mistrial.

The prosecutor usually has the right to refile charges if there is a "hung jury" regardless of what the final vote was. Lopsided votes in favor of acquittal (such as 11-1) may convince the prosecutor that the case should not be refiled. A review of what occurred at trial and interviews with cooperative jurors may give invaluable insight on how to win the case when it is retried. Some states have laws that limit the number of retrials, but these usually do not apply until the case has gone to trial at least twice.

Summary

The Sixth Amendment provides the following rights for defendants in criminal trials: speedy and public trial; impartial jury for crimes with sentences over six months; pre-trial information on the charges; in-court confrontation and cross-examination of prosecution witnesses; right to subpoena witnesses for the defense; and assistance of counsel.

A jury must be empaneled to hear the case if either the prosecution or defendant requests one. In these cases, jury selection will be the first event in the trial. Potential jurors may be excused for cause if their personal biases make it impossible for them to objectively review the evidence and apply the law the judge tells them is applicable to the case. Peremptory challenges may be used to exclude jurors based on the attorney's subjective opinions but never on account of race or gender. State law provides limits on the number of peremptory challenges each attorney may use.

The prosecutor's opening statement precedes the presentation of evidence. This speech provides an overview to help the jurors understand the "big picture" as each witness testifies. The defense may give an opening statement immediately following the prosecutor's, wait until the defense is ready to call its own witnesses, or waive the opening statement entirely. Opening statements are usually not made by either side when the case is heard by a judge without a jury.

Only relevant evidence is admissible at trial. Relevant evidence may be inadmissible under the exclusionary rule, if it is privileged, or if the judge decides it is too inflammatory, confusing or would take too much time in relation to its value. Some evidence may be relevant for one purpose but not another.

Lay witnesses may testify to what they observed with their five senses. Experts, on the other hand, are allowed to give their professional opinions. These witnesses are only allowed if the jury needs their expertise in order to understand the evidence. They are questioned on *voir dire* to establish their qualifications before they testify.

The prosecution calls its witnesses and attempts to establish the elements of the crime during its case in chief. Answers to the questions asked by the prosecutor become evidence. Objections to a question must be made immediately after the question is asked. Testimony is needed to show the relevance of each item of physical evidence and establish chain of possession. Defense attorneys are allowed to cross-examine each prosecution witness immediately after the prosecutor finishes questioning him/her. Leading questions may be used on cross-examination. The prosecutor rests after he/she believes all charges have been established beyond a reasonable doubt.

The defense's case in chief comes after the prosecutor rests. Due to the fact that the prosecution has the burden of proof, the defense is not required to present any evidence. Defense witnesses will be called if the defense attorney decides that it is necessary. They are subject to direct examination by the defense attorney followed by cross-examination by the prosecutor. The defense may call alibi witnesses and have its own expert witnesses testify. It is the defense's option to call the defendant. Jurors may not infer guilt from the fact that the defendant does not testify. The defense rests after its last witness has been called.

Witnesses may be called for rebuttal or if the judge permits an attorney to reopen the case after both sides have rested. The prosecutor may rebut testimony given during the defense's case in chief. If a new line of defense was presented, the prosecutor may be allowed to reopen the case. The defense may cross-examine when the prosector calls new witnesses at this stage and may call additional witnesses in rebuttal.

The attorneys make closing statements after all witnesses have been called. These speeches summarize the evidence and argue what inferences the jury should draw. Defense attorneys usually emphasize the heavy burden of proof the prosecution must bear. The prosector gives the first summation followed by the defense. A closing statement is made by the prosecutor.

Jury instructions are read to the jury after the speeches are finished. These instructions are prepared at a conference attended by the judge, prosecutor and defense attorneys. Instructions must cover all elements of the case including: specific elements of each crime charged; duty of jurors to deliberate; determining weight of evidence and credibility of witnesses; and burden of proof. Some states have books of approved jury instructions, others allow the judge to draft the instructions with the approval of the attorneys. The wording of jury instructions is common grounds for appeal.

Jury deliberations take place in the privacy of the jury room. The jury is instructed to select a foreman and go over all the evidence before taking any votes. They are usually given forms with each possible verdict so that they can vote on all possibilities. If questions arise during deliberations, the foreman can write a note to the judge explaining the problem. No new evidence may be introduced but the jury is entitled to have the court reporter read the verbatim transcript to them. It may be necessary for the judge to give additional jury instructions to clarify the jury's legal questions. A conference must be held with the attorneys before this decision is made.

Deliberations continue until there is a verdict, or the jurors decide a verdict is impossible, on each charge. The jury notifies the judge when it reaches a verdict. The verdict will be read in open court with the defendant and attorneys present. The defense may request that the jury be polled to give jurors one last chance to change their minds. Once this is done, the verdict is officially accepted. A mistrial will be declared if the jurors are unable to reach a verdict.

If there is a conviction, the defense attorney usually makes a motion for a new trial. Sentencing may be done at the time the verdicts are accepted. Frequently, sentencing is delayed to allow for the preparation of a probation and sentencing report. Motions may be made to permit the defendant to be free on bail or released OR during this delay.

Study Questions

1. Check your local laws and procedures on jury selection:
   a. How many jurors are required for a criminal trial?
   b. Is a unanimous verdict required? If not, how many votes are required.
   c. What are the qualifications for jury service?
   d. How does the jury commissioner select the jury pool?
   e. How many peremptory challenges are permitted:
      1) misdemeanor
      2) felony
      3) death penalty case
2. How are jury instructions selected for criminal trials in your local court:
   a. Are standardized jury instructions available?
   b. Are jurors given a printed copy of the jury instructions?
   c. Draft a set of jury instructions for the robbery case in this chapter.
3. Go to court and observe a trial. Prepare a report describing:
   a. opening statements.
   b. each prosecution witness':
      1) relevant testimony

2) impeachment
3) rehabilitation

c. each defense witness':
1) relevance
2) impeachment
3) rehabilitation

d. each piece of physical evidence's:
1) relevance
2) witnesses required to establish chain of possession

e. closing statements
f. jury instructions
g. verdict

4. Hold a mock trial on a case that is currently receiving publicity in your area. Have students play the roles of each person in the scenario or ask the acting class to play these parts. Assign students to prepare and present:
a. prosecution's opening statement
b. defense's opening statement
c. prosecution's case in chief
d. defense's case in chief
e. closing arguments
f. jury instructions

5. Rent a video of a movie that has major trial segments. Critique how accurately the movie portrays the proper handling of a trial:
a. selection of jury
b. opening statements
c. prosecutor's case in chief
d. defense's case in chief
e. closing statements
f. jury instructions
g. jury deliberations
h. entry of verdict(s)

CHAPTER 10

SPECIAL TRIALS

LEARNING OBJECTIVES

After reading this chapter, the student will be able to:

- State the standard for determining if a defendant is competent to stand trial.
- Identify the procedures for determining if a defendant is competent to stand trial.
- Explain the procedures for determining if a defendant who entered a plea of "not guilty by reason of insanity" should be acquitted.
- Describe the procedures used in capital cases to determine if the death penalty should be imposed.
- Explain procedures when a person is tried in juvenile court.
- Describe the procedures for determining whether a juvenile should be tried as an adult.
- Explain the court procedures for removing dependent children from an unfit home.

Key Terms

aggravating circumstances
competence to stand trial
- legal standard
- procedure

dependency court
dependent children
detention hearing
disposition hearing
fitness hearing
guilt phase
intake
involuntary civil commitment
jurisdiction hearing
mitigating circumstances
not guilty by reason of insanity
- legal standard
- procedure

penalty phase
petition
petitioner
respondent
sanity phase
special circumstances
sua sponte
transfer case to adult court
ward of the court

10.1 Competency to Stand Trial

The Supreme Court has held that a person must be mentally competent during all court proceedings. This rule also applies to the time of execution. This right is based on due process and is not waived if the defense fails to raise the issue: the prosecutor and judge also have an obligation to see that competency is determined if the defendant's conduct suggests a lack of competency.

Test for Competency

Competency relates to the defendant's ability to function during court proceedings. The test is composed of two separate parts: the defendant must understand the nature of the proceedings and be able to assist in his/her defense. The defendant must pass both parts of this test.

Understand the Nature of the Proceedings

The defendant must have a general understanding of the court process. Specifically, he/she must understand that the trial is being held to determine if punishment should be imposed upon him/her. Confusion about the roles of the participants in the proceedings, such as believing that a friendly prosecutor is looking out for the defendant's best interest, may also result in a ruling that the defendant does not sufficiently understand the nature of the proceedings.

Assist in the Defense

The defendant must be able to assist with the defense by conferring with his/her attorney and providing appropriate information; there is no requirement that the defendant understand the rules of evidence and criminal procedure. Two fairly common situations arise that involve this part of the competency test: lack of memory and refusal to cooperate with the defense attorney.

The courts are very suspicious of a defendant's claim of having no memory of the events in question. False claims of amnesia are easy to make and hard to disprove. In cases where amnesia is claimed, the court usually places the defendant at an in-patient mental health facility for treatment and waits for memory to return. The courts must honor permanent amnesia, however, if there is no other person available to provide details that the defense attorney needs. An example of a case where amnesia was successfully claimed involved a robbery in which the clerk, who was the only person present besides the robbers, was killed. A high-speed chase ensued in which the car driven by the robbers struck a tree killing one robber and resulting in serious head injuries to the other. Medical testimony established that amnesia resulted from head injuries sustained in the crash and there was no foreseeable chance of recovery. The court held that permanent amnesia, coupled with the lack of eyewitnesses, made a trial a denial of the defendant's due process rights.

A more common problem is the defendant's failure to cooperate with his/her attorney. Paranoid defendants frequently refuse to believe that their attorney, especially a court appointed defense attorney, represents their interests. As a result, the defendants refuse to disclose any information about the crime to the attorney; sometimes they refuse to talk to the attorney at all. A total lack of communication results in a defendant being unable to assist with the defense. Judges frequently appoint a different defense attorney in hopes that the defendant will confide in the new one. If such procedures fail, the defendant may be declared incompetent to stand trial.

Occasionally, the lack of communication is due to the defendant's physical or mental impairments. The case that was the basis for the television movie *Dummy* involved a deaf-mute who lacked the mental capacity to learn sign language. Transfer of the defendant to a training school resulted in no improvement. Finally, the case was dismissed.

Procedure for Determining Competency

The proceeding to determine competency is technically a civil hearing rather than part of the criminal trial. Once the issue of competency is raised, the criminal proceedings are suspended. The important consequence of this distinction is that it does not result in a violation of double jeopardy to return the defendant to court to face criminal charges after competency has been restored.

The question of the defendant's competency to stand trial is usually raised by a motion by the defense. If made during the pre-trial proceedings, it will usually be a formal, written motion with copies served on the prosecution before the hearing. When the issues arise during trial, an oral motion may be made in open court. The prosecutor may also make the motion; if both sides fail to notice signs of the defendant's incompetency, the judge has a duty to consider the issue ***sua sponte*** (on his/her own initiative without a motion from either side).

The judge must hold a competency hearing if there appears to be any evidence, including in-court behavior, in support of the motion. This normally requires the court to appoint mental health professionals to examine the defendant and report back to the court. The actual hearing usually does not occur immediately due to the time needed to conduct these examinations and make reports. The defense may want to have the defendant examined by its own experts during this period. A six-week delay is not unusual. The defendant may be transferred to a mental health facility or held in jail during this period. Treatment may be ordered during this delay if he/she appears to be seriously disturbed.

The competency hearing usually proceeds much like a civil trial. The expert witnesses will be subject to direct and cross-examination. While the crucial question is competency during the court proceedings, prior history of mental illness, or lack thereof, may be important. Lay witnesses may be called to testify about the defendant's conduct both before and during trial. Officers who made the arrest and those who had contact with the defendant at the jail testify as lay witnesses and may be asked about behavior they observed.

Some state laws require that a jury decide the issue of competence. The burden of proof is a preponderance of the evidence. The side raising the issue has the burden of proof; in most cases this will be the defense.

The criminal trial will resume if the verdict is that the defendant is competent to stand trial. If the delay has been minimal, the same jury that was originally empaneled may hear the case. Lengthy delays may require starting the trial over with a new jury. If there is a verdict of not competent to stand trial, the defendant is transferred to the mental health system. Typically, this means he/she will be confined in an in-patient facility for treatment; some states utilize out-patient facilities if the defendant's condition indicates this is appropriate.

State law establishes the procedures following the defendant's commitment to mental health authorities. Typically, the court must review the defendant's progress at specified intervals, such as every six months. A maximum length of confinement is usually stated; for example, three years or the maximum sentence for the crimes charged, whichever is shorter.

Some defendants can be restored to competency by the use of antipsychotic drugs such as thioridazine. Defendants may object to such treatment because the drugs have painful side effects such as severe upper body spasms; overmedication may result in drowsiness, possibly to the extent of not knowing what is occurring in court. An additional reason for declining to take these medications is the potential impact on the jury of a defendant who appears to be "normal": the jury may consider the defendant's in-court appearance of normality as an indication that the defendant was not insane at the time the crime occurred. The Supreme Court has held that a defendant can be required to take these medications against his/her will only if they are medically necessary and there is no less restrictive means to prevent the patient from harming him/herself or others. Drugs may not be administered involuntarily merely to make the patient more "manageable."

A formal hearing is triggered by one of two events: a staff report by a mental health expert indicating that the defendant has recovered, or the expiration of the maximum period for which the defendant may be held. The judge will review the staff reports and make a determination if the defendant has recovered sufficiently to stand trial. If so, a trial date will be set and the case returned to the criminal court calendar. If the maximum detention has elapsed without recovery, the judge must decide what to do: release the defendant or place him/her under a civil commitment. The minimum standard for a civil commitment is that the defendant is dangerous to him/herself or to others. The Supreme Court has held that a defendant may not be detained under involuntary civil commitment unless he/she is both mentally ill and dangerous.

10.2 SANITY PHASE OF TRIAL

The plea of **"not guilty by reason of insanity"** is separate from the consideration of competency to stand trial. The two proceedings are based on different legal definitions; they also focus on the defendant's mental state at different time periods. The insanity plea alleges that the defendant was criminally insane at the time the crime occurred; competency proceedings focus on mental capacity at each court appearance. Three possible outcomes occur: the defendant was insane at the time the crime occurred and is also incompetent to stand trial; the defendant was insane at the time the crime occurred but has recovered competency by the time of the trial; and the defendant was legally sane when committing the offense but is now incompetent.

Unlike competency to stand trial, which has no double jeopardy implications, a verdict of "not guilty by reason of insanity" has all the consequences of any other "not guilty" verdict: the defendant may not be tried again on the charges regardless of any bad faith in bringing the defense.

Procedurally, the defense must plead "not guilty by reason of insanity" before trial. State court rules usually require that the plea be entered a sufficient time period before trial to enable the prosecution to prepare to establish sanity. The normal procedure is to enter two pleas: not guilty; and not guilty by reason of insanity. A trial is held on the charges to determine if the defendant is guilty of committing the offense; this is referred to as the **guilt phase** of the trial. Only if a guilty verdict is entered is the sanity issue considered. A second proceeding, frequently called the **sanity phase**, is held to determine if the defendant was sane at the time the crime was committed.

THE INSANITY TEST

State law establishes the legal standard for insanity. The M'Naghten Rule is the most commonly used. *Black's Law Dictionary* states that the

M'Naghten Rule requires proof that, at the time the crime was committed, the defendant was

> . . . laboring under such a defect of reason from disease of the mind as not to know the nature and quality of the act he was doing, or if he did know it that he did not know he was doing what was wrong.

Other tests, such as the American Law Institute rule which requires that the defendant lack substantial capacity to conform his/her conduct to the law, are in use in some states. The Supreme Court recently declined a request to rule on whether Montana's abolition of the insanity defense was constitutional. This leaves individual states free to pass laws which refuse to allow defendants to use the insanity defense. An intermediate approach used by some states is a plea of "guilty but mentally ill." A guilty verdict results in confinement to a mental health facility; upon recovery, the defendant is returned to prison to serve any time remaining on the sentence.

Procedure for Establishing Criminal Insanity

The law presumes the defendant is sane. If the defense does not raise the issue, it will be presumed the defendant was sane no matter how irrational his/her behavior may have been. Some defendants refuse to enter an insanity plea, possibly due to the stigma society attaches to mental illness. This results in inmates being convicted and sentenced to jail or prison who are incapable of dealing with life in custody; many states maintain separate facilities for these types of inmates.

The defense must raise the issue of insanity. In addition to entering a plea of "not guilty by reason of insanity," the defense must present some evidence showing that the defendant was not sane at the time the crime was committed. The burden of going forward with evidence on the issue of sanity then shifts to the prosecution. States may assign the burden of proof on the issue of insanity differently than the burden for other issues in a criminal trial. For example, some states require the defendant to establish insanity by a preponderance of the evidence.

In most states, the sanity phase of the trial is held only after a verdict of guilty has been returned. The reason for this is two-fold: it saves the time of presenting evidence on insanity if the defendant is not guilty of committing the crime; and much of the evidence on sanity would be inadmissible, and potentially prejudicial, if presented at the trial on the issue of guilt. The sanity phase usually begins immediately after the guilty verdict is returned. Both sides have had ample notice that the issue will be considered so there is no need for a continuance. The jury that decided guilt usually determines sanity.

The focus of the insanity defense is the defendant's mental state at the time the crime was committed. Eyewitnesses can be called as lay witnesses to provide information on how the defendant behaved as well as any relevant statements made. Police officers who were present when the crime occurred or arrived shortly after the event may testify to what they observed. These lay witnesses may not state conclusions such as "He acted like a crazy person," but they may provide insight into whether the defendant's actions appeared to be rational and his/her speech coherent. Physical appearance as well as oral and written statements of the defendant are relevant.

Both the prosecution and defense have the right to have experts examine the defendant prior to trial in order to testify in court. Prosecution experts must advise the defendant of the *Miranda* rights prior to such an interview. Therapists who have previously treated the defendant may be called to testify if the defendant has a history of mental illness. While this testimony cannot establish the defendant's mental state at the time the crime was committed, jurors may infer that serious mental illness (or the lack thereof) immediately prior to the crime is indicative of the defendant's mental state at the time in question.

In many cases, the sanity phase becomes a battle of the experts. More than one expert may be called by each side, but the judge has the discretion to limit the number testifying if it appears excessive. Each side may call expert witnesses to testify regarding their opinions of the defendant's mental state at the time the crime was committed. Many states permit the court to appoint more impartial experts as well. The normal rule that experts may be asked hypothetical questions applies.

This means experts who did not personally examine the defendant may give opinions as to his/her mental state based on a review of the evidence in the case. The jury will be inundated by psychiatric opinions. Experts, including those called by the same side, frequently disagree on the seriousness of the defendant's mental disease. Diagnoses used by psychiatrists and psychologists do not directly relate to the legal definition of sanity.

Jurors, who usually have been screened by using peremptory challenges to exclude anyone with knowledge of psychiatry, are left to analyze the conflicting opinions and decide how to apply the law to the facts and opinions introduced. Jurors may conclude that a defendant is sane or insane based on testimony of lay witnesses and reject the opinions of the experts. Jurors may reject the opinions of experts if they find them implausible or if they are so technical that the jurors do not understand them. They may consider the background qualifications of each expert, the length of time the expert interviewed the defendant, whether the opinions appear to be logical, and any bias that the expert may have which might interfere with an objective analysis of the case. Two areas of impeachment frequently have major impacts: high fees paid to the expert for testifying; and a witness' history of testifying for only one side, for example, having testified as an expert in ten cases and concluded that the defendant was insane in all ten.

If the jury finds the defendant sane, the judge will proceed to sentencing, frequently after a delay to obtain a probation and sentencing report. A verdict on "not guilty by reason of insanity" is treated as an acquittal. The defendant may not be sentenced for the crimes committed. In many states, the court does have the power, however, to order the defendant detained in a mental health facility under **involuntary civil commitment** if he/she is a danger to him/herself or others. The defendant may be temporarily admitted to a mental health facility for evaluation of the need for such a commitment. Defendants confined on these grounds must be released as soon as they recover sufficiently so that the danger is over. The Supreme Court has ordered periodic reviews of the patient's progress in order to satisfy due process when involuntary commitments occur.

10.3 Penalty Phase of Death Penalty Case

The Supreme Court has spent the last 20 years trying to establish rules on the use of the death penalty. Over 100 cases have been decided and the rulings are not completely compatible with each other. Some basic rules have emerged: the jury must have controlled discretion to decide who receives the death penalty; state law must establish clearly defined "special circumstances" under which murder becomes a capital offense; jurors must be allowed to consider both aggravating and mitigating circumstances in all capital cases; the death penalty may not be automatically imposed for any crime without considering possibly mitigating circumstances.

These features of a capital murder case result in unique trial procedures. The prosecution must give the defendant notice before trial that the death penalty will be sought. Defendants in these cases have the right to additional assistance prior to trial; this usually includes hiring experts to examine the evidence and provide assistance to the defense attorney. Other issues, such as a "not guilty by reason of insanity" defense may further complicate trial procedures.

Jury selection takes on added features: jurors may be excluded based on their personal opposition to the death penalty if their beliefs would make it impossible for them to vote in accordance with the law. Additional questions are used during *voir dire* of potential jurors. Many courts try to expedite the process by having potential jurors complete printed questionnaires prior to *voir dire*. The focus on personal beliefs of the jurors requires extra time. Questions will be asked to try to distinguish between jurors who do not believe the death penalty is appropriate but will follow the law if the facts indicate the death penalty is legally required, and those who have conscientious objections to capital punishment and would not vote for death no matter what the facts are. A juror with the latter beliefs could be challenged for cause. Each side is usually given extra peremptory challenges in capital cases. The attorneys must make subjective determinations about each potential juror's reservations about the death penalty in order to exercise these challenges. Experts on jury selection may be employed to assist with this process. It may also be necessary to excuse more people than usual because the length of the trial imposes hardships beyond what jurors are normally expected to bear.

The trial is usually divided into two parts: the **guilt phase**, where the jury determines if the defendant committed the crime; and the **penalty phase**, where the jury determines if capital punishment should be imposed. The same jury normally hears both phases. In many states, the guilty verdict can be affirmed on appeal even though the penalty phase must be retried because it was found to contain reversible error.

At the guilt phase of the trial, the prosecution must establish both guilt for the murder and that at least one "special circumstance" was present. **"Special circumstances"** are listed in the capital murder statute. They can be divided into two major types: nature of the current crime (multiple murders; killing for hire; death of a peace officer the defendant knew was acting in the line of duty; gratuitous violent crimes causing excessive suffering; etc.); and the defendant's social history (prior murder convictions; history of extreme anti-social behavior, etc.). Accomplices who participate in a murder with the knowledge and intent that it be carried out under conditions amounting to "special circumstances" can also be given the death penalty.

Death penalty cases frequently result in the introduction of evidence that would normally be inadmissible at criminal trials. Some "special circumstances" relate to prior crimes, such as the defendant's conviction for a murder committed several years before the current offense. Other "special circumstances" place the defendant's mental state in issue, for example, sadistic torture. Some states permit consideration of future dangerousness to society. Expert witnesses, particularly psychiatrists and psychologists, are frequently called to testify on these issues.

The prosecution is allowed to show **aggravating circumstances** during the penalty phase; for example, the extreme brutality of the crime or the defendant's lack of remorse. The Supreme Court's holding that the defendant can submit any evidence he/she deems appropriate to show **mitigating circumstances** has resulted in a wide variety of evidence being admitted; for example, the defendant's inadequate personality, deprived childhood, low intelligence, lack of prior criminal record, and youthfulness at the time of the crime.

The jury receives a potpourri of evidence as a result of the requirement that it determine both "special circumstances" and aggravating and mitigating circumstances. Appropriate jury instructions will be given. Only two verdicts are usually allowed at the penalty phase: death or life imprisonment without possibility of parole. If no verdict is reached, some states impose life without parole; others permit the penalty phase to be retried before a different jury.

The trial judge is usually required to review the verdicts in capital cases. The death penalty verdict may be rejected if the judge finds that the evidence does not support it. Most states with capital punishment also provide for automatic review by the state's highest court, usually without prior hearings before intermediate-level appellate courts. These procedures are seen as reducing the chances of arbitrary imposition of the death penalty. A proportionality review is usually required. This means that the reviewing court compares the crime with others receiving the death penalty: if the crime appears substantially less heinous than others receiving the death penalty, the sentence should be reduced.

10.4 Juvenile Court

The juvenile court movement began in the 1890s with the purpose of rehabilitating wayward youth. A kindly, father-figure judge was seen as putting his arm around the delinquent and guiding him/her into a productive life. Over the years, the juvenile courts became more crowded and the informality envisioned by its founders resulted in denial of a fair hearing for many juveniles. Two Supreme Court cases, *Kent v. United States* 383 U.S. 541 (1966) and *In re Gault* 387 U.S. 1 (1967), require that juveniles be given many of the same procedural rights as adults: notice of charges, confrontation of witnesses, proof beyond a reasonable doubt, etc. Juveniles also have the same right to be represented by an attorney as adults do. A few rights, particularly public trial, jury and bail, have not been extended to juvenile court proceedings.

The defendant's chronological age at the time the crime was committed, not the trial date, places him/her under the jurisdiction of the juvenile court. Most states have provisions to send juvenile case to adult court for the most serious crimes or when the minor has demonstrated, by prior court records, that he/she will not benefit from the services provided by juvenile court. The maximum age limit for juvenile court is set by state law and is not always the same as the age of majority: many states use 18 but some extend the jurisdiction only to those who are under 16 or 17. Juvenile court may be a branch of the court that tries felonies; some states make it a part of family court. Juvenile courts frequently handle both misdemeanors and felonies; some also handle traffic offenses committed by juveniles.

In addition to handling criminal cases involving minors, juvenile court usually handles cases of abused, neglected and abandoned children (called **dependent children**) if it becomes necessary to remove them from the custody of their parent(s) or guardian. Sometimes this is done in a branch of the juvenile court referred to as **dependency court.** A social worker from Children's Protective Services (or a similar agency) usually conducts necessary investigation in these cases. Court-ordered outcomes in these cases can range from leaving the child in the home while the caregivers take classes to improve their parenting skills, placement of the child in foster care, and severing parental rights so the child can be placed for adoption. Many states require a separate juvenile facility for children who are being detained pending disposition by the court in these types of cases. In some states, juvenile courts also handle the trials of individuals accused of crimes in which children are the victims.

Another unique feature of juvenile court in most states is its authority over so-called status offenses: actions that make a juvenile in violation of the law but are not crimes if committed by adults. Truancy, running away from home, and curfew violations are typical examples; habitual refusal to obey reasonable commands of parents also fits into this category. Children who are under juvenile court supervision for these reasons are frequently called persons in need of supervision" (PINS), "minors in need of supervision" (MINS) or a variety of other similar titles.

Procedures When Minor Is Tried as a Juvenile

The most obvious difference in juvenile court procedure is that the names of documents and court proceedings are frequently different from those used in adult court. Some of these differences are shown in Table 10.1. The terms used are more similar to those in civil court than criminal.

The process of completing the necessary paperwork for admission to a juvenile facility is frequently called **intake** (not booking) and is done by an intake officer. Officers are required to notify the minor's parents that he/she has been taken into custody. This must be done very

Terms Commonly Used in Juvenile Court

Term Used in Adult Court	Term Used in Juvenile Court
Booking	Intake
Criminal Complaint	Petition
Plaintiff	Petitioner
Defendant	Subject or Respondent
Arraignment	Detention Hearing
Trial	Jurisdiction Hearing
Sentencing Hearing	Disposition Hearing
Convicted	Adjudicated within jurisdiction of juvenile court
Sentenced	Made a ward of the Court

Table 10.1

soon after the arrest, usually within four to six hours. State law specifies the time limits for filing the petition against a minor who is being held in custody; they are frequently shorter than for filing charges against an adult. For example, a state may require that an adult be arraigned within 48 hours but the first court appearance for a minor must be within 24 hours. Officers are usually required to notify the minor's parents of the pending court action and to keep the juvenile informed.

A **petition** is filed to start the juvenile court proceedings. The petition serves the purpose of the complaint: it must satisfy the due process requirements of giving notice of the charges; other legal requirements include establishing geographical jurisdiction of the court and showing that the statute of limitations has not run. The government may be called the **petitioner** and the juvenile referred to as the **respondent**. The prosecutor usually files the petition if the case involves criminal activity by a minor. In many states either a prosecutor or probation officer may file the petition if status offenses are involved. Social workers usually prepare the petition if the purpose of seeking court involvement is to take custody of dependent children.

The first hearing in the juvenile case is frequently called a **detention hearing**: its purpose is to determine if the child should remain in custody until the court hearing is held to determine if the acts alleged actually occurred. The judge reviews the charges to verify that juvenile court has jurisdiction and decides whether it is necessary to keep the child in custody. Options available to the judge usually include releasing the child to the parent(s) or guardian, placement in foster care, or detention in a secure juvenile facility. Attorneys will be appointed at the detention hearing. In dependency cases, the court may appoint separate attorneys for the child and the parent because their interests may not be the same: the parents want to keep custody of the child but the child's best interests may be to be removed from an unfit home.

The **jurisdiction hearing** serves the purpose of the trial: it determines whether the minor is within the jurisdiction of the juvenile court. This means the facts must place the child under the authority of the court based on age and his/her behavior or that of a parent or guardian. The time between the detention hearing and the jurisdiction hearing is frequently shorter than in adult court. Both sides have the right to call witnesses and conduct cross-examination, but the case is usually heard without a jury. Depending on state law, it will be heard by a judge, commissioner or referee. The result of the jurisdiction hearing is an adjudication, not a conviction.

A child who has been found to be within the jurisdiction of the juvenile court may be made a **ward of the court**. "Ward of the court" literally means a person is under the protection of the court. It gives the court the power to control the custody of the child. A decision will be made on whether to allow the child to stay in his/her home while on probation or send him/her to a detention facility; foster care and adoption decisions may be made in the case of dependent children. The type of detention facility must also be decided. This is done at a **disposition hearing** (similar to a sentencing hearing in adult court). Later court hearings can be used to release the juvenile from wardship or change the level of supervision.

State law may provide that the authority of the juvenile court for the purpose of punishment and rehabilitation extends past the age of minority. For example, a person who commits a crime as a juvenile may be held in the custody of the Youth Authority (or similarly named agency) until the age of 21 or longer. Without this type of provision, juveniles near the upper age limit of the juvenile court's jurisdiction would escape with little or no punishment.

Transfer of Case to Adult Court

Most states have provisions in their juvenile law to transfer serious cases to adult court. Many specify minimum age limits so that juveniles younger than 14, for example, may never be tried in adult court. The decision to transfer older juveniles is usually within the discretion of the judge. A special hearing, frequently called a **fitness hearing**, is held in juvenile court to determine which court will hear the case. Two types of factors are usually considered before a case is transferred: the nature of the current offense and the juvenile's criminal history. State law frequently includes a list of serious offenses, such as murder, rape, arson, armed robbery, etc., that are presumed to be more appropriately heard in adult court. Even so, the defense may argue that there are circumstances justifying retention of the case in juvenile court; when this approach is taken, the defense has the burden of proof. The prosecution may argue that a juvenile belongs in adult court even though the offense is not on the list of serious offenses. Criteria for a transfer on these grounds are usually designated in the statutes, and include such things as: degree of criminal sophistication exhibited; possibility for rehabilitation including consideration of failure of previous attempts to rehabilitate; previous criminal history; and circumstances and gravity of the offense. The prosecution usually has the burden of establishing that these cases should be transferred to adult court. Due to the consideration of these personal factors, it is possible to have two juveniles commit an offense together but one is tried as an adult while the other remains in juvenile court.

Cases that are transferred to adult court usually are handled in the same manner as those for adults: public trial, jury, etc. State law may provide, however, that a juvenile convicted in adult court may be sentenced to prison facilities designed for serious juvenile offenders. When this occurs, the convicted person is sent to a juvenile facility but if the maximum age for detention in such a facility is met before the sentence is complete, the person will be transferred to an adult prison to serve the remainder of the sentence. Laws in each state designate the maximum ages involved.

Making Dependent Children Wards of the Court

Children come under the jurisdiction of dependency court because they are victims of parental abuse, neglect or abandonment. A child who has been beaten by a parent is a typical case; so is an incest victim. The law is usually broad enough to allow legal intervention when a parent intentionally permits the child to be abused by another person and does nothing to intervene. Abandonment cases range from the baby left on a stranger's doorstep to children whose parent(s) have been taken into custody and therefore cannot care for them.

A social welfare agency, such as Children's Protective Services, usually handles dependency cases. Sometimes they are the first agency called; other times law enforcement officers initially handle the case and turn the children over to the social workers for placement. Most social workers operate under the premise that they are there to protect the best interest of the children. They believe, contrary to the beliefs of many police officers, that keeping the family intact serves that interest. Terminating parental rights and placing the child for adoption is considered a last resort.

Legal proceedings in this area are very involved; the code usually requires numerous hearings at specified intervals. The burden of proof usually increases as more intrusive measures are considered: less evidence needs to be produced if the court is asked to make the child a ward of the court but leave him/her in the home than is necessary to terminate parental rights. Adoption decisions typically cannot be made until two or more years after the wardship has been imposed. Parents are normally given the opportunity to redeem themselves by taking appropriate classes on child discipline and development and otherwise demonstrating the ability to care for their children. Courts usually seek placement with relatives over foster care with strangers if the child is to be removed from the home. Foster care is considered preferable to keeping the child in an institutional setting.

Dependency cases are considered civil rather than criminal. The rules of evidence involved are usually similar to those used in criminal court but the burden of proof is usually lower. Many of the hearings in dependency court have similar names to those in juvenile court (detention hearing, jurisdiction hearing, disposition hearing). Police officers may be called to testify at the jurisdiction hearing if they witnessed any events relevant to the case. The officers will be subject to cross-examination by an attorney representing the parents and possibly another attorney who represents the child.

State law may permit the social worker to make an agreement with the parents that they will be under the informal supervision of the social worker while they try to improve their behavior. When this is done, a substantial delay may exist between the date when the officers handled the case and the date it goes to court. Dependency cases may not go to court immediately if someone volunteered to take care of the children but later was unable to fulfill this responsibility. It is important that officers keep notes on these cases until the final disposition has occurred.

Summary

Due process requires that a defendant only stand trial if he/she is competent. This means the defendant must understand the nature of the proceedings and be able to assist with the defense. Either the defense, prosecution or judge may raise this issue. Criminal proceedings are suspended while civil proceedings are used to determine if the defendant is competent. A defendant who is not competent will be sent to a mental health facility for treatment. This delay does not affect the statute of limitations or double jeopardy: the trial may resume when the defendant is declared competent.

A plea of "not guilty by reason of insanity" also triggers inquiry into the defendant's mental health. Only the defense can raise this issue. When this plea has been entered, the trial is divided into two parts: the guilt phase determines if the defendant committed the crime; then the sanity phase considers whether or not the defendant is legally sane. Many states use the M'Naghten Rule to determine legal insanity. A defendant who has been found insane is acquitted and double jeopardy prevents a retrial.

Death penalty cases are usually tried in two phases: the guilt phase to determine if the defendant is guilty of the crime charged; and the penalty phase to decide if the death penalty should be imposed. The prosecution must prove that "special circumstances" exist that make the case more serious than ordinary murder. State law cannot make the death penalty the automatic punishment upon conviction for certain crimes: the defendant always has the right to introduce evidence to show what he/she believes to be mitigating circumstances.

Juvenile court is usually considered part of the civil court system. Names of procedures may be different from those used in adult court. Juvenile court may handle delinquents (those who would be charged with crimes if they were adults), status offenders and dependent children. Most of the procedural rights afforded adults now apply to juvenile court. The state sets age limits for minors to be brought before the juvenile court. Sanctions imposed by this court can range from probation to incarceration in a facility designed for young offenders.

Juveniles may be tried as adults for serious crimes. State laws designate the age groups that can be transferred to adult court and the reasons for such actions. Normally the transfer applies to only the most serious crimes or offenders who have a history of juvenile offenses without any showing of rehabilitation.

Dependency court, usually a branch of juvenile court, handles placement of abused, neglected and abandoned children. Law enforcement becomes involved in these cases when they handle reports of physical and/or sexual abuse of children. Action by this court may also be necessary when adults are taken into custody and no one is available to care for their children.

Study Questions

1. Find a case involving competency to stand trial in your local newspaper:
   a. Who brought the motion for a determination of the defendant's competency?
   b. At what phase of the criminal court proceedings was the motion made?

c. What facts were used to establish incompetency of the defendant?
d. What procedures were used to postpone criminal proceedings while competency was determined?
e. If the defendant was determined to be incompetent:
    1) What was done with him/her?
    2) Was the defendant tried on the criminal charges at a later date?

2. Search local newspapers for a case involving a plea of "not guilty by reason of insanity":
    a. When was the insanity plea entered?
    b. Was a proceeding held to determine competence to stand trial?
    c. Was the defendant found guilty of the substantive offense?
    d. What test for insanity is used in your state?
    e. What occurred at the sanity phase of the trial?
    f. Was the defendant found legally sane?

3. Use your local newspapers to follow a case in which the death penalty was sought by the prosecution:
    a. Under the laws of the state where the crime occurred, when may the death penalty be imposed?
    b. What procedures were used to select the jury?
    c. What "special circumstances" applied to the case?
    d. What facts were used to establish "special circumstances?"
    e. Was the defendant found guilty of capital murder? If so:
        1) What evidence did the prosecutor introduce at the penalty phase to show aggravating circumstances?
        2) What evidence did the defense attorney introduce at the penalty phase to show mitigating circumstances?
        3) What was the verdict from the penalty phase?

4. Check your state law and find the terminology used in your juvenile court for:
    a. criminal complaint
    b. arraignment
    c. trial
    d. sentencing hearing
    e. status offender
    f. child who is under court supervision

g. hearing to determine if juvenile will be tried as an adult
h. court handling cases involving abused, neglected or abandoned children

5. Check the laws of your state for situations involving juveniles:
   a. What is the name of the court handling juvenile cases?
   b. What is the maximum age for treatment as a juvenile?
   c. What juveniles can be tried as adults?
      1) ages
      2) types of offenses
      3) other factors considered
   d. Where are children charged with crimes detained prior to trial?
   e. Where are abused and neglected children housed?
   f. What is the maximum age for detention as a ward of the court?
   g. Where do juveniles serve their sentences if they are convicted for offenses committed as juveniles but receive sentences that extend past the time they reach the age of majority?
   h. Where juveniles are housed who are tried as adults:
      1) while awaiting trial
      2) when sentenced

Chapter 11

Sentencing Hearing

Learning Objectives

After reading this chapter, the student will be able to:

- Differentiate between determinant and indeterminant sentencing.
- Explain the sentencing options normally available to a judge.
- Explain the factors the judge considers when deciding on a sentence for a person who has been convicted of a crime.
- Identify what is included in the probation and sentencing report.
- Describe what usually occurs at the sentencing hearing.

Key Terms

aggravating circumstances
allocution
base sentence
community service order
concurrent sentences
consecutive sentences
determinant sentence
enhancements
fine
indeterminant sentence
intermittent sentence
mitigating circumstances
presumptive sentence
probation
probation and sentencing report
recidivist
restitution
sentencing guidelines
victim impact statement
work furlough

11.1 Sentencing Laws

Sentencing is a function of the judiciary, but the sentencing laws are enacted by the legislature. This creates a delicate balance between the two branches of government: the legislature sets the sentences for specific crimes, but, in most states, the judiciary retains the discretion to consider other factors besides the current conviction when imposing sentence on an individual.

Each state has its own laws governing sentencing of convicted defendants. Crimes prosecuted in federal court are governed by the United States Code and the Federal Sentencing Guidelines. A variety of different sentencing systems is used. Some states use a combination; for example determinant sentencing may be used for most crimes but indeterminate sentencing applies to non-capital murder. It is important to understand the sentencing system in use in the state where you live so that appropriate information will be retained for use at the sentencing hearing.

Indeterminate Sentencing

Indeterminate sentencing laws do not give the defendant a specific number of years in prison. The statutes usually set minimum and maximum limits but the judge is allowed to give any sentence within these ranges. For example, state law may provide that the sentence for robbery is from four to fifteen years but an individual convicted of robbery might be sentenced to serve five to ten years in state prison. How long the person actually serves is left to the discretion of the prison authorities and the parole board. The idea behind indeterminate sentencing is twofold: observations of the inmate's behavior in counseling and other prison programs provide the best indication of when the person is ready to be released; and the opportunity for early release motivates inmates to rehabilitate themselves. It is fairly common to use determinate sentences for misdemeanors in states that have indeterminate sentencing for felonies.

Determinant Sentencing

Determinate sentencing systems require the judge to impose a specific sentence, such as ten years in prison. State statutes may read like indeterminate sentencing laws (five to ten years) but the judge imposes a fixed sentence (eight years). Some state statutes provide a more structured framework for use by the judge when deciding on the sentence. There usually is a **presumptive sentence** (sometimes called a **base sentence**): it is the sentence the legislature intended for the crime but the judge can impose a shorter one if there are mitigating circumstances or a longer term if there are aggravating ones. Two examples: the penalty for robbery may be ten years but the judge can impose a different sentence if there are unusual circumstances; or the penalty for burglary might be two, four or six years with four years being the presumptive sentence, two-year sentences are imposed if there are mitigating circumstances, and six years when aggravating circumstances are present. Even within a determinant sentencing system there are usually options available to the correctional system, such as "good time," to motivate the inmate to comply with the prison rules. These are discussed in Chapter 13.

Length of Sentence

The judge starts with the length of sentence designated by the legislature. Two basic methods are used to indicate the baseline information. They can be used in both determinate and indeterminate sentencing systems.

Designating Crimes by Class

Some states organize their sentencing laws by constructing several classes for felonies and misdemeanors. When this approach is used, the definition of the crime states the class of the crime: robbery is a Class 2 felony. The code sections listing the sentences are usually in one place, frequently at the beginning of the penal code. Table 11.1 gives the sentencing ranges used in Virginia. For example, Class 1 felonies are the most serious and have sentences of life imprisonment or the death penalty; the judge can impose a 25 year sentence for a Class 2 felony, etc. Table 11.2 illustrates an indeterminant sentencing law. An Ohio judge selects a minimum term from those stated but the maximum term is set by law; for example, a person convicted of a second degree felony could receive an indeterminant sentence of four to 15 years.

Other states designate the sentence for each crime, or group of crimes, along with the definition. An example of this is a code that defines robbery and then states that the sentence for first degree robbery is 15 years and second degree robbery is punishable by 12 years in prison. There is frequently a section in the code stating the sentence for felonies and misdemeanors when nothing is stated in the defining section. Table 11.3 shows sentences for some felonies in California. The judge has a choice of three terms for each crime; as discussed later in this chapter, enhancements may be applied to increase these sentences.

Sentencing Guidelines

Judges are given guidelines to use when imposing sentences. Some, like the sentencing guidelines used by the federal courts, contain a very complex point system which the judges must use. Others involve a series of statutes which must be considered. Many states have worksheets that are used to calculate the actual sentence once the judge has decided upon all the relevant factors. Some of these systems are very complicated. Figure 11.4 shows the California worksheet for felonies. Note the numerous items that must be considered. It is important for police officers to understand what facts can be used to impose longer sentences and make sure that relevant evidence is available for the sentencing hearing.

Determinant Felony Sentencing Law

Code of Virginia Section 18.2-10

Punishment for conviction of felony. The judge must select a determinant sentence within the following authorized punishments; the judge has the discretion to impose any fine up to the maximum amount indicated in addition to the prison sentence:

Class of felony	Length of Incarceration	Maximum fine
Class 1	death or imprisonment for life	$100,000
Class 2	imprisonment for life or for any term not less than 20 years	$100,000
Class 3	not less than 5 years nor more than 20 years	$100,000
Class 4	not less than 2 years nor more than 10 years	$100,000
Class 5	not less than 1 year nor more than 10 years, or in the discretion of the jury or the court trying the case without a jury, confinement in jail for not more than 12 months	$2,500
Class 6	not less than 1 year nor more than 5 years, or in the discretion of the jury or the court trying the case without a jury, confinement in jail for not more than 12 months	$2,500

Table 11.1

Indeterminant Felony Sentencing Law

Ohio Revised Code Section 2929.11

Penalties for felonies. The judge shall impose an indefinite term of imprisonment consisting of a maximum term as provided in this section and a minimum term fixed by the court. Judge has discretion to impose a fine up to the maximum indicated below in addition to imprisonment. Convicted defendant shall be required to reimburse agencies for their investigation or prosecution costs.

Degree of Felony	Minimum	Maximum
Aggravated 1st Degree Felony		$10,000 fine
with prior conviction*	10 to 15 years	25 years
without prior	5 to 10 years	25 years
1st Degree Felony		$10,000 fine
	4 to 7 years	25 years
Aggravated 2nd Degree Felony		$75,00 fine
with prior conviction*	8 to 12 years	15 years
without prior conviction	3 to 8 years	15 years
2nd Degree Felony		$7,500 fine
	2 to 5 years	15 years
Aggravated 3rd Degree Felony		$5,000 fine
with prior conviction*	5 to 8 years	10 years
without prior conviction	2 to 5 years	10 years
3rd Degree Felony		$5,000 fine
Non-violent criminal**	24, 30, 36 or 48 months	10 years
	definite term: 12, 18 or 24 months	n/a
4th Degree Felony		$2,500 fine
Non-violent criminal**	18, 24, 30 or 36 months	5 years
	definite term: 6, 12 or 18 months	n/a

* Prior convictions utilized for this purpose include: aggravated murder, murder,or any aggravated felony of the first, second or third degree. Any crime under former Ohio law or the laws of other state or the United States that is substantially equivalent to any of these crimes is counted as a prior conviction.

** To qualify for this sentence the crime must have been committed without causing physical harm to any person or making an actual threat of physical harm with a deadly weapon, and the defendant must have no prior convictions for a violent offense.

Table 11.2

California Felony Sentences for Selected Crimes

Punishment for felonies. The judge imposes one of the three sentences listed in the penal code. The middle sentence is the presumptive sentence; the lower one is imposed if there are mitigating circumstances. Imposition of the higher one requires aggravating circumstances. Additional enhancements may be added based on the facts of the case.

Crime	Sentence
Aggravated Mayhem (PC 205)	life with possibility of parole
Kidnapping for ransom (PC 209)	life with possibility of parole, no parole if victim suffered bodily harm
Forcible rape (PC 261(a)(2))	3, 6 or 8 years
Arson of inhabited structure (PC 451(b))	3, 5 or 8 years
Kidnapping (PC 207)	3, 5 or 8 years
Robbery, first degree (PC 212.5)	3, 4 or 6 years
Burglary, first degree (PC 460(a))	2, 4 or 6 years
Mayhem (PC 203)	2, 4 or 8 years
Robbery, second degree (PC 211)	2, 3 or 5 years
Burglary, second degree (PC 459)	16 months, 2 or 3 years in prison or 1 year in jail
Forgery (PC 470)	16 months, 2 or 3 years in prison or 1 year in jail
Grand theft (PC 487)	16 months, 2 or 3 years in prison or 1 year in jail

Table 11.3

Fixed Term Worksheet

Based on California Penal Code Section 1170

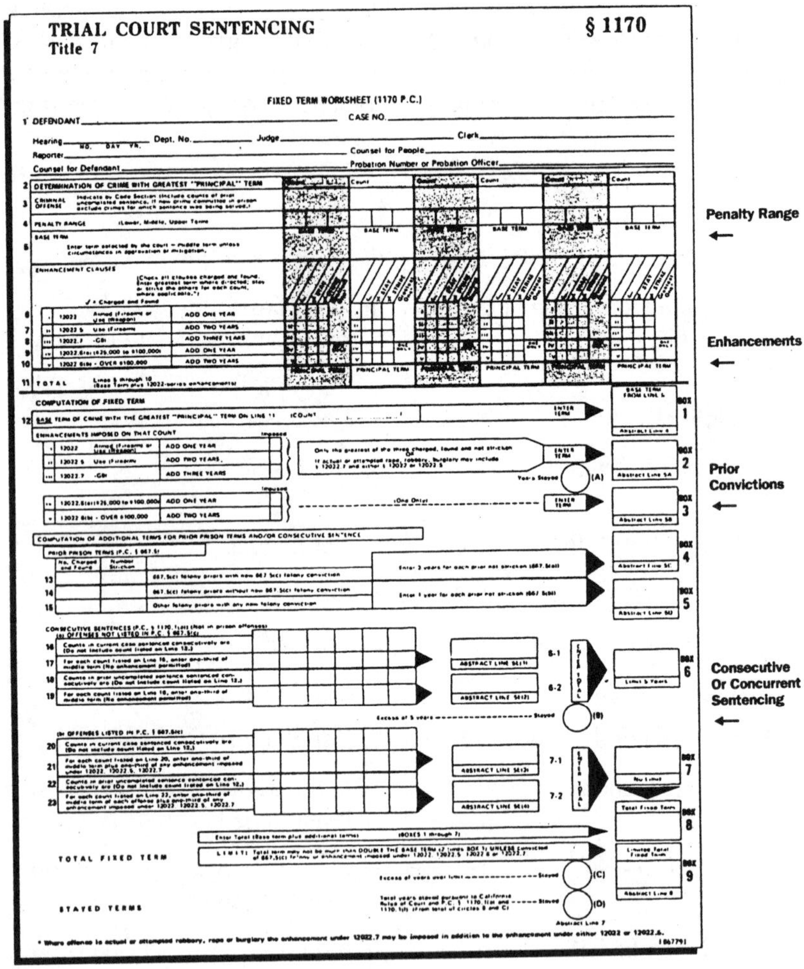

Figure 11.4

Aggravating and Mitigating Circumstances

Nearly all criminal statutes permit the judge to consider aggravating and mitigating circumstances when imposing sentence. The judge considers all facts presented at the sentencing hearing when making this decision. It is not a question of showing more items on one list than the other; for example, the judge might impose the highest possible term even though there were three mitigating circumstances (young, mentally impaired defendant who was first offender) if one aggravating factor, such as the extreme level of violence used, outweighed them. State laws may establish aggravating and mitigating factors or it may be left to the judge's discretion. Table 11.5 contains a partial list of the factors considered under Illinois law; it is typical of the laws in many states. Even when the law provides a list of factors to consider, the judge usually has the discretion to consider any facts that are unique to the case.

Enhancements

State laws frequently permit enhancement of a sentence in addition to imposing a longer term because of aggravating circumstances. Usually enhancements are imposed due to prior criminal conduct, but sometimes they relate to factors involved in the crime itself. The distinction between aggravating circumstances and enhancements is not always clear. Facts used to show aggravating circumstances normally cannot be used for enhancements, but sometimes the legislature permits use of certain facts for both purposes. This does not violate double jeopardy.

A common enhancement is for the use of a firearm or other dangerous weapon while committing the crime. This normally applies only if using the weapon involved is not part of the definition of the crime for which the defendant was convicted. For example, state law may provide a one-year enhancement for being armed; this could be used to increase the sentence of a burglar who carried a gun but not a person charged with *armed* robbery. For this reason, some states no longer have a separate crime of armed robbery; the enhancement is used to increase the sentence in much the same way as the older armed robbery code section did. The basic enhancement for being armed has been expanded due to the proliferation of assault rifles and other types

Factors Used as Aggravating and Mitigating Circumstances

Partial List of Factors Listed in Illinois Statutes 5/5-5-3.1 and 5/5-5-3.2

Aggravating circumstances the judge may consider as grounds to impose a more severe sentence or extend the term of a sentence include:

- defendant's conduct caused or threatened serious harm
- defendant received compensation for committing the offense
- defendant has a history of prior delinquency or criminal activity
- defendant, by the duties of his/her office or by his/her position, was obligated to prevent the particular offense committed or to bring the offenders committing it to justice
- the sentence is necessary to deter others from committing the same crime
- defendant committed the offense against a person 60 years of age or older or against a person under the age of 12
- defendant committed the offense against a person or a person's property because of such person's race, color, creed, religion, ancestry, gender, sexual orientation, physical or mental disability, or national origin
- defendant committed the offense while released on bail or his/her own recognizance pending trial for a prior felony
- defendant wore bullet proof vest while committing or attempting felony
- defendant had been convicted of a felony of the same or similar class or greater during the preceding 10 years excluding time in custody
- defendant committed a felony accompanied by exceptionally brutal or heinous behavior indicative of wanton cruelty

Mitigating circumstances that may be grounds for withholding or minimizing a prison sentence include:

- defendant's criminal conduct neither caused nor threatened serious physical harm to another
- defendant acted under strong provocation

- there were substantial grounds tending to excuse or justify the defendant's criminal conduct, though failing to establish a defense
- defendant's criminal conduct was induced or facilitated by someone other than the defendant
- defendant has no history of prior delinquent or criminal activity, or has led a law-abiding life for a substantial period before the commission of the present crime
- defendant's criminal conduct was the result of circumstances unlikely to recur
- defendant's character and attitudes indicate that he/she is unlikely to commit another crime
- sending the defendant to prison would entail excessive hardship to his/her dependents
- sending the defendant to prison would endanger his/her medical condition

Table 11.5

of combat weapons. Table 11.6 shows a list of some of the enhancements used for this purpose in California:

Enhancements are also enacted to cover a wide variety of situations that make the crime more serious in the eyes of the legislature. Committing a crime while out on bail or free OR frequently is considered as an enhancement. Excessive property damage during vandalism may be handled this way; usually a dollar amount is specified, for example, damage over $10,000. Most states have both misdemeanor and felony theft statutes but enhancements may be used to add punishment for an exceptionally large loss; again, dollar figures are normally included in the enhancement, such as in cases of theft over $25000, the sentence should be enhanced by a two-year term.

Table 11.7 shows Florida's approach for assaults and batteries on senior citizens. Some states use enhancements for "hate crimes" rather than enacting specific laws prohibiting criminal actions against a person on the basis of race, gender, sexual orientation, religion, etc. For example, a sentence for battery might be one year in the county jail under ordinary circumstances, but if the victim was abused primarily for racial reasons, an enhancement of two years might be added to the one year term. In other states, this same case might be

Sentencing Enhancements for Using Firearm during Crime

Partial List from California Penal Code Sections 12022 to 12022.5

Action by Defendant During Crime	Years Added to Sentence
• armed with firearm during commission or attempted commission of a felony	1 year
• armed with a firearm or deadly weapon during commission of forcible rape	2 years
• armed with assault weapon or machine gun during commission or attempted commission of a felony	3 years
• defendant or co-defendant used firearm or deadly weapon in the commission of forcible rape	4 years
• defendant personally used firearm during commission or attempted commission of felony	4 years
• armed with firearm during commission or attempted commission of felony and had ammunition in possession that is designed primarily to penetrate metal or armor	4 years
• personally used assault weapon or machine gun during commission or attempted commission of a felony	5 years

Table 11.6

Sentencing Enhancements for Battery Against a Person Over 65

West's Florida Statutes Annotated Section 784.08

Mandatory minimum sentence for aggravated assault or aggravated battery on a person 65 years of age or older, and reclassification of assaults and batteries against victims in this age group:

(1) A person who is convicted of an aggravated assault or aggravated battery upon a person 65 years of age or older shall be sentenced to a mandatory minimum term of 3 calendar years and fined not more than $10,000 and shall also be ordered by the sentencing judge to make restitution to the victim of such offense and to perform up to 500 hours of community service work. Restitution and community service work shall be in addition to any fine or sentence which may be imposed and shall not be in lieu thereof.

(2) Whenever a person is charged with knowingly committing an assault or aggravated assault or a battery or aggravated battery upon a person 65 years of age or older, the offense for which the person is charged shall be reclassified as follows:

(a) In the case of aggravated battery, from a felony of the second degree to a felony of the first degree.

(b) In the case of aggravated assault, from a felony of the third degree to a felony of the second degree.

(c) In the case of battery, from a misdemeanor of the first degree to a felony of the third degree.

(d) In the case of assault, from a misdemeanor of the second degree to a misdemeanor of the first degree.

(3) Notwithstanding the provisions of s. 948.01, adjudication of guilt or imposition of sentence shall not be suspended, deferred, or withheld.

Table 11.7

handled as a battery with aggravating circumstances instead of using enhancements.

Recidivist Laws

A recidivist is a person who has a prior conviction. Recidivists frequently receive longer sentences. Depending on how the legislature worded these provisions, the prior convictions may be considered enhancements, aggravating circumstances, or trigger recidivist laws. Some states consider juvenile convictions for this purpose. Table 11.8 shows New York's approach to this problem. Note that the sentencing pattern is more severe for recidivists who have convictions for violent crimes.

Some states make a second conviction for selected misdemeanors a felony; this is common with petty theft. Another approach is to leave the offense a misdemeanor but increase the fine and/or make a minimum jail sentence mandatory if there is a second conviction; spousal battery is treated this way in some states. A few statutes recognize the fact that some defendants have been convicted more than twice for the same crime and include progressively longer mandatory minimum sentences for each subsequent conviction.

The legislature has a great deal of leeway in designing recidivist laws. They may require a prior conviction for the same offense, or a similar group of offenses such as violent sex crimes. Some are more general, such as those that impose a longer sentence if the defendant has any prior felony convictions. Sometimes these laws apply only if the person served a prison sentence for the prior conviction. Another approach is to give the longer sentence only if the current offense occurred within a stated period, such as ten years, after the first conviction or the date the person was released from prison on the previous conviction. The sentencing guidelines used by the federal courts contain an elaborate combination of these approaches. The worksheet illustrated in Figure 11.9 is used to calculate the points that will be added to the federal defendant's "score" for purposes of deciding what sentence should be imposed.

"Three strikes and you're out" has become the catchy phrase for imposing life sentences on defendants with three felony convictions. This type of sentencing law was reviewed twice by the United States Supreme Court in the early 1980s. It held that such laws are constitutional even though each prior felony was a non-violent

Sentences for Recidivists

Persistent Criminal Laws

Penal Law 70.08 and 70.10 of McKinney's Consolidate Laws of New York

Persistent felony offender is defined as a person, other than a persistent violent felony offender, who stands convicted of a felony after having previously been convicted of two or more felonies. A previous felony conviction, as used for this purpose, is a conviction for a felony committed in New York or any other state, provided:

(i) that a sentence to a term of imprisonment in excess of one year, or a sentence to death, was imposed therefore; and

(ii) that the defendant was imprisoned under sentence for such conviction prior to the commission of the present felony; and

(iii) the defendant was not pardoned on the ground of innocence.

Persistent violent felony offender is defined in a similar manner except that both prior convictions for which prison sentences were served must have been for violent felonies (code lists specific offenses that apply).

Authorized sentence:

Persistent Felon. Judge has ***discretion*** to impose sentence the same as for Class A-I felony (15 to 25 years in prison) upon findings that:

- defendant is persistent felon AND
- the history and character of the defendant and the nature and circumstances of his criminal conduct indicate that extended incarceration and life-time supervision will best serve the public interest

Persistent Violent Felon. Judge is ***mandated*** to impose an indeterminate sentence:

- Class B felony — life imprisonment with judge to set minimum sentence between 10 and 25 year.
- Class C felony — life imprisonment with judge to set minimum sentence between 8 and 25 years.
- Class D felony — life imprisonment with judge to set minimum sentence between 6 and 25 years.

Table 11.8

property crime but that giving "life without parole" was too harsh. The statutes reviewed imposed a life term on the third or fourth felony conviction. Due process requires states to clearly identify which crimes are eligible for treatment in this manner and notify the defendant that the longer sentence will be sought. Case law on other recidivist laws has held that using convictions for crimes that occurred before the recidivist law was enacted does not violate the prohibition against ex post facto laws.

Other Sentencing Options

A wide variety of other sentencing options is usually available to the judge. Many of them can be combined, such as imposing a fine as well as a jail sentence. The penal code may contain a comprehensive provision, such as a statement that a judge may impose a fine of up to $1,000 for any misdemeanor conviction, or individual sections may specify what additional punishments may be imposed.

Probation

Probation was originally instituted to give first offenders convicted of minor crimes an opportunity to demonstrate that they could conform to society's norms. Probation officers supervised them, gave direction and counseling, and if necessary, brought the case back to court because the defendant did not comply with the conditions of probation. Today, probation is used in both misdemeanor and felony cases. State laws establish the maximum period of probation for a given offense. Defendants who do not comply with the conditions of probation may be required to serve time in jail or prison.

The judge normally tries to select defendants who are most likely to benefit from probation, but jail and prison overcrowding has resulted in many repeat offenders being placed on probation. Some legislatures have tried to control the judge's discretion in sentencing defendants to probation. Laws may be enacted making a person convicted of certain crimes ineligible for probation. "Use a gun go to jail" laws deny the judge the option of giving probation if the defendant used a gun while committing the offense for which he/she was convicted. Judges sometimes avoid this consequence by striking the allegation that the defendant used a firearm. A less severe legislative

Federal Worksheet C (Criminal History)

WORKSHEET C (Criminal History)

Defendant ______________________ **Docket Number** ______________________

Date Defendant Commenced Participation in Instant Offense (Earliest Date of Relevant Conduct) ______________

1. **3 POINTS** for each prior **ADULT** sentence of imprisonment exceeding ONE YEAR and ONE MONTH imposed within 15 YEARS of the defendant's commencement of the instant offense OR resulting in incarceration during any part of that 15-YEAR period. (See §§4A1.1(a) and 4A1.2.)

2. **2 POINTS** for each prior sentence of imprisonment of at least 60 DAYS resulting from an offense committed **ON OR AFTER** the defendant's 18th birthday not counted under §4A1.1(a) imposed within 10 YEARS of the instant offense; and

   2 POINTS for each prior sentence of imprisonment of at least 60 DAYS resulting from an offense committed **BEFORE** the defendant's 18th birthday not counted under §4A1.1(a) from which the defendant was released from confinement within 5 YEARS of the instant offense. (See §§4A1.1(b) and 4A1.2.)

3. **1 POINT** for each prior sentence resulting from an offense committed **ON OR AFTER** the defendant's 18th birthday not counted under §4A1.1(a) or §4A1.1(b) imposed within 10 YEARS of the instant offense; and

   1 POINT for each prior sentence resulting from an offense committed **BEFORE** the defendant's 18th birthday not counted under §4A1.1(a) or §4A1.1(b) imposed within 5 YEARS of the instant offense. (See §§4A1.1(c) and 4A1.2.)

   NOTE: a maximum of 4 POINTS may be imposed for the prior sentences in Item 3.

Date of Imposition	Sentence Status*	Offense	Sentence	Release Date **	Criminal History Pts.

* Sentence status, juvenile (J) or adult (A), required on sentences if offense committed prior to age 18.

** A release date is required in only three instances:

1. When a sentence covered under §4A1.1(a) was imposed more than 15 years prior to the commencement of the instant offense but release from incarceration occurred within such 15-year period;

2. When a sentence counted under §4A1.1(b) was imposed for an offense committed prior to age 18 and more than 5 years prior to the commencement of the instant offense, but release from incarceration occurred within such 5-year period; and

3. When §4A1.1(e) applies because the defendant was released from custody within 2 years of the instant offense or was still in custody at the time of the instant offense.

Total Criminal History Points for §§4A1.1(a), 4A1.1(b), and 4A1.1(c) (Items 1, 2, 3) ☐

Rev. 11/1/91

Figure 11.9

approach to restricting the use of probation is to require the judge to state in open court the reasons for his/her choice of sentence.

Probation is normally considered an alternative to incarcerating a defendant. This is not always the case: a jail term may be made a condition of probation. Recent trends include requiring a mandatory minimum jail sentence, frequently 48 hours to 30 days, for persons placed on probation after conviction for driving while under the influence of alcohol.

A defendant who is placed on probation must comply with the conditions of probation imposed by the judge. These frequently include mandatory periodic meetings with a probation officer, attending counseling, maintaining a good job/school record, not associating with known criminals, no substance abuse, and a curfew. Agreeing to abide by these conditions is a prerequisite to being placed on probation. The judge must select a different sentence if a defendant refuses. Procedures to remove a defendant from probation because of failure to comply with the conditions imposed are discussed in Chapter 13.

Work Furlough

Work furlough programs permit an inmate to maintain a job outside the jail facility. Typically, the inmate goes to work on his/her normal schedule but spends remaining hours in jail. This arrangement allows inmates to keep jobs and support their families. Frequently, it keeps the family off welfare. It also makes the transition back into the community easier after the sentence has been served because the inmate is employed. Sometimes, inmates are allowed to go to vocational or college classes under arrangements similar to work furloughs. Only defendants who are not considered escape risks are placed on this type of program because they are usually not accompanied by a guard from the time they leave for work until they return to the jail. Defendants convicted of drug use or dealing drugs are usually not allowed on work furlough because of the potential risk they pose.

Operating work furlough programs requires a great deal of cooperation by the correctional facility staff. Schedules must be coordinated so that the inmates can go to work on time. Meals at unusual hours and sack lunches to take to work may be required. Inmates returning from work must be searched to make sure that contraband will not enter the facility. Larger jails may house work furlough inmates in a separate area to make this special handling easier.

Intermittent Sentences

Another approach used to help persons with fairly short sentences retain their jobs is intermittent sentencing. When defendants are given **intermittent sentences**, they are allowed to serve their sentence a few days at a time. Intermittent sentences are frequently referred to as serving "weekends" because the defendant typically works at a job from Monday through Friday and spends the weekend in jail. Many jails can accommodate people with other days off. This approach can also be used for other reasons, such as allowing a defendant to continue going to school while serving a jail sentence.

In some states, the judge sentences the defendant to a three month intermittent sentence which means every weekend for three months will be spent in jail; other states impose a sentence, such as 30 days, with the provision that the defendant can spend each weekend in jail until a total of 30 days has been served. Intermittent sentences, like work furlough, require extra effort by jail personnel to handle the unique requirements of these inmates and the extra record keeping involved. Some state laws specifically provide for weekends. In other areas, jail and judicial personnel have made the necessary arrangements so that it can be offered.

Fines

In most cases, the judge has the authority to fine a defendant who is convicted. A fine can be combined with other sentencing options or be the sole punishment for the crime. It is common to have standard fines, such as $1,000 for misdemeanors and $10,000 for felonies. Statutes may regulate the maximum and minimum amount that can be imposed. Judges usually have the discretion to impose fines based on the circumstances, including the income of the defendant. Some states also have laws raising the amount of the fine if the defendant profited financially from the crime; for example, in felony fraud cases the fine may be $10,000 or three times the victim's loss, whichever is greater.

Equal protection prohibits sending people to jail because they are unable to pay fines. This applies to decisions made at the sentencing hearing and also to revoking probation because a defendant has not paid a fine. The rule only applies to a person who in good faith is unable to pay. A person who is unwilling to pay but has the financial ability, or one who refuses to look for a job so that he/she will not have the money, can be sent to jail for not paying a fine.

Restitution

A recent trend is to require the defendant to pay restitution to the victim. This is separate from imposing a fine: the fine goes to the government, restitution money goes to the victim; fines are usually set by the legislature based on the severity of the offense (felony or misdemeanor) while restitution is based on the victim's financial losses. State laws regulate what types of losses are covered. Typically, they include medical bills, lost wages, and damage to property. The actual amount of these losses must be established at the sentencing hearing. Table 11.10 shows the type of form a judge uses when determining the amount of restitution the defendant must pay.

Case law has not clearly established the point yet, but it appears that equal protection prohibits restitution orders against defendants who in good faith cannot pay. It is possible, however, to extend the time for payment to allow the defendant to find a job or otherwise obtain the funds needed; installment payments are also a common method used to facilitate collection of court-ordered restitution.

Community Service Orders

Some states permit the sentencing judge to make a community service order that requires the defendant to perform volunteer work for the benefit of the community. Other states permit community service in lieu of paying fines. The code usually indicates the maximum number of hours that can be required. One thousand hours is the equivalent of working full-time for six months. The defendant usually works a few hours a week until the mandated total is reached.

A variety of approaches is used. The defendant may be allowed to select any non-profit agency that provides services to the public. There may be a local agency, such as a volunteer center, which matches the defendant's abilities with agencies in need of help. Sometimes the judge orders the work done at an agency that assists victims of crimes similar to those committed by the defendant; for example, a person convicted of spousal abuse may be required to do maintenance work at a shelter for battered women. The defendant may have to work for a government agency; an example of this is California's program which requires persons convicted for driving under the influence of alcohol who cannot pay their fines to help the Department of Transportation pick up trash along the freeway.

RESTITUTION ORDER

Based on Florida Rule 3.986

By appropriate notation, the following provisions apply to the sentence imposed in this section:

___ Restitution is not ordered as it is not applicable.
___ Restitution is not ordered due to the financial resources of the defendant.
___ Restitution is not ordered due to ____________________.
___ Due to the financial resources of the defendant, restitution of a portion of the damages is ordered as prescribed below.
___ Restitution is ordered as prescribed below.
___ Restitution is ordered for the following victim. (Victim refers to the aggrieved party, aggrieved party's estate, or aggrieved party's next of kin if the aggrieved party is deceased as a result of the offense. In lieu of the victim's address and phone number, the address and phone number of the prosecuting attorney, victim's attorney, or victim advocate may be used.)

______________ ______________________________
Name of victim Name of attorney or advocate if applicable
Address ______________________________
City, State, and Zip Code ______________________________
Phone Number ____________________

___ The sum of $____ for medical and related services and devices relating to physical, psychiatric, and psychological care, including non-medical care and treatment rendered in accordance with a recognized method of healing.
___ The sum of $____ for necessary physical and occupational therapy and rehabilitation.
___ The sum of $____ to reimburse the victim for income lost as a result of the offense.
___ The sum of $____ for necessary funeral and related services if the offense resulted in bodily injury resulting in the death of the victim.
___ The sum of $____ for damages resulting from the offense.
___ The sum of $____ for ______________________________.

It is further ordered that the defendant fulfill restitution obligations in the following manner:

___ Total monetary restitution is determined to be $____ to be paid at a rate of $___ per (check one) __month __week __other (specify) ____ and is to be paid (check one) ____ through the clerk of the circuit court, ____ to the victim's designee, or ____ through the Department of Corrections, with an additional 4% fee of $____ for handling, processing, and forwarding the restitution to the victim(s).

___For which sum let execution issue.

Table 11.10

Court Costs

Court costs may be assessed against the defendant who is convicted. Usually, there is a set schedule used rather than actually trying to calculate the time expended by the judge and other court personnel. The amount imposed needs to be related to the expense to the taxpayers.

The United State Supreme Court upheld an Oregon law that allowed the judge to require a convicted defendant, as a condition of probation, to pay the cost incurred by the county in prosecuting the case. The court mandated protection of the defendant from undue hardship and suggested that procedures similar to those used to protect a creditor from excessive wage garnishment be used. Some states have become innovative in this area and try to collect the cost of incarcerating the defendant and/or investigating the case.

Concurrent and Consecutive Sentences

When the defendant has been convicted of more than one crime, the judge is usually given the discretion to decide if the sentences will be concurrent or consecutive. **Concurrent sentences** can be served at the same time; for sentences imposed at the same time this means that when the longest sentence has been served the defendant is released because the shorter ones are also complete. Sometimes, a judge rules that a sentence can be served concurrently with one the defendant received in an unrelated case. Concurrent sentences may become important if one, but not all, of the convictions are reversed on appeal. When this happens, the defendant can be required to serve the sentences for the convictions that were affirmed.

Consecutive sentences are served in sequential order: the defendant serves all of the time imposed for one crime before starting to serve the sentence for another offense. This results in a longer prison term than would have been served if concurrent sentences were given. Factors frequently considered by the judge when deciding to impose consecutive sentences include: whether the objectives of the crimes were predominantly independent of each other; whether the crimes involved separate acts of violence; whether the crimes were committed so close together that a single period of aberrant behavior is indicated. The criteria to be considered may be listed in the sentencing law or the court's rules.

Some states mandate consecutive terms for specific crimes. Extra time imposed for enhancements or recidivism may also be required to be served consecutively. A few states have mathematical formulas which require the defendant to serve part, but not all, of the normal sentence for crimes when consecutive sentences are imposed. For example, California requires the defendant to serve the full term for the first crime and one-third of the presumptive term for each consecutive sentence.

11.2 Probation and Sentencing Report

The probation and sentencing report provides the judge with relevant background information about the defendant. It is usually prepared by a probation officer or another officer of the court. Most judges request the report after the verdicts are read. There are two main reasons for delaying the preparation of the report until this time: reports are only prepared for defendants who are convicted, thus saving the staff time required to investigate and write reports on defendants who are acquitted; and the person writing the report can interview the defendant and include his/her statements in the report because the defendant can no longer claim the Fifth Amendment as a grounds to refuse to discuss the case. When the probation and sentencing report is not requested until after the verdict is entered, a continuance is necessary before the sentencing hearing. Six weeks may be allotted for this purpose.

As Section 11.1 has demonstrated, many factors are considered by the sentencing judge in addition to guilt of the offense charged. For this reason, the probation and sentencing report must contain information on many things that were not introduced into evidence at trial. It contains a social history of the defendant. This includes a brief biographical summary of the defendant's success (or lack thereof) in school and his/her behavioral problems. Attention will be focused on the defendant's prior convictions as either an adult or juvenile. If the defendant has ever been on probation, the report will indicate the outcome: revoked, revoked but reinstated, or successfully completed. The number of times probation has been imposed and the defendant's success are important considerations if probation will be an option when the judge imposes the current sentence. Prior convictions, particularly those for which the defendant served time in prison, frequently are grounds for imposing a more severe sentence.

The facts of the current case are summarized. The impact of the offense on the victim may be discussed, particularly if the victim was injured, left fearful of future harm, or suffered financial hardship due to the crime. Other aggravating and mitigating facts are included. Probation and sentencing reports usually end with a recommendation to the judge on the sentence to impose. If prison is recommended, the report will suggest the length of the term. When probation is recommended, the report usually states the length of the probation and the conditions of probation that should be imposed. In states that have a sentencing worksheet for the judge to use to calculate the sentence, the probation and sentencing report usually contain a worksheet with the necessary computations completed.

The probation and sentencing report is submitted to the judge. Many courts consider the report confidential and do not make it part of the public record, but both the prosecutor and defense attorney are usually entitled to copies. They may want to dispute facts stated in the report or urge the judge to draw different conclusions. This is normally done by oral argument but documents, including a private probation and sentencing report prepared by a consultant for the defense, may be filed with the court. Any such documents must be served on the opposing side before the hearing to permit time to prepare to discuss them in court.

11.3 Procedures at the Sentencing Hearing

The sentencing hearing is a formal court hearing. The defendant, prosecutor and defense attorney are present. It is usually presided over by the judge that accepted the guilty plea or heard the trial and is normally held in the courtroom where these events occurred. Most sentencing hearings are brief and consist of little more than the presentation of the probation and sentencing report and a statement by the defendant. In major cases, particularly death penalty trials, the hearing may last for a week or more.

The normal rules of evidence usually apply to the sentencing hearing although the hearsay rule may be relaxed to admit evidence discussed in the probation and sentencing report. Evidence may be admissible at the sentencing hearing that was inadmissible at trial since the issues are different; therefore, items that are relevant at the sentencing hearing may have been irrelevant at trial. For example, the defendant's prior criminal record is relevant when deciding if probation should be imposed but it is not relevant in determining guilt for the offense; the amount of the victim's hospital bill is relevant when computing a restitution order but not relevant on the question of guilt for committing battery. Evidence that was not admissible at trial because of the exclusionary rule may be used at the sentencing hearings except when it was seized specifically to enhance the sentence.

In many states, the hearing begins with the testimony of the person who made the probation and sentencing report. The information in the report may be repeated from the witness stand and the prosecutor and defense attorney given the opportunity to ask questions. The judge is also allowed to ask questions.

Witnesses may be called if it is necessary to present evidence not introduced at trial. This is organized much like a trial with one side, usually the prosecution, calling all of its witnesses before the opposing side presents testimony. All witnesses are subject to cross-examination. The judge decides what weight, if any, is to be placed on the testimony of each witness except when a jury is assigned the task of deciding the sentence.

Three unique situations occur at sentencing hearings: the defendant has the right of allocution; private probation and sentencing reports may be introduced and victims may make statements. *Black's Law Dictionary* defines **allocution** as: "Formality of court's inquiry of prisoner as to whether he has any legal cause to show why judgment should not be pronounced against him on verdict of conviction." In practice, the right of allocution is the defendant's opportunity to make a speech during the sentencing hearing. As with other rights, it can be waived if the defendant does not wish to exercise it. Defendants who exercise this right usually express remorse for their actions and ask the judge for a lighter sentence.

Some states allow the defense to introduce a private probation and sentencing report. Consultants usually prepare the reports. Many times, the consultant is a former probation officer or a psychologist. The purpose of this report is to summarize the facts, including the defendant's background and potential for rehabilitation, in a manner favorable to the defense. Normally, mitigating circumstances and ways to rehabilitate the defendant are stressed. A treatment program with little or no time in custody is usually recommended. The person who prepared the report frequently testifies. The testimony is usually handled much as an expert witness would be at trial. The prosecutor has the right to cross-examine on the person's professional qualifications as well as the facts and opinions expressed.

Many states now give the victim input at the defendant's sentencing hearing. This is frequently called a **victim impact statement**. Some states allow the victim to submit written material, others require oral testimony; sometimes the victim is given a choice of either method of participation. Family members of a victim who died as a result of injuries inflicted during the crime are usually allowed to testify. Some states allow the victims to give their views on what sentence should be imposed. Two reasons buttress the use of the victim impact statements: they give crime victims a greater input into the criminal justice system; and they provide information for the judge on the mental, physical and financial suffering caused by the defendant.

After all the evidence is admitted, the prosecutor and defense attorney present arguments regarding the sentence that should be imposed. As with the closing arguments at trial, each side will attempt to portray the evidence in a light most favorable to their view. If the state's sentencing laws are complex, this may include very detailed analysis of what code sections are mandatory and which ones the judge has the option to ignore.

The judge must make the final decision on what sentence to impose. If the defendant is being placed on probation, it is also necessary to include the conditions of probation. Worksheets are frequently used to calculate the sentence. A standardized form is usually used if state law requires additions and/or subtractions for aggravating circumstances, mitigating circumstances, prior convictions, and enhancements. Some of the forms are very complicated. See Figure 11.4.

The final action at the sentencing hearing is usually the judge's oral pronouncement of sentence. Many states require the judge to give reasons for the sentence that is being imposed if it deviates from the base sentence. The judge usually gives a short speech summarizing the facts that were considered as aggravating and/or mitigating, and if the defendant was convicted for committing more than one crime, stating whether the sentences will run concurrently or consecutively. This statement by the judge may provide the grounds for an appeal if the factors stated do not coincide with what the law allows the judge to consider or if the mathematical computations are not correct.

SUMMARY

Sentencing laws vary a great deal from state to state and between the states and the federal system. It is important for the officer to understand what factors are considered when sentences are imposed so that relevant evidence will be retained for presentation at the sentencing hearing.

Sentences are either determinant (judge imposes specific sentence) or indeterminant (judge imposes range and defendant's performance in prison determines when he/she will be released). Many states use determinant sentences for some crimes while giving indeterminant sentences for others.

Statutes set the length of sentence for each crime but many factors are considered when sentencing the defendant. Most states have a range of potential sentences for a crime and the judge selects a sentence based on a combination of the crime charged, aggravating and mitigating circumstances, defendant's prior criminal record, and other enhancements approved by the legislature. If the defendant is convicted of more than one crime, it is also necessary to decide if the sentences will be concurrent (served at same time) or consecutive (one starts after prior sentence has been completed).

Judges usually have a variety of options available: prison, jail, probation, fines, community service, restitution, and paying court costs. The sentencing laws usually state which of these can be combined, for example, two years in jail plus a fine and restitution. There may be options available for those who will be incarcerated such as intermittent sentences or work furlough.

Many judges request a probation and sentencing report to assist them in making sentencing decisions. The report summarizes the defendant's social history as well as facts relating to the current crime. It normally discusses the defendant's potential for rehabilitation and recommends a sentence. The issues will be further explored at the sentencing hearing where both the prosecution and defense have the right to call witnesses and make arguments in favor of their view of what is an appropriate sentence. After hearing all the evidence, the judge will impose the sentence. Many states require the judge to explain any deviations from the base sentence.

STUDY QUESTIONS

1. Which crimes in your state have determinant sentences? Which ones have indeterminant sentences?
2. Check the laws of your state and explain:
   a. What aggravating circumstances may the judge consider when imposing sentences?
   b. What mitigating circumstances may the judge consider when imposing sentences?
   c. What, if any, other enhancements are authorized?
   d. What special sentencing rules apply to recidivists?
3. Check the laws of your state and explain the rules for including the following as part of a sentence:
   a. fine
   b. restitution
   c. community service
   d. court costs
4. What are the rules in your state for utilizing the following sentences:
   a. jail
   b. intermittent sentence
   c. work furlough
   d. prison
5. Attend a sentencing hearing and report on the following:
   a. What crime(s) was the defendant convicted for?
   b. Was a probation and sentencing report prepared? If so, summarize its content if it was discussed in court.
   c. Was a private probation and sentencing report prepared? If so, summarize its content.
   d. Were witnesses called? If so, summarize the testimony of each one.

e. Were victim impact statements presented? If so, summarize each one.
f. Did the defendant exercise the right of allocution? If so, summarize what he/she said.
g. Summarize the arguments of prosecutor and defense attorney.
h. What sentence was imposed? Summarize the judge's rationale for giving this sentence.

Chapter 12
Appeals

Learning Objectives

After reading this chapter, the student will be able to:

- Describe the court procedures used when an appeal is taken.
- Explain the defendant's right to counsel and other necessary services when appealing a conviction.
- Identify when the defense and prosecution are permitted to appeal before trial begins.
- Explain when a defendant is permitted to appeal after pleading guilty.
- Describe the process for a direct appeal after a conviction.
- Describe the appellate process after a judge has imposed the death penalty.
- Identify the process used when a person convicted in state court appeals his/her case to the United States Supreme Court.
- Explain the procedures used to obtain a writ of *habeas corpus*.

KEY TERMS

advance sheets
amicus curiae
appellant
appellant's opening brief
appellant's reply brief
automatic appeal
clerk's transcript
collateral attack
direct appeal
discretionary appeal
motion to proceed in *forma pauperis*
petition for writ of *certiorari*
petition for writ of *habeas corpus*
prayer
reporter's transcript
respondent
respondent's opening brief
slip opinions
writ of *certiorari*
writ of *habeas corpus*

12.1 THE APPELLATE PROCESS

The American justice system assigns the task of assessing credibility of witnesses to the jury, or to the judge if the case was heard without a jury. For this reason, it is very rare for an appellate court to become involved in the issue of whether the jury correctly weighed the evidence in a case except when the court finds that there was no credible evidence to support an element of the crime. If there are witnesses giving different versions of the facts, the appellate court defers to the judgment of the jury (or trial judge) who observed the behavior of the witness as well as heard what was said. Occasionally, an appellate court will rule that the testimony of a witness was so inherently improbable that it was not worthy of belief. This usually occurs when the timing of the events testified to, or the physical layout of the scene, makes it impossible for the events to have occurred or for the witness to have observed them.

The appellate process is designed to review the legal issues of a case. This usually relates to legal documents filed and arguments made at the pretrial hearings and trial. The judge's rulings during trial on objections made by the attorneys are also potential issues on appeal. Extensive documentation is needed because the judges who will hear the appeal were not present during the trial. Two documents are used for this purpose: the clerk's transcript and the reporter's transcript.

The federal rules of appellate procedure require these transcripts to be combined in one appendix with consistent page numbering to make referencing them easier.

The **clerk's transcript** contains all the documents used in the case: warrant applications and warrants (if any) with proof of service and inventory of items seized; criminal complaint; indictment (if any);

A 68 375

A L B E R T S T E I N E R, called as a witness having

10 been first duly sworn by the Clerk of the Court, testified as follows:

DIRECT EXAMINATION

BY MR. LEVIN-EPSTEIN:

Q Good morning, ladies and gentlemen. Good morning, Mr. Steiner?

A Good morning.

Q For the record and so the jurors at this end can hear you clearly, will you once again state your full name?

A Albert Steiner.

Q Mr. Steiner, at this time, are you employed?

A No, sir, I'm retired.

Q How long have you been retired?

A Approximately three years.

Q Prior to the time that you entered retirement, were you employed?

A I was.

Q What was your occupation, sir?

A I was in the fuel oil and oil burner business.

Q In the fuel oil and oil burner business, did you have your own company or were you employed by someone else?

A No, I had my own company.

Q What was the name of that company?

Figure 12.1 - Sample of Reporter's Transcript

motions to suppress evidence; discovery motions; clerk's minutes (also called docket entries) regarding what occurred on each court day; information on jury selection; jury instructions (if pre-printed instructions are used); verdicts; and notice of appeal. The **reporter's transcript** contains a verbatim account of what was said in court. What the attorneys say, the judge's comments, and the testimony of the witnesses are recorded. In lower courts, such as those handling misdemeanors, the reporter's transcript may be replaced by a statement, agreed to by both attorneys, which summarizes the facts. Reporter's transcripts may also be available for grand jury proceedings, preliminary hearings, and suppression hearings. Figure 12.1 shows a sample page from a reporter's transcript.

These transcripts are necessary to challenge rulings the judge made on oral objections. They will show whether the objection was made in a timely fashion and if the attorney stated the correct grounds for the objection. Where legal rulings depend on the facts of the case, such as a question of whether an item was legally seized without a warrant, the reporter's transcript is needed to determine what the officers testified that they did. The clerk's transcript is also needed because the appellate court will review the points and authorities submitted to the judge at the suppression hearing to determine whether the argument for suppression was correctly made. To facilitate review of the record, the appellate court usually requires the attorney appealing an issue to cite the page numbers for any relevant information in the clerk and reporter's transcripts.

The first document filed in an appeal is the notice of appeal. This may be a pre-printed form. Strict rules govern when the notice of appeal may be filed; for example, many states require it to be filed within 30 days of the sentencing hearing but prohibit filing appeals before the final judgment is entered. Failure to file on time waives the right to appeal. The primary function of the notice of appeal is to alert court personnel to prepare the necessary documents and to transfer the files to the appellate court. Figure 12.2 shows a typical format for a notice of appeal.

A copy of the notice of appeal is normally served on the opposing party; court rules may also make it the duty of the person appealing to notify the court reporter that transcripts will be needed. The notice of appeal may include a request for the court to appoint an attorney to handle the appeal because the defendant does not have the financial

Notice of Appeal

STATE OF MINNESOTA COUNTY COURT

COUNTY OF ______________________

	)	NOTICE OF APPEAL, BY
	)	DEFENDANT, ON THE
________________,	)	RECORD TO DISTRICT
Plaintiff,	)	COURT FROM COUNTY
	)	COURT
vs.	)	
	)	
________________,	)	
Defendant.	)	County Court File No. ______

TO: the Clerk of the above-named County Court, and the Prosecuting Attorney

PLEASE TAKE NOTICE that the above-named Defendant hereby appeals on the record to the District court for the above-named County from the following Judgment or Orders of the above-named County Court:

_____Final Judgement of Conviction, entered on the ___ day of _________, 19__.

_____Order refusing or imposing conditions of release, entered on the ___ day of _________, 19__.

Dated: ____________ ________________________

(Attorney for Defendant)

Name:

Title:

Address:

Telephone No.:

Figure 12.2

resources to do so. Figure 12.3 shows the Michigan form used by the judge to grant the appeal, appoint an attorney and notify the court reporter to prepare the transcript. A defendant who files the notice may abandon the appeal later.

Frequently, the attorneys that handle the trial do not process the appeal. Many attorneys specialize in either trial or appellate work because the skills involved are quite different. The trial attorney focuses his/her efforts on preparing the case for trial, presenting evidence, examining witnesses and making appropriate objections. Public speaking skills are important. The appellate attorney reviews the transcripts and focuses on researching the legal issues and writing persuasive briefs. Some states have the attorney general's office handle appeals in criminal cases instead of the local prosecutor's office; this is more common with felony appeals than for misdemeanors. There may be a statewide public defender's office to handle the appeals for cases in which the defendant cannot afford to hire a lawyer.

The side filing the appeal, called the **appellant**, prepares a brief stating all the legal issues involved in the appeal. This is called the **appellant's opening brief**. It starts with a summary of the case. The legal maneuvers in the case will be summarized: charges defendant was arraigned on; charges the defendant was held to answer on after the preliminary hearing; any charges dismissed before trial; and charges on which the defendant was convicted. Relevant dates for these actions are usually included along with references to the page of the clerk's transcript for each. The second part of the summary is a statement of the facts (e.g., at 6:35 p.m. on September 4, 1994, John Jones returned home after work and discovered that his home had been broken into and his stereo was missing, etc.). These facts must be supported by references to testimony in the reporter's transcript.

The legal arguments are the heart of the appellate brief. Figure 12.4 shows a page from an appellant's opening brief. Each issue is usually set out under a separate heading.

Each issue is fully developed citing the facts, U. S. Constitution and Bill of Rights, state constitution and statutes and relevant case law. Citations for all statutes and cases are required. Failure to raise an issue in the opening brief waives the right to appeal on that point of law. The brief ends with a "**prayer**" which is a request for appellate court action, usually the reversal of the conviction. State law usually sets a time limit, such as 60 days, for the appellant to file an opening brief. This

Criminal Procedure **Rule 6.425**

Approved, SCAO

Copies to: Trial Court, Court Reporter(s)/ Recorder(s), Appointed Counsel, Defendant, Prosecutor, Court of Appeals, and MAACS

STATE OF MICHIGAN JUDICIAL CIRCUIT COUNTY	CLAIM OF APPEAL AND ORDER APPOINTING COUNSEL	CASE NO.

Court address — Court telephone no.

THE PEOPLE OF THE STATE OF MICHIGAN

v

Defendant name, address, date of birth, and inmate no (if known)

OFFENSE NAME	MCL CITATION	SENTENCE(S)

1. The defendant claims an appeal from a final judgment or order entered on ____________ (Date) in the ________ Circuit Court, ____________ County, Michigan by Judge ____________

____________ Bar no.

Copies of the final judgment or order being appealed are attached for the Court of Appeals and appointed counsel.

2. On ____________ (Date) the defendant filed a request for appointment of counsel and a declaration of indigency.

IT IS ORDERED:

3. ☐ The State Appellate Defender Office, 1200 Sixth Avenue, Third Floor North Tower, Detroit, MI 48226 (313) 256-2814
   OR
   ☐ ____________
   Name of Appellate Counsel — Address
   ____
   City, state, and zip — Telephone no. — Bar no.

   is appointed counsel for the defendant in post-conviction proceedings. If appointed counsel cannot or will not accept this appointment, counsel shall notify the court immediately.

4. The court reporter(s)/recorder(s) shall file with the trial court clerk the transcripts checked below and any other transcripts requested by counsel in this case not previously transcribed. Transcripts shall be filed within 28 days for pleas or 56 days for trials from the date ordered or requested. [MCR 7.210(B)] Reporter(s)/recorder(s) shall be paid as provided by law.

TRANSCRIPT ORDERED	REPORTER/RECORDER NAME, DESIGNATION, AND NUMBER	DATE(S) OF PROCEEDING
☐ a. Jury trial ☐ b. Bench trial ☐ c. Plea		
☐ Probation Violation ☐ d. Plea ☐ e. Hearing		
☐ f. Sentence ☐ g. Resentence		
☐ h. Other (specify)		

5. The clerk shall immediately send to counsel a copy of the docket entries and the transcripts ordered above or requested by counsel as they become available. The clerk shall also forward documents upon request by counsel. [MCR 6.433]

Date — Judge — Bar no.

PROOF OF SERVICE

On this date I served a copy of this claim of appeal on appointed counsel, defendant, court reporter(s)/recorder(s), prosecutor, Court of Appeals, and the Michigan Appellate Assigned Counsel System. I also served a copy of the final judgment or order being appealed on appointed counsel and the Court of Appeals and a copy of the defendant's request for appointment of counsel on appointed counsel, the prosecutor, and the Michigan Appellate Assigned Counsel System.

Date — Signature

CC 403 (12/89) **CLAIM OF APPEAL AND ORDER APPOINTING COUNSEL** MCR 6.425(F), MCR 6.433, MCR 7.210(B)(3)

Figure 12.3

time runs from the time the notice of appeal was filed or the date the transcripts are ready. Continuances may be sought if there is good cause for the delay. The appellant's opening brief is filed with the clerk of the appellate court. Copies are usually served on the opposing party and the trial judge.

The **respondent**, which is the opposite side from the appellant, must respond to the appellant's opening brief. If the criminal defendant appeals, the prosecutor or attorney general's staff handles the appeal on behalf of the government. This is true even when the appeal is from a court ruling rather than for something that the prosecutor did. The **respondent's opening brief** is filed to refute the legal claims made in the appellant's opening brief. It normally begins with a summary of the case but the respondent can accept the one prepared by the appellant. The respondent must counter each issue raised by the appellant; it does not, however, need to raise any additional issues. Figure 12.5 shows the first page of the reply to the issue raised in the case shown in Figure 12.4.

The respondent's brief usually takes one of three approaches: it argues that the facts do not support the appellant's argument; cases may be cited that the appellant did not mention; or arguments may be made that the cases appellant cites are not applicable to the facts of the case. A combination of these approaches is frequently used. Citations for all cases and statutes are required. State law usually establishes a deadline for filing respondent's opening brief; it may be 30 days from receipt of appellant's opening brief. The appellate court has the authority to grant continuances. The brief is filed with the court and copies are served on the opposing side and the trial judge. Upon receipt of respondent's opening brief the clerk of the appellate court usually schedules the case for oral arguments.

Most states permit the appellant to respond in writing to arguments made by the respondent. The brief prepared for this purpose is called **appellant's reply brief**. It is usually optional. Figure 12.6 shows a page from the appellants reply brief in the same case shown in Figures 12.4 and 12.5. New arguments are not usually permitted at this point. State law establishes the time limit for filing this document; it is usually shorter than the time allotted for the opening brief. Local rules may permit the respondent to file a reply brief.

Oral arguments are usually optional at the appellate level. Local custom usually indicates whether an attorney should prepare for them

Appellant's Opening Brief

JUDITH A. HAILS
ATTORNEY AT LAW
15751 BROOKHURST STREET • SUITE 113
WESTMINSTER, CALIFORNIA 92683
(714) 531-1722

ARGUMENT

I

DENIAL OF MOTION TO SEVER
WAS PREJUDICIAL ERROR AND
DEPRIVED DEFENDANT OF HIS
RIGHT TO A FAIR TRIAL

On January 21, 1977, defendant's motion for severance of the four counts of the Information was heard. After argument by both sides, the motion was denied. (RT1 2-13, CT 20) It is maintained that under the circumstances of the case and in view of the testimony before the court, denial was prejudicial error.

It is recognized that the granting of a motion to sever is within the sound discretion of the court and that the court was entitled to consider the interplay of evidence between multiple occurrences. Normally the objectivity of the jury is considered properly guarded by appropriate jury instructions, (People V. Blalock 238 Cal.App. 2d 209, 222 (1965)) but a strong showing to the contrary can overcome the presumed effect of the jury instruction. (People v. Chambers 231 Cal.App. 2d 23 (1964)) The court in Chambers concluded:

> That we speak in terms of possibilities is no answer. We do not know of course what actually motivated the guilty verdict. Where fundamental demands for the individual adjudication of personal guilt may have been violated, we cannot take refuge in threadbare presumptions that the jury resolutely ignored inflamatory, irrelevant evidence and hewd strictly to the letter of its instructions. Instead we remand the matter to provide an opportunity for the defendant's retrial under more acceptable circumstances. (231 Cal.App. 2d at 34)

While the court in Chambers was dealing with the denial of a motion to sever the trials of co-defendants, arguments by the prosecutor at the hearing on the motion indicates that the

21

Figure 12.4

Respondent's Opening Brief

ARGUMENT

I

THE TRIAL COURT DID NOT ABUSE ITS DISCRETION IN DENYING APPELLANT'S MOTION TO SEVER

Appellant argues the trial court prejudicially abused its discretion when it refused to sever the four counts of the information. (AOB 21.) Appellant contends had the four counts been severed and tried separately, not guilty verdicts would have been returned on each. Appellant notes the deputy district attorney himself argued that if the jury was unaware of appellant's repeated attacks on women, it would be difficult to convict him of any one of those assaults. (RT LF 1-13.)[4/] Appellant argues joinder for that purpose is improper and the trial court abused its discretion in refusing to sever.

Penal Code section 954 allows the joinder of two or more offenses connected in their commission or offenses that are of the same class of crime. The section likewise authorizes severance if good cause is shown and if done in the interest of justice. The denial of the motion to sever is within the sound discretion of the trial court. Denial of the motion will be disturbed only for abuse of

---

4. RT LF refers to the Reporter's Transcript prepared by Court Reporter Louis Frank.

Appellant's Reply Brief

IN THE COURT OF APPEAL OF THE STATE OF CALIFORNIA
FOURTH APPELLATE DISTRICT
DIVISION TWO

THE PEOPLE OF THE STATE OF CALIFORNIA, Plaintiff and Respondent, v. TY GLEN CLAYTON, Defendant and Appellant.	4 Crim. No. 9747 (Sup.Ct.No. C-36468)

APPEAL FROM THE SUPERIOR COURT OF ORANGE COUNTY

Honorable Mason L. Fenton, Judge Presiding

APPELLANT'S REPLY BRIEF

ARGUMENT

I

DENIAL OF MOTION TO SEVER WAS PREJUDICIAL ERROR AND DEPRIVED DEFENDANT OF HIS RIGHT TO A FAIR TRIAL

Respondent argues that severance would cloak defendant in an aura of credibility to which he is not entitled. This ignores the fact that the prosecution admitted, on the record, that in all probability the defense would be successful if severance was granted. Appellant does not seek unfair advantage but merely the protection of the rights to which each person charged with a crime is entitled, namely, that prosecution bear its burden of proving each essential element of each crime (People v. Francisco 228 Cal.App. 2d 355, 358 (1964)) and that

1

Figure 12.6

or submit a waiver. The length of oral arguments also varies with some courts allocating only five minutes per attorney while others are more generous.

When oral arguments are scheduled, the appellate judges normally review the briefs before the case is heard. In some courts, staff attorneys assist with this process and may even prepare a draft opinion before the case is heard. Some judges listen passively to what the attorney wants to present while others aggressively ask questions. The judges usually meet after the day's oral arguments have been heard. A vote is taken on each case. One judge from the majority is assigned to write the court's opinion; other judges may write their own opinions either concurring with the outcome but stating different reasons for doing so or dissenting and stating reasons why the case should have been decided differently. Many states have laws that require appellate judges to issue the opinion within a fixed time, such as 90 days, after oral arguments. The opinion is filed with the clerk of the appellate court and copies are sent to the attorneys for each side and to the trial judge. A copy also goes to the official publisher of the state's appellate opinions.

Only published opinions become precedent. Some states allow the judges to vote on whether an opinion will be published. This is done to reduce the volume of cases in the official reports. An unpublished opinion is still filed in the court record and served on the attorneys and trial judge. It is binding on the parties to the case but cannot be cited by attorneys arguing other cases. The most common reason for not publishing an opinion is that it contains no new issues and the fact pattern has been adjudicated in the past. Many states vacate an opinion if the case is accepted for hearing by a higher court; this leaves only the final decision in the officially published reports.

12.2 Defendant's Constitutional Rights on Appeal

There is no mention in the Constitution or Bill of Rights of a right to appeal. The Supreme Court has noted, however, that all 50 states and the federal system provide for appeals after convictions. In recognition of the universality of the right to appeal in the American judicial system, the Supreme Court has extended the right to counsel through the first post-conviction appeal. This means that an indigent defendant is entitled to have an attorney appointed to handle the first appeal. The standard for determining if a defendant is indigent is the same as it was at trial: can the person afford to hire an attorney in light of the cost of legal representation for this type of case and the number of dependents that the defendant is supporting? This test is applied at the time appellate counsel is requested. Defendants who paid lawyers to represent them at trial may have exhausted their financial resources and be indigent as far as the appeal is concerned. For this reason, it is more common to find court-appointed counsel handling cases on appeal than it was at trial.

The Supreme Court has held that a defendant's appeal cannot be blocked due to his/her inability to pay fees or purchase documents necessary for the appeal. Some unique features of the appellate process make this decision necessary if the defendant is to be able to pursue an appeal. Many courts have filing fees ranging from $100 to $500 for an appeal. Being required to pay this fee would mean many indigent defendants would forego an appeal; therefore, the filing fee must be waived for them. The transcripts are necessary in many cases because an attorney who did not represent the defendant at trial is appointed to handle the appeal. The documents are frequently lengthy and expensive: the clerk's transcript may cost $1 per page and the reporter's transcript as much as $5 per page. If the rules mandate references to these documents, it is necessary for the government to provide copies to the attorney representing the defendant on appeal. A fourth expense on appeal involves the printing of the briefs. Some courts have rules that require the briefs to be printed — not xeroxed. Again, it becomes necessary to pay for the printing of briefs for the indigent or, as an alternative, the appellate rules may permit indigent briefs to be xeroxed or prepared by some other less expensive process.

Not every conviction merits an appeal. Sometimes there were no errors committed at trial serious enough to be grounds for reversal. On the other hand, the Supreme Court has been reluctant to let appointed attorneys be the sole arbitrator of whether the defendant's case will be heard at the appellate level. This has been reinforced by several cases that have been reversed after an attorney wrote a letter stating that the case had no merit. The Supreme Court ruled that an attorney must file a brief discussing all arguable issues prior to requesting to be removed from the case. The appellate court is required to review the brief and appoint another attorney if there are arguable claims of error. Failure to follow this procedure is a prejudicial error which warrants a new appeal. Figure 12.7 shows the form used by the United States Court of Appeal for the Seventh Circuit when at attorney has asked to withdraw from the case because he/she does not believe there are appealable issues involved. Note the procedures the defendant can follow to obtain another attorney.

In some cases, a defendant whose case is on appeal may be allowed to remain free on bail or OR. This rarely occurs if the defendant was in custody while awaiting trial. Most states leave the decision to release the defendant to the trial judge. The convicted defendant is usually seen as a flight risk and must show a strong justification for being allowed out of jail at this point. If the defendant was given a sentence that did not include incarceration, the judge is not likely to require him/her to return to jail pending appeal.

12.3 Pretrial Appeals

State laws vary, but some legal issues can be raised on appeal before trial. The advantage of the appeal at this stage is that the issue can be settled before trial, thus avoiding problems with double jeopardy. Even if double jeopardy would not be a problem, early resolution of the issue saves the cost of a second trial if the conviction is reversed due to the erroneous ruling of the lower court judge. Delays caused by good faith appeals cannot be used as a grounds for dismissal for lack of speedy trial.

All of the actions discussed in this section are appealable, but some states require the appeal to be made before trial, others want the issue raised in the direct appeal that follows conviction, while a few permit an appeal at either time. Attorneys handling the case must check the local rules and determine when to file the appeal. Failure to file the appeal in a timely manner may result in the court's refusal to consider the issue later.

Pretrial appeals challenge the rulings of judges presiding over arraignments, preliminary hearings, and pretrial proceedings. Sometimes, they also challenge the actions or composition of the grand jury. Either the defense or prosecution can appeal these actions because

FORM OF NOTICE FOR DEFENDANT COUNSEL'S MOTION FOR LEAVE TO WITHDRAW UNDER CIRCUIT RULE 51(a)

To: ______________________________
(Name)

____
(Street Address or Prison Box)

____
(City, State, Zip Code)

You are the appellant in a case now pending in this court: Case No. __________

____
v.
____

Your attorney filed a brief on ____________, 19 ___, stating a belief that your appeal is frivolous and requesting permission to withdraw from the case. Please be advised as follows:

1) You have 30 days from the date this notice was mailed in which to raise any points that you choose which show why your conviction should be set aside.
2) If you do not respond within 30 days, the court may affirm or dismiss your appeal. An affirmance or dismissal would mean that your case would be finally decided against you.
3) If you want to make a showing why the court should not affirm or dismiss your appeal and believe that there is a very good reason why you will not be able to file your objections with the court within the 30-day limit, you should *immediately* write to the court and ask for additional time up to 30 days. If additional time is granted, you must file your reasons why the court should not affirm or dismiss your appeal before your additional time expires.
4) You do not have a right to another attorney unless this court finds that your showing requires that your case be further briefed or argued. If the court finds that your case should be further briefed or argued, an attorney will be appointed for you who will argue your appeal.

If you want to write to this court, you should address your letter to:

Clerk of the Court
United States Court of Appeals
219 South Dearborn Street
Chicago, Illinois 60604

Be sure, when writing, to show clearly the name and number of your case.

Notice mailed ____________, 19 ___

____

Deputy Clerk, U.S. Court of Appeals
Attorney for appellant

____
(Name)

____
(Street Address)

____
(City, State, Zip Code)

____
(Area Code and Telephone Number)

Figure 12.7

double jeopardy has not attached at this stage of the proceeding. Although the case may list the court as a party, such as Jones v. Superior Court, the arguments made on appeal are handled by the prosecution and defense. If the prosecution appeals, the defense must file a brief in support of the action taken by the judge. The opposite is true if the defense appeals: the prosecution files a brief arguing that the judge's ruling was correct.

The most common issues appealed after the arraignment deal with the wording of the criminal complaint: jurisdictional facts; statute of limitations; and stating a cause of action. Section 7.4 discusses many of these issues. No one testifies before the appellate court. The defense must raise the issue by filing a motion in the court where the arraignment occurred. If denied, it may appeal. If the motion was granted, the prosecution may appeal. The clerk's transcript, which contains the complaint and other documentation from of the arraignment, as well as the dialogue contained in the reporter's transcript, is important for these appeals. An appeal normally goes to the next higher court. For this reason, pretrial appeals in felony cases are frequently heard by a lower level court than would hear the appeal of a conviction. For example, if arraignments are held in Municipal Court and felony trials in Superior Court, the appeal from a ruling made at the arraignment in Municipal Court would be heard in Superior Court rather than the Court of Appeals that hears challenges to convictions from Superior Court trials.

Holding the defendant to answer at the end of the preliminary hearing can be challenged before trial in some states. In addition to the issues that can be raised to challenge the complaint, the defense can allege that there were insufficient facts presented to establish a *prima facie* case. The verbatim transcript of the testimony at the preliminary hearing is crucial for this purpose. Occasionally, the prosecution files an appeal from a ruling at this stage of the case. Pretrial appeals from the preliminary hearing are usually heard in the same court that hears challenges to the criminal complaint.

Many states permit Fourth and Fifth Amendment challenges to the evidence before the trial begins. Section 7.5 discussed many of these issues. For example, the defense may claim the murder weapon was unconstitutionally seized or that the confession was obtained in violation of the defendant's *Miranda* rights. A motion requesting a hearing on these issues must be filed. Depending on the time of the motion, it may be filed in the court that handled the arraignment or, in felony cases, the court that will hold the trial. The judge's ruling on the motion can be appealed by either side. Five things are usually important for use on this type of appeal: verbatim transcript of preliminary hearing for witnesses involved in the search or obtaining the confession; verbatim transcript of suppression hearing for testimony regarding how the evidence or confession in question was obtained; points and authorities submitted before the suppression hearing by both sides; oral arguments made by both sides at the suppression hearing; and the judge's ruling, including any written opinion, giving reasons for his/her resolution of the matter.

12.4 Appeal After Guilty Plea

A defendant has the right to counsel when entering a guilty plea. The issue of inadequate representation can be raised in a plea bargain case based on the same standard it would be if a trial had occurred: defendant was entitled to a competent counsel; reversal is required only if having competent counsel would have altered the outcome. Important constitutional rights must be waived when the judge accepts the plea: trial by jury; confront and cross-examine witnesses; and proof beyond a reasonable doubt. The defendant is entitled to withdraw a plea if he/she did not knowingly waive these rights. Coercion is also raised occasionally.

It is generally agreed that the defendant has the right to the plea bargain that he/she agreed to. If the judge rejects the agreement, the defendant has the right to withdraw the plea. Refusal to permit the defendant to do so is grounds for reversal on appeal. In many courts, it is recognized that the judge retains discretion to impose sentence and the plea bargain can only cover the charges involved. When this is incorporated in the bargain the defendant cannot appeal because of the sentence imposed.

The dialogue of what occurred in court on the day the plea bargain was entered is crucial to determining whether errors occurred. The verbatim transcript of the hearing becomes the key evidence on appeal. If the issue is incompetence of counsel, the transcript frequently provides insufficient information on why the attorney performed in the manner he/she did. A writ of *habeas corpus* is needed to determine this issue. Section 12.8 discusses how *habeas corpus* is handled.

Some states have a seemingly contradictory procedure: a defendant whose motion to suppress evidence is unsuccessful can enter a guilty plea and still appeal the ruling on the suppression motion. This saves trials in many cases: defendants whose only defense rested on the suppression of evidence do not take up court time with trials in order to retain the right to appeal Fourth and Fifth Amendment issues. The transcript of the suppression hearing is usually the key to the appeal in these cases.

12.5 Direct Appeal of Conviction

The appeal from a conviction that is taken immediately following sentencing is referred to as a **direct appeal**. To obtain further appeals after that time, the defendant must petition the court for its permission to appeal. These are called **discretionary appeals**. The constitutional right to have an attorney appointed if the defendant is indigent applies to direct appeals but not discretionary appeals.

A direct appeal is limited to issues presented in the trial record (clerk and reporter's transcripts). The most common issues relate to jury instructions which tell the jury how to apply the law to the facts. Search and seizure issues and *Miranda* questions are common. Local laws may state that issues raised on pretrial appeals cannot be relitigated as part of the direct appeal. There are also issues that may be non-appealable unless specific procedures, such as filing an exception to the admission of evidence, were complied with at trial. The contemporaneous objection rule applies to many things that occur at trial and prohibits appeal regarding evidence that was admitted at trial without an objection.

Some issues cannot be raised on direct appeal because there is nothing in the trial record about them. Incompetence of counsel is a good example. The trial record contains verbatim accounts of what was done but usually does not show whether the attorney was following a tactical plan or was unprepared or unaware of the issues involved. *Habeas corpus* is the appropriate procedure to raise these issues. Section 12.8 explains procedures that are used to obtain a writ of *habeas corpus*.

Nearly all appeals following convictions are taken by defendants. Double jeopardy does not protect a convicted defendant from being retried on the same charges if he/she wins a direct appeal. There is one exception: cases in which the appellate court held that there was insufficient evidence to support a conviction. On the other hand, if the jury finds the defendant not guilty or the judge orders an acquittal, the prosecution cannot refile the charges no matter what happens on appeal. Perjury or subordination of perjury can be filed if the defendant lied under oath or had other witnesses do so during the trial, but the charges the defendant was acquitted on cannot be refiled.

Occasionally, the prosecution will appeal to settle a point of law, usually because the trial judge directed a verdict of acquittal based on an unusual interpretation of how the law applied to the facts of the case. These appeals may be important because of the legal precedent that they set, but they have no effect on the defendant because double jeopardy protects him/her from being tried again.

12.6 Appeals When Death Penalty Has Been Imposed

Many states set up different appellate procedures if the defendant was convicted of a capital crime and sentenced to death. The first step is usually to require the trial judge to review the case more carefully and grant a motion for a new trial if he/she believes that reversible error occurred. The judge may also have the authority to enter the conviction for murder but disregard the jury's verdict recommending the death penalty. These actions are done before the case is transferred to the appellate court.

State law frequently designates one court to hear all death penalty appeals. The state's highest court is commonly used for this purpose and the intermediate-level appellate courts are bypassed. When this is done there is only one appeal within the state court system but it is more thorough than what normally occurs. Many states also make review by this appellate court mandatory, sometimes called an **automatic appeal**, if the death penalty has been imposed.

Greater care is usually exercised when appointing an attorney to handle the appeal. In many states, a special list of appellate attorneys is used for this purpose. Unlike the average case where any licensed attorney may be appointed, the court may require proof that the attorney has sufficient experience to adequately handle the life-and-death issues to be addressed. More time may be authorized for the preparation of the appellant's briefs. Any page limits that apply to appeals are usually waived so that the attorney may devote as much space to each argument as he/she believes necessary.

Courts that hear death penalty appeals usually take more time considering them than they do other cases. The opinions are usually longer and demonstrate more detailed application of the law to the particular facts of the case. Many states require the court to consider proportionality of the sentence as well as the defendant's guilt. This means the judges are to compare the current case with other capital punishment cases they have reviewed: they should reverse the sentence if it seems disproportionately harsh compared to the facts of other death penalty cases they have affirmed.

12.7 Discretionary Appeals

All appeals after the direct appeal are discretionary. The normal process is for the side that lost the direct appeal to file a petition asking the higher court to take the case. If a conviction was reversed on direct appeal, the higher court can reverse the first appellate court, thereby reinstating the conviction, without violating double jeopardy. The justices review these petitions and decide which ones will be heard. Usually, a positive vote of nearly a majority of the justices is needed before the petition is granted. This process is followed in many states and also for most cases heard by the United States Supreme Court.

Most defendants face two problems when seeking a discretionary appeal: they do not have an attorney to handle the case and they cannot afford the fees involved (filing fees, printing costs, etc.). Defendants cannot invoke the Sixth Amendment or equal protection as grounds for the courts to provide the services they seek. The right to counsel ended with the direct appeal. States are free to address these issues as they wish so long as they do not totally cut off access to the courts. At a minimum, they must provide law libraries in the prisons, appropriate writing materials and postage to mail legal documents. "Jailhouse lawyers," inmates who help other inmates with legal matters, cannot be prohibited unless other forms of assistance are available.

Due to the fact that defendants frequently write their own petitions for discretionary appeals, many courts have accepted petitions that the clerk's office otherwise would refuse to file. Many are handwritten. The legal issues may be poorly worded. If the justices vote to hear the case, an attorney may be appointed by the state even though the federal constitution does not mandate it.

State defendants can petition the United States Supreme Court to hear their cases on the grounds that there was a constitutional error. The first step usually is a **motion to proceed *in forma pauperis*** such as the one shown in Figure 12.8. The literal meaning of *in forma pauperis* is "like a poor person." Granting of this motion excuses the defendant from paying filing fees and complying with some of the court rules, such as the one that mandates all briefs be printed.

Once the motion has been granted, the defendant can file a **petition for writ of *certiorari*** such as the one shown in Figure 12.9. The **writ of *certiorari*** is the document the court issues accepting a case on discretionary appeal. The petition must state constitutional grounds for the appeal and convince the justices to hear the case. The petitions are reviewed in conference and votes taken. At least four of the nine United States Supreme Court justices must vote in favor of issuing the writ of *certiorari*. This does not mean that the defendant is assured of winning the case: two justices may have voted to hear the case because they wanted to affirm the conviction while two others voted for it so they could reverse it. The grant of *certiorari* states what issues will be heard. Occasionally, the justices will ask the parties for supplemental briefs on additional issues. Once the Supreme Court grants *certiorari*, it appoints an experienced attorney to prepared the necessary briefs and pays for printing briefs and other expenses.

The Supreme Court works on a yearly term which begins the first Monday in October and closes the last week in June or first week in July. The parties file briefs similar to those used for direct appeal in state court. Figure 12.10 shows the introduction to a petitioner's brief in a recent case. The prosecution's brief is usually prepared by the state attorney general's staff.

One or more ***amicus curiae*** may also file briefs. *Amicus curiae* means friend of the court. An *amicus curiae* brief is filed by someone (a person, organization, or governmental entity) that wishes to present a viewpoint for the justices to consider. The party wishing to participate files a petition requesting the court's permission to do so. After the request is granted, a brief is filed which is usually in the same format as the opening brief of the side the *amicus* supports. Examples of *amicus curiae* in criminal cases include the International Association

Motion for Leave Proceed in Forma Pauperis

No. ____________ ORIGINAL

IN THE

SUPREME COURT OF THE UNITED STATES

October Term, 1992

PAUL PALALAUA TUILAEPA,

Petitioner, 93-5131

vs.

THE STATE OF CALIFORNIA,

Respondent.

Supreme Court, U.S.
FILED
OFFICE OF THE CLERK

MOTION FOR LEAVE TO PROCEED

IN FORMA PAUPERIS

The petitioner, PAUL PALALAUA TUILAEPA, requests leave to file the accompanying petition for writ of certiorari, without prepayment of costs and to proceed in forma pauperis. Petitioner has been granted leave to so proceed before the California Supreme Court. Petitioner's affidavit in support of this motion is attached hereto.

Dated: 7/6/93

Respectfully submitted,

Howard W. Gillingham
4370 Tujunga Avenue
Suite 105
North Hollywood, CA 91604

Counsel for Petitioner

Figure 12.8

of Chiefs of Police filing a brief supporting what the police did and the American Civil Liberties Union filing a brief in support of the defendant's allegations that the police actions were unconstitutional. The justices consider these briefs when deciding the case.

Oral arguments before the Supreme Court are very formal. Specific time limits are set and strictly enforced. Justices interrupt the attorney's speech to ask questions. The justices meet in conference

Petition for Writ of *Certiorari*

No. ____________________

(Application # A898)

IN THE

SUPREME COURT OF THE UNITED STATES

October Term, 1992

PAUL PALALAUA TUILAEPA, Petitioner,

v.

THE STATE OF CALIFORNIA, Respondent.

PETITION FOR WRIT OF CERTIORARI TO

THE SUPREME COURT OF CALIFORNIA

RECEIVED
JUL 8 1993
OFFICE OF THE CLERK
SUPREME COURT, U.S.

HOWARD W. GILLINGHAM
4370 Tujunga Avenue
Suite 105
North Hollywood, California 91604
(818) 763-4775
[Fax (818) 763-5822]

Lawyer for Petitioner

Figure 12.9

once a week and discuss the cases that they have heard. A vote is taken. Someone from the majority is assigned to write the opinion. The draft opinion is circulated to the other justices and those that agree with it sign it. Justices also have the option of writing their own opinions. A justice may sign more than one opinion, for example a justice might sign the majority opinion because of agreement with the outcome of the majority opinion (conviction affirmed) but disagree on the legal

BRIEF FOR PETITIONER

CITATION TO OPINION BELOW

The opinion of the California Supreme Court is reported as *People v. Tuilaepa*, 4 Cal.4th 569, 842 P.2d 1142 (1992), and is located in the Joint Appendix, pages 68-105 (hereinafter "JA ___").

JURISDICTION

The judgment of the California Supreme Court was entered on December 28, 1992. A petition for rehearing was denied on March 10, 1993. The petition for writ of certiorari was filed on July 8, 1993, and granted on December 6, 1993. This Court's jurisdiction is invoked pursuant to 28 U.S.C. § 1275(a).

CONSTITUTIONAL AND STATUTORY PROVISIONS INVOLVED

1. This case involves the Eighth Amendment to the United States Constitution, which forbids the infliction of "cruel and unusual punishment."

2. It also involves the Fourteenth Amendment to the United States Constitution, which provides in pertinent part that no state may "deprive any person of life-. . . without due process of law. . . . "

Figure 12.10

rationale and write a concurring opinion. Dissents are also written, sometimes with justices signing more than one. An opinion may be both (i.e., it may concur with part of the majority opinion and dissent as to other parts of it).

Opinions by the Supreme Court are read aloud in court on the day they are released. Copies, called **slip opinions**, are given to the parties and distributed to those who subscribe to this service. Opinions also become available across the country by electronic mail almost immediately. The official version may not appear in *United States Reports* for nearly two years but other publishers issue **advance sheets** within a few weeks containing the text of the opinion.

12.8 *Habeus Corpus*

Article I, Section 9, paragraph 2 of the United States Constitution provides:

> The privilege of the Writ of *Habeas Corpus* shall not be suspended, unless when in Cases of Rebellion or Invasion the public Safety may require it.

The **writ of *habeas corpus***, sometimes called the "great writ," is used to challenge illegal confinement. This writ orders a governmental agency to bring the petitioner to court and explain the legal basis for the detention. It can be used to challenge confinement in jail or prison due to: illegal arrest; denial of reasonable bail for a bailable offense; illegally obtained conviction; conviction due to incompetent representation of counsel (either at trial or on appeal); or failure to release person after sentence has been served. *Habeas corpus* has also been used to challenge inhumane prison conditions. It can also be used to challenge involuntary confinement in a mental hospital. One prerequisite is that the person still be in custody when the petition is sought. Some courts consider a person in custody for the purpose of challenging an illegal arrest or conviction if he/she still has charges pending or is on probation or parole. Inmates may be able to use *habeas corpus* to secure reversals of their convictions even though they have unsuccessfully raised the issue on direct appeal if an appellate court decision in another case involving issues raised in their case was applied retroactively.

Habeas corpus is considered a civil action, therefore the inmate does not have the constitutional right to have an attorney appointed to handle the case. It is referred to as a **collateral attack** on a conviction, meaning that it is not part of the normal appellate process. Both state and federal laws provide for *habeas corpus* although it is sometimes classified as one of several post-conviction remedies and the name *habeas corpus* is not used. Normally, the case must proceed through the state courts before it can be filed in the federal system. Inmates who are in custody for breaking a state law whose constitutional rights were violated can file the federal equivalent of *habeas corpus* in the United States District Court. In recent years, the federal courts have imposed a variety of restrictions to reduce the number of cases heard in this manner. The most common one is that inmates cannot proceed in federal court if they have had a full and fair hearing on the same Fourth Amendment issues in state courts. This is a procedural approach: the opportunity to be heard on the issue is controlling, not whether the judge made the correct decision on the constitutionality of the police action.

The first document filed with the court in a *habeas corpus* proceeding is the **petition for a writ of *habeas corpus***. This is frequently a pre-printed form such as the one in Figure 12.11. Many jails and prisons keep copies of the form on hand for inmate use.

The person filing this petition must allege facts that indicate that he/she is being illegally confined. The court assigns a judge to review the petition. The writ of *habeas corpus* will be issued if the judge determines that the facts, if true, indicate illegal confinement. This document, as shown in Figure 12.12, orders the person holding the inmate in custody to bring the petitioner to court for a hearing.

The writ of *habeas corpus* is directed at the sheriff if the inmate is being held in county jail; for inmates in state prison, the writ usually names either the warden of the prison or a high-ranking official in the state's Department of Corrections. The court clerk serves the writ on the appropriate person.

A return is usually filed to the writ of *habeas corpus*. The return is the written reply by the person who is holding the petitioner in custody. It states the legal grounds for the confinement and includes appropriate documentation such as a copy of the conviction. The return is filed with the court and a copy served on the petitioner.

Petition for Writ of *Habeas Corpus*

11-6.5

ATTORNEY OR PETITIONER WITHOUT ATTORNEY *(Name and Address)*: TELEPHONE NO.: PETITIONER'S BIRTH DATE:	*FOR COURT USE ONLY*
SUPERIOR COURT OF CALIFORNIA, COUNTY OF	
IN THE MATTER OF *(NAME)*: Petitioner	CASE NUMBER:
PETITION FOR WRIT OF HABEAS CORPUS—Penal Commitment	

1. Petitioner is being unlawfully restrained of liberty at *(specify name of treatment facility)*:
   by *(specify name of persons having custody, if known)*:

2. Petitioner was admitted to the treatment facility on *(date)*: and is currently detained pursuant to:
   - ☐ Penal Code § 1026 (not guilty by reason of insanity)
   - ☐ Penal Code § 1026.5(b) (extended commitment)
   - ☐ Penal Code § 1370 (incompetent to stand trial)
   - ☐ Penal Code § 2684 (prisoners transferred to state hospital)
   - ☐ Penal Code § 2962 (mentally disordered offender)
   - ☐ Former W & I § 6300 (MDSO)
   - ☐ Other *(specify)*:

3. **Check at least one box:**
   a. ☐ Petitioner is illegally confined for the following reason:

   b. ☐ Petitioner has been denied the following rights without good cause (Penal Code section 2600):

4. Petitioner has no adequate and speedy remedy at law.

5. Have you made any previous requests for relief from this confinement? ________ *If your answer is yes,* state the nature and grounds for your request, the date it was made, and the result:

6. Petitioner requests that this court *(check all that apply)*:
   a. ☐ Issue a Writ of Habeas Corpus to the director of the facility named in item 1, commanding that the petitioner be brought before this court at a specified time and place.
   b. ☐ Order the facility personnel to release petitioner from said restraint.
   c. ☐ Order that all rights to which petitioner is entitled as a patient be observed.
   d. ☐ Grant such other relief as this court deems appropriate.

I declare under penalty of perjury under the laws of the State of California that the foregoing is true and correct.
Date:

(TYPE OR PRINT NAME) ▶ (SIGNATURE OF PETITIONER OR PERSON REQUESTING WRIT ON PETITIONER'S BEHALF)

Form Approved by the Judicial Council of California MC-270 (New January 1, 1994)

PETITION FOR WRIT OF HABEAS CORPUS—Penal Commitment (Mental Health)

Calif. Rules of Court, rule 260

Figure 12.11

Writ of *Habeas Corpus*

Special Proceedings **Rule 3.303**

Approved, SCAO

ORIGINAL - COURT
1ST COPY - CUSTODIAL OFFICER
2ND COPY - TRANSPORT OFFICER
3RD COPY - PROSECUTOR
4TH COPY - RETURN

STATE OF MICHIGAN JUDICIAL DISTRICT JUDICIAL CIRCUIT	WRIT OF HABEAS CORPUS	CASE NO.

Court address

Court telephone no

IN THE NAME OF THE PEOPLE OF THE STATE OF MICHIGAN:

TO ______ THE AGENCY OR PERSON HAVING

CUSTODY OF ______ (Name) ______ (I.D. no.) ______ (Date of birth)

☐ To bring prisoner to court in the case of:
People of
v

☐ To inquire into detention/custody of:

YOU ARE ORDERED to:

1. ☐ Answer this writ, stating the authority under which you ☐ restrain the named prisoner. ☐ exercise custody over the minor child.
   File your answer with the ☐ court ☐ judge by ______ (Date).
2. ☐ Deliver the person named in this writ into the custody of ______ (Name/Title/Agency)
   for the following purpose: ______ (To testify, for preliminary examination, trial, to be held pending court appearance, etc.)
   Immediately after the prisoner completes his/her appearance, the prisoner shall be returned to your custody.
3. ☐ Bring the person named in this writ before the Honorable ______
   at ______ (Location of court), on ______ (Date) at ______ m. (Time)
   Bring this writ with you.

Clerk of the Court

______ (Date) By: ______

CERTIFICATE OF ALLOWANCE OF WRIT

I, ______ (Name of Judge), P. ______ (Bar no.), certify that the above writ of habeas corpus was allowed by me on ______ (Date). ☐ Fees are allowed in the amount of $ ______.

______
Judge

MC 203 (11/85) WRIT OF HABEAS CORPUS MCLA 600.4301 et seq.; MSA 27A.4301 et seq., MCR 3.303, 3.304

Figure 12.12

A hearing will be held on the writ of *habeas corpus*. Witnesses testify under oath and are subject to cross-examination. If the issues raised center on releasing the petitioner on bail or failure to release the defendant at the end of a sentence, testimony of jail or prison officials may be required at the hearing. If the allegation is incompetency of counsel, the hearing centers around testimony of the allegedly incompetent attorney. Challenges to police conduct may require testimony of the law enforcement officers involved.

If the petitioner establishes his/her case at the *habeas corpus* hearing, the judge has the authority to discharge the inmate. In most cases, this means to release the person from jail/prison; in cases challenging prison conditions, it may be an order to improve the deficient conditions or transfer the inmate to an appropriate facility. The inmate may be arrested before leaving the custodial facility if the prosecution intends to refile the charges.

SUMMARY

The appellate process provides an opportunity to correct mistakes made in the trial courts. Rulings on the admissibility of evidence may be reversed if they were raised in a timely fashion at trial. It is rare for an appellate court to reverse a conviction due to insufficient evidence unless no testimony was presented about at least one element of the crime: decisions on the credibility of the witnesses are left to the jury.

Direct appeals are based on the record of what occurred at pretrial hearings and the trial. A notice of appeal is filed with the trial court. The attorney for the appellant reads the clerk's and reporter's transcripts to find issues, researches relevant law and prepares the appellant's opening brief. The opposing party's attorney prepares the respondent's opening brief which addresses each issue raised by the appellant. The appellant may file a reply brief to respond to statements in the respondent's brief. Oral arguments are heard and the judges write an opinion in the case. Opinions that appear in the officially published reports become precedent for future cases.

A defendant who cannot afford to hire an attorney has a constitutional right to have one appointed to represent him/her through the end of the direct appeal. This includes obtaining copies of necessary documents, such as the clerk's and reporter's transcripts, and waiving filing fees for the appeal. An appointed attorney who wishes to withdraw must file a brief discussing all possible issues before being dismissed from the case. Another attorney must be appointed to complete the appeal if the court believes there are any non-frivolous issues.

In some states, appeals may be taken before the trial starts. This usually occurs when there are serious legal questions regarding dismissal of the charges (or failure to do so), constitutionality of a search, or appropriate use of *Miranda* warnings. Some states allow the defendant to enter a guilty plea but retain the right to appeal search and seizure issues. Failure of the judge to honor a plea bargain agreed to by the defense and prosecution may also be appealed.

The appeal that normally follows immediately after the conviction is called a direct appeal. It is limited to items that can be determined by reading the transcripts of the case. *Habeas corpus* must be used if it is necessary to call witnesses. Time limits are usually set for direct appeals and if no action is taken the defendant is deemed to have waived this right. Most appeals to higher courts, such as the state's highest court or the United States Supreme Court, are considered discretionary appeals because the judges have the discretion to grant or deny requests for an appeal to be heard.

Death penalty cases are frequently an exception to the normal appellate rules: many state statutes designate the state's highest court as the court to hear the direct appeal if the death penalty was given by the trial judge. The court may be required to consider whether the death penalty was imposed in what appears to be an arbitrary manner. Proportionality may be considered, i.e., whether the current case represents as serious an offense as other cases in which the death penalty has been affirmed.

A defendant who appeals waives double jeopardy and submits to a second trial unless the conviction is reversed for insufficient evidence. Prosecution appeals cannot reverse acquittals but they can prevent rulings of a lower court judge from becoming established precedent. The prosecution can seek discretionary review when the direct appeal results in the reversal of a conviction, and if successful, the original conviction will again become effective. Pretrial appeals by either side do not affect double jeopardy: charges that have been dismissed can be refiled and evidence that was ruled inadmissible can be admitted if the appellate court rules the lower court acted incorrectly.

The United States Supreme Court hears most of its criminal cases via writs of *certiorari*. The party seeking review presents a petition trying to persuade the justices to hear constitutional issues in the case. At least four justices must vote in favor of considering the case. Once the writ is granted, briefs will be filed by both sides and other parties, called *amicus curiae*, who are interested in the case. Formal oral arguments are heard. The opinion normally is issued during the term in which the oral arguments were heard.

Habeas corpus is used to challenge illegal confinement ranging from pretrial detention due to false arrest to unconstitutionally inhumane prison conditions. The initial petition must state sufficient facts to show that a legal issue is involved. If so, a writ of *habeas corpus* is issued directing the custodial authorities to bring the petitioner to court for a full hearing. In recent years, federal court rules have become more restrictive in order to prevent state inmates from using *habeas corpus* to relitigate Fourth Amendment issues that were previously decided in state courts.

Study Questions

1. Check the laws of your state and explain:
   a. The time limit after a conviction for filing a direct appeal.
   b. How the defendant's appellate attorney is selected.
   c. How much time the appellant is given to file an opening brief.
   d. How much time the respondent is given to file an opening brief?
   e. What time limits are imposed on reply briefs.
   f. When oral arguments are held.
   g. What, if any, time limits apply to issuing an opinion in the case.
2. Check the rules for your local court and explain:
   a. What court hears pretrial appeals:
      1) felony cases.
      2) misdemeanor cases.
      3) other grounds for determining the appropriate court.
   b. What documents are required for pretrial appeals.
   c. What court hears appeals from misdemeanor convictions.

d. What documents are required for a misdemeanor appeal.
e. What court hears appeals from felony convictions.
f. What documents are required for a felony appeal.

3. If possible, go to oral arguments before your local appellate court. Prepare a report on one case you heard argued. The report should describe:
   a. charges
   b. facts of case
   c. legal issues raised
   d. oral arguments by attorneys
   e. interaction between justices and appellate attorneys

4. Check the laws in your state and describe how an appeal is taken to the state's highest court:
   a. How does a defendant petition the high court for a hearing?
   b. How many justices must vote to accept the case?
   c. If the case is accepted, is an attorney appointed to present the case to the high court?
   d. What time limits apply to preparing briefs by each side?
   e. Where are oral arguments held?
   f. Are there time restrictions on oral arguments? If so, what are they?
   g. Are there time restrictions on how soon the opinion must be issued after oral arguments? If so, what are they?

5. Check the laws in your state regarding *habeas corpus*:
   a. What forms or other paperwork requirements apply to filing a Petition for Writ of *Habeas Corpus*?
   b. Which court reviews these petitions?
   c. Are there restrictions on the types of cases that can be heard via *habeas corpus*? If so, explain.
   d. How long does the respondent have to reply to the petition?
   e. How soon after filing the reply is a hearing held on the petition?
   f. How does a state inmate file a *habeas corpus* petition in your local federal court?

Chapter 13

Corrections

Learning Objectives

After reading this chapter, the student will be able to:

- Explain four rationales for punishing convicted criminals.
- Explain the factors a judge considers when placing a person on probation.
- Describe at least five common conditions placed on probationers.
- Describe the procedures that must be complied with to revoke probation.
- Explain how parole dates are established and changed.
- Explain how inmates accumulate "good time" and how it can be lost.
- Describe the inmate's due process rights at jail or prison disciplinary hearings.
- Explain how parole functions.
- Describe what occurs at a parole revocation hearing.
- Describe three recent innovations in corrections.

Key Terms

boot camp
conditional discharge
conditions of probation
day fine
death warrant
general deterrence
halfway house
ignition interlock device
incapacitation
informal probation
intensive probation
Interstate Agreement on Supervision of Probationers and Parolees
Interstate Corrections Compact
preliminary revocation hearing
probation
rehabilitation
retribution
return on death warrant
revocation hearing
specific deterrence
suspended sentence
technical violations

13.1 Rationales for Corrections

The criminal justice system revolves around the concept that a person can control his/her behavior and those that do not conform to the criminal law should be punished. The type of punishment imposed varies with the severity of the offense and the level of the defendant's blameworthiness, but also depends on the reasons for punishment. Four main rationales are used; sometimes more than one of these is in use at the same time. Other considerations, such as the high cost of incarceration and prison overcrowding, also play important roles in these decisions. Historical trends can be discerned; no one rationale stays in fashion. Which ones are currently utilized is normally determined by the local legislature.

Retribution

Criminal punishments in primitive societies were usually a family matter: the family of the victim took revenge on the offender. It frequently took a symbolic form, such as the proverbial "eye for an eye, and a tooth for a tooth." For more serious offenses retribution was carried out at the tribal level. As societies became more civilized, the government assumed the function of retribution: it imposed punishment for the injuries inflicted on innocent people. In doing so, it prohibited individual members of society from extracting their own vengeance. The victims' rights movement which has emerged in recent years is a modified version of retribution: the victim is entitled to have the criminal punished.

DETERRENCE

Deterrence is based on the concept that punishment will deter criminal activity. It has two interrelated concepts: specific deterrence and general deterrence. **Specific deterrence** punishes a person in order to deter that individual. In other words, if John Jones is sent to jail for petty theft, he is unlikely to steal again. If it is determined that the individual will respond to less severe punishment, for example probation, then it is not necessary to incarcerate the defendant.

General deterrence punishes a person as an example to society. There needs to be some reason to believe that others would be deterred by the punishment imposed. Publicizing the punishment may serve this purpose. John Jones is sent to jail for petty theft as an example to all thieves in hopes that it will deter them from stealing. This approach would find it necessary to punish John Jones for being a thief, even if it could be determined that he would never steal again, if others would interpret a lenient sentence as an indication that they could "get away with" stealing.

REHABILITATION

Rehabilitation is based on the idea that the defendant's behavior can be changed. It usually emphasizes counseling and job training so that the person will not want to commit additional crimes and will be able to be gainfully employed. It places heavy reliance on psychologists and other counselors. Rehabilitation is frequently linked to indeterminate sentencing so the inmate can be kept in custody until he/she displays appropriate behavior and attitudes. It is more likely to be used in prisons than jails because of the length of time needed to affect these change(s). A diagnostic study is usually done shortly after the defendant enters prison to determine psychological problems the defendant may have as well as job skills that are needed. Inmates who want to become productive members of society can benefit from this. On the other hand, many inmates become savvy to what is expected and quickly learn to say and do what their counselors want in order to gain early release. Inmates who do not want to be rehabilitated and refuse to cooperate serve the longest sentences.

Incapacitation

Incapacitation is based on the idea that keeping criminals off the streets makes society safer. It does not pretend to change long-term behavior, nor does it consider whether the sentence will deter crime. Studies of individuals who support themselves by robbery, burglary and theft show that hundreds of crimes can be prevented by keeping these offenders in prison for long terms. The logic of incapacitation does not fit cases in which the defendant was convicted for an isolated offense and is not likely to commit other crimes.

13.2 Probation

Probation, **suspended sentences**, and **conditional discharges** involve releasing the convicted offender into the community, frequently without serving time in jail. For convenience, all three will be referred to as probation in this chapter. Some defendants are released with little or no supervision, sometimes called **informal probation**; others report regularly to probation officers. A condition of all of these releases is that the person commit no new crimes. A new offense, or a violation of other conditions placed on the release, will result in incarceration without a new trial.

Most state sentencing laws are written so that the judge has the option to place the defendant on probation unless the code section contains specific language restricting this discretion. This allows the judge to consider both the defendant's background and the current offense when deciding whether probation should be imposed. Figure 13.1 gives lists of factors that are typically considered. Some code sections prohibit the use of probation. An intermediate approach

Factors Considered When Deciding Whether to Place Defendant on Probation

Based on Rule 414 of California Rules of Court

Facts relating to the crime, including:

1. The nature, seriousness, and circumstances of the crime as compared to other instances of the same crime.
2. Whether the defendant was armed with or used a weapon.
3. The vulnerability of the victim.
4. Whether the defendant inflicted physical or emotional injury.
5. The degree of monetary loss to the victim.
6. Whether the defendant was an active or passive participant.
7. Whether the crime was committed because of an unusual circumstance, such as great provocation, which is unlikely to recur.
8. Whether the manner in which the crime was carried out demonstrated criminal sophistication or professionalism on the part of the defendant.
9. Whether the defendant took advantage of a position of trust or confidence to commit the crime.

Facts relating to the defendant, including:

1. Prior record of criminal conduct, whether as an adult or a juvenile, including the recency and frequency of prior crimes; and whether the prior record indicates a pattern of regular or increasingly serious criminal conduct.
2. Prior performance on probation or parole and present probation or parole status.
3. Willingness to comply with the terms of probation.
4. Ability to comply with reasonable terms of probation as indicated by the defendant's age, eduction, health, mental faculties, history of alcohol or other substance abuse, family background and ties, employment and military service history, and other relevant factors.

5. The likely effect of imprisonment on the defendant and his or her dependents.
6. The adverse collateral consequences on the defendant's life resulting from the felony conviction.
7. Whether the defendant is remorseful.
8. The likelihood that if not imprisoned the defendant will be a danger to others.

Figure 13.1

appears in some codes: the statute states that probation is prohibited except in unusual circumstances where the interest of justice would be served by not incarcerating the defendant. Prior to granting probation under one of these laws, the judge usually must state on the record what the unusual circumstances are that justify placing the defendant on probation.

State law usually specifies the length of probation that a judge may impose. Some states standardize the length of probation, such as one year for misdemeanors and three years for felonies. Others allow the judge to impose probation for any length of time up to the maximum length of incarceration that could have been imposed.

Conditions of Probation

Probation serves two purposes: it gives the probationer the opportunity to demonstrate that he/she can be rehabilitated while, at the same time, it gives the court the authority to impose sanctions without a new trial if the defendant fails to abide by the conditions of probation. In addition to forbidding the commission of new crimes, most probationers are required to comply with a list of rules imposed to assist in rehabilitation. Two legal restrictions apply to imposing conditions of probation: the condition must be related to rehabilitation and/or supervision of the probationers; and it must be authorized by state law. Figure 13.2 shows a sample list taken from Arkansas statutes. The restrictions, called **conditions of probation**, fall into several general categories: commit no crimes; earn an income and support family or go to school to learn job skills; participate in counseling program;

Conditions of Probation

Based on Arkansas Code 5-4-303

If the court suspends imposition of sentence on a defendant or places him/her on probation, it may, as a condition of its order, required that the defendant:

1. Support dependents and meet family responsibilities;
2. Work faithfully at suitable employment;
3. Pursue a prescribed secular course of study or vocational training designed to equip him/her for suitable employment;
4. Undergo available medical or psychiatric treatment, and enter and remain in a specified institution, when required for that purpose;
5. Participate in a community-based rehabilitative program or work-release program. The court may impose reasonable fees on the defendant to be used in support of said programs;
6. Refrain from frequenting unlawful or designated places or consorting with designated persons;
7. Have no firearms in his/her possession;
8. Make restitution to victim in an amount defendant can afford to pay, for the actual loss or damage caused by his/her offense;
9. Post bond, with or without surety, conditioned on the performance of prescribed conditions;
10. Satisfy any other conditions reasonably related to the rehabilitation of the defendant and not unduly restrictive of his/her liberty or incompatible with his/her freedom of conscience.

As condition of probation the court may also require that the defendant:

1. Report as directed to the court or probation officer and permit the probation officer to visit him at his place of employment or elsewhere;
2. Remain within the jurisdiction of the court unless granted permission to leave by the court or the probation officer;
3. Answer all reasonable inquires by the court or probation officer and promptly notify the court or probation officer of any change in address or employment.

Figure 13.2

avoid persons and places associated with the commission of crimes; and make restitution.

Two more conditions are added in many states: submit to searches and seizures, and undergo drug testing. The search and seizure restriction is considered important for detecting criminal activity by the probationer. When these conditions are included, accepting probation is tantamount to waiving Fourth Amendment rights. The main questions regarding this condition are: who is authorized to conduct the search? and under what circumstances? Some states only allow probation officers to conduct these searches. Others permit police officers who encounter probationers in the field to search them. Sometimes a computerized database must be checked prior to the search to verify that the person has the search and seizure condition. Some states require that a police officer have at least a suspicion that the probationer is involved in criminal activity before a search is permitted unless the probation officer is present. The search and seizure condition usually applies to search of the probationer's residence; some states permit unannounced entry to conduct residential searches while others do not waive "knock-notice." It is important for police officers to know the law of the state they work in so evidence found when searching probationers will be admissible in court.

Drug testing usually is made a condition of probation if the conviction was for drug-related charges, the defendant was under the influence of drugs at the time of arrest or has a history of drug abuse. Some programs require routine testing at every visit to the probation officer. Others use random testing; some use both. Precautions must be instituted that protect privacy while the urine sample is given, but, at the same time, insure that the probationer will not submit "clean" urine obtained from a person who does not use drugs. Careful labeling of urine specimens and accurate testing are also necessary.

Probationers can be required to pay the cost of supervision and counseling programs that they attend. Repayment of court costs as well as the expenses incurred for a public defender can be added. Installment payments are frequently established to facilitate collection of these fees. Equal protection prohibits incarceration for failure to pay these expenses if the person was legitimately unable to pay. Prior to revoking probation because complete payment was not made on time, the court must inquire into the facts to establish whether the probationer made good faith efforts to do so.

Jail can be made a condition of probation. For example, the sentence might be one year probation with the condition that the defendant serve 30 days in jail. When this is done, the defendant usually serves the jail term first and then is placed on probation. In most states, judges retain the discretion to permit the jail time to be served as "weekends" or in some other manner. Mandatory jail as a condition of probation, meaning that the judge is required to impose the jail term, has become a popular approach to sentencing in driving under the influence and spousal battery cases, particularly if the defendant has already been placed on probation for a prior conviction for the same crime.

The probation department is usually organized at the same level as the court of general jurisdiction (i.e., the county or similar political boundaries). When a defendant is convicted for a crime committed in the county the case is normally supervised by a probation officer employed by that county. The conditions of probation frequently require the probationer to obtain permission before leaving the jurisdiction. Juveniles may need a transfer to another county because their parents are moving there. Employment opportunities, family responsibilities, and other situations may make it desirable for adult probationers to move to another part of the state. State laws or administrative regulations usually specify a procedure to permit probation officers in another part of the state to supervise the case. For example, New York Criminal Procedure Law §410.80 allows the judge to designate any other probation department in the state to handle the case. Under this law, the sentencing court has the option to retain jurisdiction over the case for revocation proceedings or delegate it to the court where the case is transferred. The laws usually specify which county is responsible for the expenses incurred in supervising the probationer.

Some states permit early termination of probation. For example, Arizona Rule 27.3 permits the judge to terminate probation at any time upon motion of the probation officer or the judge's own motion. A hearing is held after such a motion is made and the prosecutor has the opportunity to make arguments in favor of continuing probation. If the motion is granted, the probationer is unconditionally discharged in the same manner as if the entire sentence had been served.

Supervision of Probationers Who Move Out of State

In some cases, it may be desirable for the probationer to move out of state before the end of his/her sentence. The **Interstate Agreement on Supervision of Probationers and Parolees** is an agreement signed by all 50 states, the District of Columbia, Puerto Rico, the Virgin Islands and the United States Congress (for federal probationers). For ease of discussing this Interstate Agreement, the jurisdiction in which the original conviction occurred will be called the "sending state" and the one where the person wishes to be transferred will be called the "receiving state;" "probation" will be used although the Interstate Agreement applies to both probation and parole; and "probationer" will be used to refer to both persons on probation and parole.

The Interstate Agreement permits transfer if the probationer is a resident of, or has family residing in, the receiving state and can obtain employment there; or the receiving state accepts supervision of the person asking for the transfer. The receiving state has the right to investigate the probationer's proposed home and prospective employment before accepting a transfer. Once a person has been accepted, supervision will be done under the same standards as apply to probationers who were convicted in the receiving state.

Officers of the sending state have the right to arrest their probation violators in the receiving state. The decision of the sending state to revoke probation is not reviewable by the receiving state. The right to challenge extradition is waived but the probationer still has the right to a full revocation hearing. The receiving state has the right to block return of the probationer to the sending state if there are any criminal charges pending against the probationer or if he/she is suspected of having committed a crime within the receiving state. The probationer must be returned after prosecution is complete and/or the probationer has served his/her sentence in the receiving state.

Revocation Hearings for Probationers

Probation can be revoked for a violation of any condition placed on the defendant. These fall in two categories: an arrest for another crime or violation of a condition that is not itself criminal (sometimes called a **technical violation**). The probation officer usually has authority to arrest for any violation of the conditions of probation. He/ she may also obtain a warrant for the arrest of the violator; such warrants can usually be served by both probation officers and police. A typical law authorizing arrest for violation of probation is shown in Figure 13.3.

To revoke probation, the violation must be established at a hearing which is usually held before a judicial officer. In *Gagnon v. Scarpelli*, 411 U.S. 778, 36 L.Ed. 2d 656, 93 S.Ct. 1756 (1973), the Supreme Court held that due process rights apply to revocation of probation. In this context, due process does not encompass all of the rights afforded the accused at a criminal trial. The Court viewed a two-phase system as adequately protecting the defendant's rights. A **preliminary revocation hearing** must be held soon after the person is arrested for violating a condition of probation unless he/she is legally in custody on other grounds, such as being charged with a new crime. The Court did not set specific deadlines, such as within 48 hours, but state law may provide limits. The probationer must be given notice of the time and place of the hearing as well as what conditions of probation allegedly have been violated. The defendant has the right to be present at the hearing, confront witnesses and present evidence on his/her own behalf. Normal rules of evidence do not apply to these hearings and both sides can introduce testimony and documents that normally would not be allowed at trial. Unlike a trial, the right to confront and cross-examine may be restricted in some situations; the Court used the example of a hearing officer determining that the informant would be subjected to risk of harm if his/her identity were disclosed as a reason to deny confrontation and cross-examination. At the end of the preliminary hearing, the fact finder must make a written report on the evidence presented and decisions made. The basic standard for detaining a person in custody is that there was probable cause that a probation violation occurred.

The preliminary revocation hearing focuses on the facts showing a violation; the probation **revocation hearing** has a wider purpose: it must review the facts and determine whether probation should be revoked. The same basic procedural safeguards apply: notice of charge, notice of time and place of hearing, right to present evidence, and confrontation and cross-examination unless the judge determines there is a valid reason to limit it. The key difference is that the judge

Arrest for Violation of Probation

Based on Connecticut Penal Code Section 53a-32(a)

1. Arrest based on warrant issued by judge:
   - At any time during the period of probation, the court or any judge thereof may issue a warrant for the arrest of a defendant for violation of any of the conditions of probation, or may issue a notice to appear to answer to a charge of such violation, which notice shall be personally served upon the defendant.
   - Any such warrant shall authorize all officers named therein to return the defendant to the custody of the court or to any suitable detention facility designated by the court.

2. Warrantless arrest by probation officer or upon request of probation officer:
   - Any probation officer may arrest any defendant on probation without a warrant or may deputize any other officer with power to arrest to do so by giving him a written statement setting forth that the defendant has, in the judgment of the probation officer, violated the conditions of his probation.
     - Such written statement, delivered with the defendant by the arresting officer to the official in charge of any correctional center or other place of detention, shall be sufficient warrant for the detention of the defendant.
     - After making such an arrest, such probation officer shall present to the detaining authorities a similar statement of the circumstances of violation.
   - Provisions regarding release on bail of persons charged with a crime shall be applicable to any defendant arrested under the provisions of this section.
   - Upon such arrest and detention, the probation officer shall immediately so notify the court or any judge thereof.

Figure 13.3

may conclude a violation occurred but the defendant's rehabilitation would be best served by permitting him/her to remain on probation. It is common for a judge to require the defendant to serve a short time in jail before reinstating probation. Figure 13.4 shows a state law providing for revocation hearings that comply with current Supreme Court decisions.

Some states have a procedure whereby the judge places the defendant on probation without sentencing him/her. The defendant is sentenced only if probation is violated. When this type of procedure is used, the hearing at which the sentence is imposed has all the procedural safeguards of a sentencing hearing held after the verdict comes in; the defendant has a Sixth Amendment right to be represented by counsel and the government must provide one at no charge for indigent defendants. The Supreme Court concluded that appointing an attorney is ordinarily not necessary at the preliminary and final revocation hearings in cases where the defendant has already been sentenced. The judge should review each case involving indigents and appoint an attorney if the following factors indicate legal counsel is needed: probationer denies committing the alleged violation or asserts that there were substantial reasons justifying what was done or mitigating guilt; complex cases whose facts are difficult to develop or present; and cases involving probationers who are not capable of speaking effectively. Many states now appoint counsel automatically for the poor in revocation proceedings even though the Supreme Court has not required it.

A probationer may leave the state without permission and be arrested for committing a crime or violating probation while in another state. If so, it may be necessary to institute extradition proceedings unless the case was transferred to the state where he/she was arrested under the Interstate Agreement on Supervision of Probationers and Parolees. See Chapter 2 Section 2 for a discussion of the extradition process. In these cases, the probationer may be tried on the crime committed in the state where he/she was arrested before being returned to face revocation proceedings. Authorities from both states usually discuss the potential consequences of a trial on the new charges versus revocation of probation and decide which best suits the case. If revocation is instituted, the preliminary revocation hearing is held in the state where the new offense occurred to facilitate presentation of evidence on the violation.

Probation Revocation Hearing

Based on Arkansas Statutes 5-4-310

Preliminary hearing shall be held to determine whether there is reasonable cause to believe that there has been a violation of a condition of probation except when probationer has been found guilty in an independent criminal proceeding or the revocation hearing is held promptly after arrest:

1. Hearing is conducted by court having original jurisdiction to try criminal matters as soon as practicable after arrest and reasonably near the place of the alleged violation or arrest.
2. Defendant must be given prior notice of time and place of preliminary hearing, the purpose of the hearing, and the conditions of probation he/she is alleged to have violated.
3. Defendant shall have right to hear and controvert evidence against him/her and to offer evidence in his/her own behalf but court, for good cause, may refuse to allow confrontation. Court may permit introduction of any relevant evidence of the alleged violation, including letters, affidavits, and other documentary evidence, regardless of its admissibility under the rules governing the admission of evidence in a criminal trial.
4. If judge presiding over hearing finds that there is reasonable cause to believe that the defendant has violated a condition of probation, it shall order the defendant held for further revocation proceedings before the court that originally placed defendant on probation. If court does not find reasonable cause, it shall order the defendant released from custody but such release does not bar the court that imposed probation from holding a hearing on the alleged violation.
5. Court holding preliminary revocation hearing shall prepare and furnish to the court that placed defendant on probation a summary of the hearing, including the responses of the defendant and the substance of the documents and evidence given in support of revocation.

Revocation hearing must be held prior to revoking probation:

1. Revocation hearing shall be conducted by court that placed defendant on probation within a reasonable time, not exceeding 60 days, after the defendant's arrest.
2. Defendant shall be given prior written notice of the time and place of the revocation hearing, the purpose of the hearing, and the condition of probation allegedly violated.
3. Defendant has same right to hear and controvert evidence as at preliminary revocation hearing (Item 3 above).
4. If probation is revoked, the court shall prepare and furnish to the defendant a written statement of the evidence relied on and the reasons for revoking probation.

Figure 13.4

13.3 Jail and Prison Sentence

In many states, the judge sentences the defendant to serve time in prison but leaves decisions on which facility will be used to the correctional authorities (referred to here as the state's Department of Corrections). The Department of Corrections normally transfers all new inmates to a diagnostic unit where interviews are conducted and necessary tests performed to determine any special needs of the inmates. Classification is done according to security risks and other criteria and assignments to appropriate prison facilities made unless state law or regulations provide otherwise. Inmates may normally be reclassified based on their behavior while in custody. Transfers to another facility may be made for disciplinary reasons or to avoid overcrowding.

Good Time

"Good time" credit is frequently given to inmates who abide by prison rules. The formula used to compute "good time" is set by either the state legislature or Department of Corrections. Some states offer one day "good time" credit for every two days in custody. How "good time" is used is established by law: it usually reduces the amount of time spent in custody by either shortening the sentence or making the inmate eligible for parole sooner. Other incentives, such as credits for inmates who work, go to school or participate in medical research while in custody, are used in some states.

Disciplinary Hearings

Hearings are not required prior to disciplining an inmate if the relevant statute gives correctional administrators discretion to make a choice, such as assigning an inmate to a specific prison. A hearing is required to satisfy Due Process if the disciplinary action will inevitably affect the duration of the inmate's sentence or result in a major change in the conditions of confinement. Regulations must be posted for inmates to read that specify what conduct will trigger disciplinary action and what punishment will be given. For example, a rule might prohibit assaults on fellow inmates and state that up to 90 days of good time can be lost for a single incident of misbehavior that could be prosecuted as a misdemeanor. Loss of good time is an administrative procedure and provides no double jeopardy protection against criminal charges for offenses committed in custody.

Emergency measures, such as transfer of inmates immediately after a riot, may be done without a hearing, but punishment can be imposed only after a hearing. The Supreme Court in *Wolff v. McDonnell*, 418 U.S. 539, 41 L.Ed. 2d 935, 94 S.Ct. 2963 (1974), established minimum procedural safeguards for prison disciplinary hearings. Written notice of the alleged violation must be given at least 24 hours before the disciplinary hearing. In an effort to accommodate the security needs of jails and prisons, the Court held that the inmate should be allowed to call witnesses and present documentary evidence in his/her defense as long as doing so was not unduly hazardous to institutional safety or correctional goals. Prison authorities have the right to refuse to call witnesses that may create a risk of reprisal or undermine authority, as well as to limit access to other inmates for the purpose of collecting statements or compiling documentary evidence. Correctional officers who submit the charges do not have to testify in the presence of the inmate. Inmates have no constitutional right to cross-examine witnesses.

Hearing officers at the disciplinary proceeding need to be impartial. The Court permitted use of correctional officers for this purpose as long as they are not involved in the incident the inmate is being disciplined for. Their decisions must not be arbitrary. The fact finder is required to make a written statement regarding evidence relied upon and the reasons for the disciplinary action taken. Inmates have no right to have an attorney present at disciplinary hearings even if they can afford to hire one. Assistance in the form of a fellow inmate or staff person should be provided for illiterate inmates or where the complexity of the issues make it unlikely that the inmate will be able to adequately collect and present evidence.

Interstate Corrections Compacts

Sometimes it is desirable to transfer an inmate to a facility in another state. Two common reasons for this are: overcrowding of one state's prisons and the need to send an inmate to a specialized rehabilitation or treatment facility, including mental health institutions, not available in the state. The Interstate Corrections Compact, and some regional compacts such as the Western Interstate Corrections Compact, were designed to make it easier for states to transfer prisoners. Inmates sent to another state remain within the jurisdiction of the court where the conviction was entered and that state has the right to demand their return. The sending state is financially responsible for the expenses of the inmate. The receiving state must provide regular written reports on the inmates in its care. When it is time to release the inmate, he/she must be returned to the sending state unless the inmate agrees to be released at another location.

The Interstate Corrections Compact makes no mention of inmate consent to the transfer. The Supreme Court reviewed the case of an inmate who was convicted in Hawaii and had been transferred to another state. It determined that the language of the Hawaii statute left sufficient discretion with the administrators so that a hearing was not constitutionally required. Some states have made consent a prerequisite to an out of state transfer. For example, California Penal Code §11191 requires that the inmate be informed of his/her rights and be given the opportunity for a private consultation with his/her attorney or a public defender before giving consent; it also gives the inmate the right to revoke consent at any time after five years has elapsed.

Interstate Agreement on Detainers

An inmate may be wanted by authorities in another state due to an outstanding warrant, violation of probation or parole, or escape from jail or prison. The Interstate Agreement on Detainers permits a hold to be placed on the inmate so that the other state may take the inmate into custody before he/she is released from custody. These holds are usually grounds to deny parole. The Interstate Agreement allows the inmate to request that the out of state charges be adjudicated prior to his/her scheduled release from custody. Chapter 2 Section 2 discusses these procedures in detail.

Pardons and Commuting Sentences

Most state governors have authority to grant pardons to convicted persons and commute sentences. These acts are usually based on two distinctly different grounds: the defendant was wrongly convicted or the defendant has led an exemplary life since conviction. The parole board is frequently directed to forward case files to the governor if it deems a pardon appropriate. Individual inmates may submit their own cases. State law usually establishes procedures that must be followed. Pardons based on living an exemplary life usually require the person to wait at least ten years after release from custody before applying.

13.4 Parole

Parole in many ways resembles probation. It releases an offender into the community under supervision but the freedom can be rescinded without a conviction for committing a new crime. Unlike probation, parole comes at the end of a prison sentence. The inmate normally has to earn the right to be released on parole. Failure to satisfactorily complete parole usually results in return to prison to complete the time remaining on the term. The process of parole, from determining release dates through revocation of parole, is usually administered by the Department of Corrections or another state agency rather than the courts.

ELIGIBILITY

State law establishes when an inmate will be released and whether or not the inmate will be on parole. A variety of approaches is used. Determinate sentencing states may impose a fixed length of parole, such as one year, at the end of every sentence. Parole is more likely to be used in conjunction with indeterminate sentencing with behavior in prison being considered when setting a release date; when released, the inmate may be on parole for the entire time remaining on the original sentence. Some states have abolished parole.

State law establishes minimum eligibility for parole, such as first offenders must serve one-third of the maximum sentence and one-half of the maximum sentence must be served by second offenders. State law indicates whether "good time" credits are applied when determining the earliest date an inmate is eligible for parole.

Occasionally, parole is granted for humanitarian reasons. State law may provide detailed guidance for the parole board or it may be left to their discretion. For example, New York Executive Law Section 259-r, which was in effect from 1992 to 1994, permitted parole if the inmate has been "certified to be suffering from a terminal condition, disease or syndrome and to be so debilitated or incapacitated as to create a reasonable probability that he or she is physically incapable of presenting any danger to society" and such release "will not depreciate the seriousness of the crime as to undermine respect for the law." Inmates convicted of murder and manslaughter were not eligible for this type of release. The inmate must remain under doctor's care in a hospital, hospice or other medically appropriate placement. Parole under these circumstances in New York was for four months and could be renewed.

HEARINGS TO SET RELEASE DATES

Setting a parole date is an administrative function. In states with indeterminate sentencing, release dates are usually set by an agency, referred to here as the parole board, which is separate from the staff of the prison. The inmate is normally given an opportunity to appear before the parole board and make a statement; disciplinary records and other staff input are also considered. Some states permit victims, or families of victims who died as a result of the crime, to submit material for consideration and/or appear and make a statement. The trial judge and prosecutor may also be given an opportunity to input information for consideration by the parole board. Predictions of the inmate's behavior after release are also considered. For example, laws of Connecticut (§54-125), Massachusetts (127 § 130) and other states require the parole board to consider two factors: if there is a reasonable probability that the inmate will live and remain at liberty without violating the law and whether release is compatible with the welfare of society. If parole is denied, the inmate is usually entitled to a new hearing; for example, state law may require a hearing every two years.

Once the parole date has been set, it can still be revoked if the inmate does not maintain a good disciplinary record or if the parole board discovers additional evidence indicating parole is not appropriate. The Supreme Court has viewed the setting of parole dates as a discretionary function. As a result of this distinction, there is no right to a hearing and to present witnesses if a parole date is revoked or changed. Decisions to revoke the parole date cannot be arbitrary. A few states allow the governor to intervene to block the release of an inmate from custody. This type of intervention may be restricted to a few specified offenses, such as murder and forcible rape.

Conditions of Parole

When a person is released on parole, he/she remains under the jurisdiction of the state agency that operates the prisons. This gives the state the right to dictate conditions of release and to require the parolee to return to prison if the conditions are violated. One of the most common restrictions relates to residence. The parolee may be required to live in one county; changes can be made but only with consent of the parole officer. The right to control where the parolee lives is also used to place the inmate in a halfway house immediately after release from prison. **Halfway houses** are residential facilities in the community which provide a higher level of supervision for parolees than a parole officer can give. Parolees usually stay for one to six months during which time they look for employment and begin jobs. Drug testing, curfews, and other conditions may be attached to living at the facility. Inmates usually pay a fee to help cover the cost of operating the halfway house.

Other conditions of parole are usually imposed to assist the inmate's return to society. The universal one is that the parolee commit no new crimes. Many conditions are similar to the conditions of probation discussed in Section 13.2. The parolee is required to meet regularly with a parole officer to discuss progress. Gainful employment or satisfactory progress in vocational training are normally required. Association with known criminals and habituating places where undesirable people congregate are usually forbidden. Drug tests may be required; excessive alcohol consumption is prohibited.

Some states now refuse to permit rapists, child molesters and some other criminals to be paroled in the area where the crime victim resides. Some communities have successfully petitioned the parole board to deny permission for a parolee to move to their area even though the offense did not occur there. Requiring the Department of Corrections to notify the victim when the inmate is released is also becoming common.

Supervision of Parolees Who Move Out of State

Parolees may have a legitimate need to move to another state. The Interstate Agreement on Supervision of Probationers and Parolees establishes the legal framework for this to occur. When the Interstate Agreement is used, parole supervision is assumed by authorities in the state where the person relocates. See Section 13.2 for a detailed discussion of this Interstate Agreement.

Revocation of Parole

A violation of a condition imposed on a parolee can result in revocation of parole. Not all violations are handled in this manner because some violations are minor and do not warrant return to prison. The Supreme Court in *Morrissey v. Brewer*, 408 U.S. 471, 33 L.Ed. 2d 484, 92 S.Ct. 2593 (1972), established the requirements for parole revocation hearings. In most respects, they are the same as those for the preliminary and final revocation hearings discussed in Section 13.2 for probation violators: notice of charges; notice of date and place of hearing; confront and cross-examine witnesses in most instances; present evidence on own behalf; and written statement by fact finder. A subsequent case clarified that the right to appointed counsel does not automatically apply, but parolees who are unable to represent themselves, either due to illiteracy or the complexity of the case, are entitled to some form of help.

One major difference between probation and parole revocation hearings is the agency that presides over the hearings. Since the parolee is still under the jurisdiction of the department of corrections, the case does not return to court; someone within the Department of Corrections or parole agency makes the decision. The Supreme Court noted that this needs to be an impartial fact finder. The parole officer initiating the revocation proceedings and any supervisors who reviewed the decision before it was finalized do not qualify. Other parole officers may judge whether revocation is justified.

The result of revocation is return to prison, usually to serve out the remainder of the original sentence. A variety of circumstances can alter this outcome. State law must provide for each. If a parolee is arrested on new charges, a determination is usually made whether to revoke parole or prosecute the new offense. Revocation has the advantage of being quicker and having a lighter burden of proof. It is frequently used if the parolee would serve a longer term when returned to prison than the new crime has or if there are problems with the evidence in the new case. The lower burden of proof for revocation makes it possible to revoke parole even though there was an acquittal on the new charges. Figure 13.5 shows a typical statute dealing with these issues.

13.5 Execution of Death Sentences

Death penalty cases are among the most complex and time-consuming matters handled by the courts. Inmates sentenced to die are usually isolated on "death row" for many years while the direct appeal is taken and numerous collateral attacks on the conviction are attempted. Clemency petitions are presented to the governor after all tactics utilizing the courts have been exhausted. Assuming none of these are successful, a death warrant will be issued. The **death warrant** is the official document, signed by the governor, ordering the execution. The date and approximate time for the execution are specified. After it has been signed by the governor, it is delivered to the head of the Department of Corrections

Computation of Parolee's Sentence after Revocation of Parole

Based on Massachusetts Statutes 127 § 149

Arrest and Detention:

If a permit to be at liberty has been revoked, the parole board may order the arrest of the holder of such permit by any officer qualified to serve civil or criminal process in any county, and order the return of such holder to the prison or jail to which he was originally sentenced. A prisoner who has been so returned to prison or jail shall be detained therein according to the terms of his original sentence.

Computation of Period of Confinement:

- In computing the period of his confinement, the time between the day of his release upon a parole permit and the day of issuance of a parole violation warrant shall be considered as part of the term of his original sentence.
- The time between the day after the issuance of the parole violator warrant until the service of said warrant shall not be considered as any part of the term of his original sentence.
- Service of the parole violation warrant shall be made effective forthwith upon arrest and imprisonment of the parole violator unless he is convicted of commission of a crime or found guilty of violating the conditions of federal or another state's parole or probation, then service of said parole violation warrant shall not be effective until the expiration of any additional sentence by parole or otherwise.
- If the parolee is found not guilty of the additional crimes charged or not guilty of violating the conditions of parole or probation then service of the warrant on the parolee shall be made effective on the date of this issuance of said warrant and the time served by him as a result of the parole violation warrant lodged as a detainer shall be considered as part of the original sentence.
- If the disposition of the new criminal charges or charges of violation of probation or parole is without a finding of guilt, the parole board may retroactively serve the parole violation warrant.
- The provisions of this section shall not be deemed to preclude the board from withdrawing a parole violation warrant at any time. In computing the period of the parolee's confinement, the time between the day after the issuance of the parole violation warrant until the withdrawal of said warrant shall not be considered as any part of the term of the parolee's original sentence.

Figure 13.5

who also signs it and forwards it to the warden of the prison in which the execution will take place. If the execution is delayed due to legal maneuvers or other technical problems, a new death warrant must be issued. After the execution a document, known as the **return on death warrant**, must be completed stating the exact date and time the execution took place and other details. The return is filed with the court and becomes part of the case file.

Last-minute appeals and stays of execution by federal judges have become very common in death penalty cases. It is therefore imperative that prison staff have absolutely up-to-date records on the status of each legal challenge pending as the scheduled time of execution approaches. Two common-law rules also must be noted because they have become part of our legal system. One tradition is that pregnant women cannot be executed. This merely requires postponement of the execution until after the baby is born.

A person must be sane, at the time of the execution. This rule apparently was based on the idea that the defendant might provide some information at the last minute that would demonstrate innocence and result in a reprieve. Due to this tradition, it is necessary to have a mental health expert evaluate the inmate's sanity shortly before the execution. If the inmate is not sane, the execution must be postponed. Court proceedings to declare mental incompetence are normally instituted and treatment provided. After the court determines the inmate is again sane, a new death warrant can be sought. Incurable insanity permanently blocks the execution.

The extraordinary number of legal maneuvers by most death row inmates has led some to question the sanity of any inmate who refuses to allow appeals on his/her behalf. As long as the person is determined to be sane there is no legal basis for forcing an inmate to permit others who oppose capital punishment to petition the courts on his/her behalf.

13.6 Innovative Sentencing

Correctional administrators and legislators frequently initiate new programs aimed at reducing recidivism, alleviating overcrowding and/or curtailing the cost of incarceration. Penitentiaries were colonial America's attempt to improve corrections; probation was one of the contributions of the late nineteenth century. More recent additions include electronic monitoring, which was discussed in Chapter 7, and a variety of other alternatives reviewed in Chapter 11 ("three strikes and you're out," "use a gun, go to jail," work furlough, intermittent sentencing, community service orders and restitution for the victim). This section will briefly cover a few more recent techniques.

Driving under the influence of alcohol (DUI) has gained recognition as a serious social problem. A variety of approaches has been taken including increasing the fines, mandatory suspension of driver's license, and making a short jail sentence a mandatory condition of probation. Requiring convicted DUI defendants to install **ignition interlock devices** is one of the newer approaches for keeping drunk drivers off the roads. The driver must breathe into the interlock device before starting the engine. The car will not start if the sensor in the interlock device detects alcohol above a predetermined percentage. The defendant must pay for the equipment and installation and have it calibrated frequently. Periodic reports to probation officers are also required. Figure 13.6 shows the form used by California courts to order installation of such devices.

Intensive probation gives the probation officer a reduced caseload so that more time can be spent with each client. It is usually used for juveniles who are not capable of performing well under normal supervision. The time that the probation officer spends with each client, sometimes as much as ten hours per week, is designed to accomplish several purposes: provide additional guidance so the client will not become a habitual criminal; supervise activities in the community so the client will develop contacts with law abiding people and avoid known criminals; and monitor behavior so that probation can be revoked and the client placed in custody if it appears that criminal activity is occurring. Reducing caseloads so that this type of supervision can occur increases the cost of probation but the expense is still considerably less than what incarceration would cost. Success in reducing recidivism also greatly reduces the long range cost to society.

Boot camp refers to a recent approach to treating first offenders, particularly juveniles. It is a special jail program, sometimes run by the Probation Department, which is modeled after military boot camp. Strict discipline, exhausting routines, and emphasis on personal hygiene and maintenance of the housing areas are stressed. The purpose of boot camp is to instill good habits in offenders and increase their self-esteem. Pride instilled by hard work will, it is hoped, carry

Order to Install Ignition Interlock Device

Based on California Vehicle Code Sections 23246 and 23235

NAME AND ADDRESS OF COURT:

FOR COURT USE ONLY

NAME OF DEFENDANT:
STREET ADDRESS:
MAILING ADDRESS:
CITY AND ZIP CODE:
HOME TELEPHONE NO.:
WORK TELEPHONE NO.:
DATE OF BIRTH:
SOCIAL SECURITY NO.:
DRIVER'S LICENSE NO.:

DATE OF COURT ORDER:

CASE NUMBER:

ORDER TO INSTALL IGNITION INTERLOCK DEVICE

THE COURT ORDERS under Vehicle Code section ☐ 23246 ☐ 23235

1. Defendant *(name)*: shall not drive a motor vehicle unless it is equipped with a functioning ignition interlock device.
2. Devices shall be installed on the following vehicles owned or operated by defendant:

	Make	Model	Year	Color	License Plate No.	V.I.N.
a.						
b.						
c.						

3. Installation shall be no later than *(specify date no later than 30 days from date of conviction)*:
4. Defendant shall present this form to the installer at the time of installation.
5. Defendant shall return completed Ignition Interlock Installation Verification form to the ☐ court ☐ probation department no later than *(specify date no later than 30 days from date of conviction)*:
6. Defendant shall take vehicles to the installer for calibration ☐ every 60 days ☐ *(other frequency—specify)*: following the date of installation.
7. ☐ Defendant shall make payments directly to the installer and shall adhere to the following payment plan for installation of the ignition interlock device:
8. Without a court order, the devices may not be removed before *(specify date one–three years for § 23246, three–five years (period of probation) for § 23235)*:
9. ☐ Defendant's employer requires defendant to drive a vehicle owned by the employer within the course and scope of defendant's employment. Defendant shall provide the employer with the Notice to Employers of Ignition Interlock Restriction form no later than *(date)*: and keep a copy of the notice in defendant's possession or keep the original or a copy in the employer's vehicle.
10. Defendant shall maintain current insurance and registration on all vehicles owned.
11. Defendant shall surrender his or her driver's license to the court (if driving privilege not suspended or revoked) until proof of installation is submitted to and verified by the ☐ court ☐ probation officer.
12. Defendant shall report on the operation of each ignition interlock device installed to the ☐ court ☐ probation officer at least ☐ once every six months (§ 23246) ☐ once each year (§ 23235) or ☐ *(other greater frequency—specify)*:
13. For proceedings under Vehicle Code section 23235, defendant shall pay a fine of *(specify amount—not more than $1,000 for convictions under Vehicle Code § 23152; not more than $5,000 for convictions under Vehicle Code § 23153, punishable under § 23185 or § 23190)*: $
14. Other *(specify)*:

Date:

▶ ______________________________
JUDGE

Defendant: Call installer within 48 hours of this order to arrange for installation of devices. The court will provide you with a list of certified installers.

Distribution: Court, Probation Department, Defendant

(Continued on reverse)

Form Approved by the
Judicial Council of California
ID-100 [New July 1, 1993]

ORDER TO INSTALL
IGNITION INTERLOCK DEVICE
(Ignition Interlock Device)

Vehicle Code, § 23235 et seq. and § 23246 et seq.

Figure 13.6

over to their lives outside of custody. As with intensive probation, boot camp is more expensive than traditional jails but is designed to have a greater positive impact on the lives of those who complete the course.

Day fines have been used in England and Europe for over twenty years. A **day fine** makes the fine proportional to the defendant's income. The purpose of day fines is to make the deterrent value of a fine the same for rich and poor defendants. For example, rather than setting a fine at $100 for everyone, the fine is set at one day's wages; a rich person might pay $500 and a poor person only $20.

SUMMARY

Punishing convicted offenders is based on several rationales: retribution, deterrence (both specific and general), rehabilitation and incapacitation. A combination of these is probably in use in your state today.

Probation was designed to give offenders a second chance. It is now widely used in both misdemeanor and felony cases. A person who is placed on probation must agree to comply with the conditions the court places on his/her release. The Interstate Agreement on Supervision of Probationers and Parolees can be used to transfer a case to another state if a person under supervision has a valid reason to move there.

Violation of the conditions of probation can result in the offender serving time in jail. Probation cannot be revoked without formal hearings to determine whether the probationer committed the alleged offense, and if so, whether revocation is merited. Minimum due process rights for a hearing to revoke probation require: hearing shortly after the probationer is taken into custody, notice of alleged violation as well as time and place where hearing will be held; presentation of evidence of violation and opportunity to cross-examine witnesses in most cases; right to present evidence on own behalf; and impartial fact finder who makes written report on hearing. The final hearing has similar procedural rights but must also consider what action should be taken against the violator. There is a right to counsel only if the probationer denies the charges or otherwise appears unable to present the case him/herself. It will also be necessary to institute extradition proceedings if the probationer fled the state without permission and is arrested in another state.

Defendants sentenced to incarceration are usually evaluated when they first arrive at a jail or prison in order to determine what special needs they have. Inmates may be transferred to other facilities for a variety of administrative reasons including reducing overcrowding at specific prisons. "Good time" and credits for other activities are earned by inmates and applied toward their release dates. A disciplinary hearing is required if the punishment will inevitably affect the inmate's release date or result in a major change in the conditions of confinement. Minimum due process requirements for these hearings include: notice of time and place of hearing; notice of charges; right to be present and present evidence except that prison officials may limit the right to call witnesses if necessary for institutional security; impartial fact finder and written report on disciplinary action taken and reasons for doing so. Cross-examination by the inmate may be denied. There is no right to counsel at these hearings but illiterate inmates and others with problems have the right to be assigned another person to assist them.

State law specifies when an inmate is eligible for parole. The case is heard by the parole board. A parole date will be set if it is decided that the inmate should be released; this date may be changed without a hearing. When the inmate is paroled, he/she will be subject to conditions similar to those placed on probationers. A violation subjects the parolee to return to prison to serve time remaining on the original sentence. Revocation cannot occur without hearings similar to those used to revoke probation. These hearings are usually held before fact finders designated by the parole board or parole officers rather than a judge. As with probation, the final decision may be that the parolee should remain in the community rather than be returned to prison even though the violation did occur.

After the appeals have been completed in death penalty cases, a death warrant must be issued authorizing the execution. This warrant, signed by the governor, gives the date for the execution. Delays caused by last minute appeals may make it necessary to issue another death warrant at a later date. After the execution, the return on the death warrant is completed and sent to the court.

New approaches are frequently tried. Some of the more recent ones include: electronic monitoring, work furloughs, intermittent sentencing, community service orders, restitution, "three strikes and you're out," "use a gun, go to jail," ignition interlock devices for drunk drivers, intensive probation, boot camp and day fines. Other innovations will constantly change the operation of corrections.

Study Questions

1. Check the laws of your state regarding probation:
   a. How long is the probation for a misdemeanor?
   b. How long is the probation for a felony?
   c. What crimes are ineligible for probation?
   d. What crimes have a mandatory jail sentence as a condition of probation?
   e. What standard conditions of probation are imposed?
   f. Are probationers required to submit to searches? If so:
      1) Under what circumstances?
      2) What level of suspicion is required?
      3) Who is authorized to conduct the searches?
   g. Are probationers required to submit to drug testing?
2. Attend a probation revocation hearing. Prepare a report explaining:
   a. What were the original charges for which the defendant was placed on probation?
   b. What did the defendant do that resulted in the revocation proceeding?
   c. What evidence was presented at the hearing?
   d. Was it determined that the defendant violated probation?
   e. Was probation revoked?
   f. Did the judge reinstate probation? If so, under what conditions?
3. Check the laws of your state to see if inmates are released on parole. If so:
   a. Are there any offenses for which parole is not granted?
   b. What agency is responsible for setting parole dates?
   c. When does an inmate become eligible for parole?
   d. Is a parole hearing held? If so, when and where?
   e. Once parole is granted, how long will the inmate remain on parole?
   f. What agency is responsible for supervising parolees?
   g. What conditions are usually placed on the parolee?

4. If parole is used in your state, determine the procedures used for revoking parole:
   a. Who has the authority to arrest a parolee for a violation?
   b. Where is the preliminary revocation hearing held?
   c. Who acts as fact finder at the preliminary revocation hearing?
   d. Where is the parolee detained between the time the preliminary revocation hearing is held and the revocation decision is made?
   e. What is the maximum time allowed between the preliminary and final revocation hearings?
   f. Where is the final revocation hearing held?
   g. Who acts as fact finder at the final revocation hearing?

5. Check with your local probation department, county jail, parole officer, and state prison and determine which of the following programs are in use in your area:
   a. boot camp
   b. community service orders
   c. day fines
   d. electronic surveillance
   e. halfway houses
   f. ignition interlock devices
   g. intensive supervision
   h. intermittent sentencing
   i. restitution
   j. "three strikes and you're out"
   k. "use a gun, go to jail"
   l. work furlough
   m. describe other innovative programs in use

CHAPTER 14
CIVIL SUITS

LEARNING OBJECTIVES

After reading this chapter, the student will be able to:

- Explain how sovereign immunity applies to civil suits against governmental agencies.
- Differentiate between torts and crimes.
- Describe at least three torts that can be filed against police officers for acts done in the line of duty.
- Explain the purpose of wrongful death lawsuits.
- List the types of monetary damages that can be awarded in civil suits.
- Explain how the federal Civil Rights Act applies to actions of law enforcement officers.
- Give examples of police activities that can result in Civil Rights Act suits against police officers.
- Explain defenses police officers have against Civil Rights Act suits.
- Explain the types of legal relief available to a plaintiff who successfully pursues a Civil Rights Act suit.
- Describe the purpose of forfeiture proceedings against a criminal defendant.

Key Terms

answer
civil forfeiture proceedings
Civil Rights Act
class action
color of state law
compensatory damages
consent decree
constitutional tort
demurrer
deposition
general damages
in propria persona
injunction
intentional tort
interrogatories
judgement on the pleadings
lis pendens
negligent torts
plaintiff
preponderance of evidence
punitive damages
res judicata
sovereign immunity
strict liability torts
summary judgment
tort
tort claims act
wrongful death

14.1 Civil Suits Under State Law

Civil law permits an individual to recover from harm done by another. These suits provide monetary compensation for wrongful conduct. Some actions, such as assault and battery, are covered by both the civil law and criminal law. The individual who was harmed must institute the civil suit; the state handles the criminal proceedings. This does not violate double jeopardy even if part of the defendant's sentence included paying restitution.

Types of Torts

A **tort** is a civil wrong that does not arise out of a contract. Torts range from damage to a car during an automobile accident to killing someone. The amount of money that a victim can recover due to a tort depends largely on the financial loss involved and the intent of the person who caused the harm. There are three basic classifications of torts: intentional, negligent, and strict liability. **Intentional torts** result from an intentional act: the person intended to do the act but may not have intended to harm anyone. Intentional acts done in bad faith result in the payment of higher damages to the victim.

Negligent torts are based on carelessness: a person did not comply with the standard of care required by law. For this type of tort to arise, there must be a duty. Normally, a person is not required to do anything, but if he/she decides to act, due care must be taken not to injure others. There are some situations, such as seeing a neighbor's child playing in the street, that signal danger but do not impose a duty to act. The law may impose a duty to act, such as the parents' responsibility for the safety of their children, which results in liability when nothing is done. The child playing in the street is an example of this: a parent or babysitter who allows the child to play in a hazardous place may be liable for injuries.

Strict liability torts are the result of social policy that imposes an absolute duty. These torts normally involve public health and safety. Restaurants may be strictly liable if they serve contaminated food; manufacturers may have strict liability for distributing hazardous products. The party that brings a strict liability suit does not have to show that the defendant had knowledge that his/her conduct was wrongful or that there was any intent to harm others.

Tort Claims Acts

The doctrine of **sovereign immunity** protects governmental agencies from civil suits. Most states have enacted laws, frequently referred to as **tort claims acts**, permitting suits in specified situations. There is also a federal tort claims act that applies to damages caused by federal employees. Normally, these laws permit civil suits against the state, city or other governmental entity under the same circumstances. People who wish to sue the government must be able to point to specific laws that authorize their suits. Sometimes the state statutes have separate sections for different functions, such as operating motor vehicles or managing jails; if so, the appropriate one must be cited. For convenience, this chapter will refer to all claims as if they were filed against a city police department. Figure 14.1 shows two typical state laws that waive sovereign immunity.

Two Sample Tort Claims Acts

Based on Alabama Statutes 11-47-190

No city or town shall be liable for damages for injury done to or wrong suffered by any person or corporation, unless said injury or wrong was done or suffered through the neglect, carelessness or unskillfulness of some agent, officer or employee of the municipality engaged in work therefor and while acting in the line of his duty, or unless the said injury or wrong was done or suffered through the neglect, carelessness or failure to remedy some defect in the streets, alleys, public ways or buildings after the same had been called to the attention of the council or other governing body or after the same had existed for such unreasonable length of time as to raise a presumption of knowledge of such defect on the part of the council or other governing body and whenever the city or town shall be made liable to an action for damages by reason of the unauthorized or wrongful acts or the negligence, carelessness or unskillfulness of any person or corporation, then such person or corporation shall be liable to an action on the same account by the party so injured.

Based on Texas C.Pr.& R. 101.0215

(a) A municipality is liable under this chapter for damages arising from its governmental functions, which are those functions that are enjoined on a municipality by law and are given it by the state as part of the state's sovereignty, to be exercised by the municipality in the interest of the general public, including but not limited to:

(1) police and fire protection;
(2) health and sanitation services;
(3) street construction and design;
(4) bridge construction and maintenance and street maintenance;
(5) cemeteries and cemetery care;
(6) garbage and solid waste removal, collection, and disposal;
(7) establishment and maintenance of jails;
(8) hospitals...

Figure 14.1

Tort claims acts frequently require that a claim be submitted to the city within a designated period, such as 100 days after the event in question, which is much shorter than the statute of limitations. Cities are usually given a specified number of days to take action. Many cases are settled in this manner. A person who accepts the city's offer cannot sue the city based on the same facts. A lawsuit can be filed only after a claim has been made in a timely fashion and either rejected or the city failed to take any action at all. These cases must be filed in the appropriate civil court before the expiration of the statute of limitations for the type of action involved.

Civil Procedure

The person who files a civil lawsuit, called a **plaintiff**, either hires a private attorney to handle the lawsuit or proceeds ***in propria persona*** (also referred to as *in pro per*), which means the plaintiff handles the case without an attorney. The complaint is served on the defendant who must file a formal written reply, called an **answer**, within the period set by state law, typically 30 days. Each side is entitled to discovery of evidence in the hands of the other side and may take the deposition of anyone with information about the case. At a **deposition,** an attorney from each side is present along with a court reporter. The witness is given an oath to tell the truth and asked questions by the attorney who requested the deposition. The attorney for the opposing side can object to questions but usually is not allowed to cross-examine. The deposition provides useful information when preparing for trial. The transcript may be admitted at trial under the former testimony exception to the hearsay rule if the witness becomes unavailable; it may be used at trial for impeachment if the person making it testifies. **Interrogatories**, or written questions, can be served on the other side and must be answered under oath. Depositions and interrogatories are the main methods used to discover facts needed to go to trial in the case.

Pretrial motions can be made to dismiss the case. A **demurrer** challenges the complaint's technical merits. It is equivalent to a motion to dismiss the complaint in a criminal case. A **judgment on the pleadings** looks at both the complaint and answer and asks the judge to rule that one side has established its case. To win, the pleadings must establish the case without the need for the testimony of witnesses. For example, if one side alleges that the offense occurred and the answer

Notice Requirement for Filing Claims Against the Government

Based on Texas C.Pr.&R 101.101

(a) A governmental unit is entitled to receive notice of a claim against it under this chapter not later than six months after the day that the incident giving rise to the claim occurred. The notice must reasonably describe:

(1) the damage or injury claimed;

(2) the time and place of the incident; and

(3) the incident.

(b) A city's charter and ordinance provisions requiring notice within a charter period permitted by law are ratified and approved.

(c) The notice requirements provided or ratified and approved by Subsections (a) and (b) do not apply if the governmental unit has actual notice that death has occurred, that the claimant has received some injury, or that the claimant's property has been damaged.

Figure 14.2

filed by the opponent does not deny it or raise a defense, judgment on the pleadings in favor of the plaintiff would be correct. **Summary judgment** is based on the pleadings, legal points and authorities, and documents containing sworn testimony (depositions and interrogatories). The judge grants a summary judgment only if there is no doubt that the case has been established. If there is a question regarding credibility of the sworn testimony or witnesses have conflicting versions of the facts, the case will not be decided before trial. Settlement conferences are used extensively in civil court to try to save the time and expense of trials.

Civil trials proceed much like criminal trials. The burden of proof in civil cases is a **preponderance of the evidence** which means that it is more likely than not that an event occurred. The burden of proof may be allocated so that the plaintiff must prove some issues and the defendant must carry the burden on others. Either side can call the opponent to testify. The Fifth Amendment privilege against self-incrimination applies to civil proceedings to the extent of allowing a witness to refuse to answer if the testimony would subject him/her to criminal prosecution. Answering questions that are the key to financial liability for a civil judgment is not protected. In tort cases, either side has the right to request a jury trial. Most states do not require unanimous verdicts in civil cases; many use smaller juries in civil cases than they do in criminal cases.

Either side can appeal after a civil judgment is entered. The losing side may appeal much the same as a defendant does in a criminal case. The winning side sometimes appeals because the jury instructions resulted in too small of a verdict. Double jeopardy does not apply to civil cases, but there is a similar doctrine called ***res judicata*** which prohibits relitigating issues that have already been settled by a final judgment.

Torts Found in Police Activity

Officers are civilly liable for their intentional wrongful acts. Police are required to act with due care. Failure to conform to these standards may result in intentional and negligent torts. Strict liability torts usually do not apply to police conduct. The most common torts resulting from police activity are covered in this section. They can be the subject of civil suits only if sovereign immunity has been waived.

Assault and Battery

The intentional tort of battery closely resembles the crime by the same name; the tort of assault usually requires that the victim was placed in fear or apprehension of immediate battery. Battery involves unconsented touching; any force used beyond what is legally justified is also considered a battery. When a suspect alleges the police used excessive force, the case is usually filed as the torts of assault and battery. These cases depend on the credibility of the witnesses and the officers; therefore, pretrial motions to dismiss are usually to no avail. The crux of the determination of what was excessive force is what a reasonable officer would do under the same circumstances; deadly force is authorized only if someone's life is being threatened. The jury (or judge if the case is tried without a jury) must examine the facts as they existed moment by moment. The plaintiff's version of the facts usually differs substantially from the officer's. Most courts permit introduction of prior false claims filed by the plaintiff and past incidents of improper use of force by the officers. The plaintiff's history for assaultive behavior may also be introduced if the officers claim they were trying to subdue the plaintiff. Both the officer's personal history for violence and truthfulness and the department's reputation are extremely important. The verdict usually goes to the side that presents the most credible witnesses.

False Imprisonment

Civil false imprisonment is an intentional tort which covers confinement against a person's will whether done by physical or psychological force. This applies to cases of false arrest in addition to kidnapping. Failure to release an inmate when his/her sentence expires is also false imprisonment. Unlawful arrest cases usually include civil battery: since there was no right to make the arrest, any force used was unlawful.

Property Damage

Property damage can come under the intentional tort of trespass to chattels or be the result of negligence. Probably the most frequent property damage claims against police departments are the result of vehicular accidents ranging from backing into a mailbox to a collision during a high speed chase. The state tort claims act may require the police department to pay for the mailbox, but frequently the government is exempt from damages for incidents arising from legal pursuits.

One key question in the pursuit cases is whether the officers followed all regulations regarding emergency vehicles. In many states, a police car, fire engine or ambulance is exempt from the normal rules of the road only when using both red lights and siren; under these laws, the city is not exempt if officers are involved in collisions while driving over the speed limit or violating other traffic laws with only their red lights on.

Negligent Conduct

Even when there is no intent to harm, officers are civilly liable for both physical injuries and property damage caused by conduct that falls below the standard of care required of them under the circumstances. This lack of care, called negligence in legal terms and carelessness in everyday language, applies to everything that an officer does. Negligently firing a gun is an example; so is carelessly administering first aid. Reckless driving in situations not qualifying for exemptions afforded emergency vehicles can also result in liability.

Sometimes officers help someone when they are not required to do so. When they do this, they can be sued for resulting injuries they carelessly caused even though they had no duty to give assistance. Another problem arises when officers decide to "be nice" to a drunk driver and allow him/her to drive home instead of booking the driver and impounding the car. A number of courts have held that the officers are liable if the drunk causes an accident and injures someone after being released in this manner. Here the duty was to protect the public, not a particular individual.

Other

There are many other torts. Malicious prosecution can be brought if false charges are knowingly filed against an innocent defendant. Public statements that damage a person's reputation can result in a case for defamation; truth is a total defense in these cases. Invasion of privacy applies to both true and false statements that result in publicity about a person's private life unless there is a valid reason for releasing this information to the public. Theft is classified as the tort of conversion of chattels. Inflicting emotional distress is actionable when done intentionally or, under some circumstances, negligently. Some states allow a person who witnessed unjustified injuries to a close family member to recover based on emotional distress. Sovereign immunity applies to all of these torts unless it has been waived by the legislature.

Liability of the City

An employer is usually liable for actions of its employees that it authorizes or condones. This is true for governmental agencies as well as private companies except when sovereign immunity applies. This type of liability only arises if it is shown that an employee did something wrong. To do so, it is necessary to include both the employee and the employer as defendants in the suit. The main reason for trying to hold the city liable is that it makes it possible to recover more money. Grounds for the city's liability include: inadequate training, failure to supervise, negligent pre-employment screening, and policies that tolerate wrongful conduct.

Class Action Suits

A **class action** is a civil suit brought on behalf of a large number of plaintiffs who allege that they have suffered the same wrong. No minimum size is mentioned in most state statutes but the judge is given discretion to certify a case as a class action if the number of plaintiffs involved is too large to be handled individually. Once certified, the case proceeds with one or more attorneys representing all potential plaintiffs. State laws regulate procedures for class actions. It may be necessary to advertise in newspapers to locate all potential plaintiffs so their rights can be protected and give them an opportunity to share in the money recovered. Some states allow individuals to opt out of the class action and proceed with separate lawsuits.

A class action must have at least one named plaintiff who suffered the purported wrong. The suit alleges that many others have been mistreated in a similar manner. Racial discrimination by national restaurant chains and price-fixing by major clothing manufacturers are examples of class actions filed without knowing who all the potential plaintiffs are. Occasionally, a class action is brought against a police department that is alleged to have a policy condoning excessive force. Employment discrimination suits against a law enforcement agency have also been handled as class actions.

Types of Damages in Civil Suits

One of the basic tenets of torts is that you "pay for what you break." In other words, you must reimburse the victim if you wrongfully cause personal injuries or property damage. Another tenet is that the person who in bad faith causes these damages should be punished; this is accomplished by imposing additional monetary damages.

Compensatory Damages

Compensatory damages merely reimburse the victim for his/her expenses. For this reason, they are sometimes called "out of pocket" damages. Expenses that can be included range from medical bills to car repairs; necessary adaptive devices such as wheelchairs and constructing ramps to allow the wheelchair to enter the house are included. The victim usually can recover for lost wages. This applies even if the victim received paid sick leave while recovering because the sick leave utilized in this manner reduces benefits available in the future. Some states permit the victim to recover for medical bills even though an insurance company paid them; others require reimbursement for these expenses to be paid directly to the insurance company.

Receipts are usually required for compensatory damages. An exception to this is when the victim suffered injuries that will require treatment in the future. Part of the judgment can provide funds to pay these bills. For example, the attorney would ask the jury to award $52,000 for treatments costing $100 each which are required once a week and are anticipated to be needed for the next 10 years ($100 x 52 x 10 = $52,000). Opposing attorneys would try to convince the jury that the treatments are either not needed, less expensive, or not likely to be required for such a long period of time.

General Damages

General damages, sometimes referred to as "pain and suffering" damages, compensate the victim for inconvenience and pain caused by the tort. Injuries that are more painful or take longer to heal result in higher awards. Those that leave scars, particularly disfiguring ones, also merit higher awards. The highest awards usually go to injuries that will result in painful, permanent impairments. For example, if the victim sustained a broken leg that did not heal correctly the attorney might argue:

> You've seen the plaintiff walk. She limps badly. Walking is slow and painful. It throws her spine out of line and causes constant backaches. She will never be able to participate in sports. She will have trouble playing simple games with her children in the park. She will not be able to keep up with her toddler. I think $100 a day is a fair value to put on this severe handicap.
>
> You heard the doctor say that this condition cannot be corrected. This means it will make every step she takes every day of her life more difficult. The actuary testified that the victim has a life expectancy of 43.7 years. She should be compensated for every day she suffers during those 43 years.

If the jury decides to calculate damages for the broken leg according to this attorney's formula, the general damages would be $1,595,050 ($100 x 365 x 43.7). Juries are free to develop their own formulas as long as they are logically related to the facts. The judge can reduce a verdict that is excessive. Another procedural device available to the judge is to inform the parties that a new trial will be ordered unless they accept what the judge believes is a more reasonable verdict.

Punitive Damages

Punitive damages are designed to punish a defendant who acted in bad faith or intentionally harmed someone. Without punitive damages, some people and businesses would intentionally ignore potential danger to others because many victims would not complain, and settling with those who did sue was not likely to be expensive.

The jury proceeds on a three-step process: (1) did the defendant do the alleged wrongful act; (2) if so, was it done in bad faith; (3) if so, how large a verdict is necessary to make an impact on his/her future conduct. The amount of punitive damages is only indirectly related to the general damages; it is more closely tied to the defendant's ability to pay. For example, most college students would be deterred by having to pay $100; some large companies would consider awards less than $100,000 a victory. The defendant's financial records are admissible if the case gets to the question of how large the punitive damages should be.

Wrongful Death

If someone is killed by a tortious act, the person responsible must compensate the family. Two items relating to the victim are considered: income from all sources and life expectancy. Anticipated promotions and adjustments for inflation may be considered by the jury. History of unemployment and/or failure to support dependents may also be considered. The award resulting from the death of a 30-year-old junior executive currently making $50,000 and considered likely to become CEO might be $12,000,000 (30 years x $50,000 with 10% raise and inflation adjustment per year plus ten years of retirement at 50% of salary for last year worked); but an award of $60,000 (5 years x $12,000 social security) might be justified for the death of a 70-year-old man even though the actions causing the deaths were the same. The family's emotional distress and loss of companionship are calculated separately.

Limitations on Amount of Recovery

Some states have enacted tort reform laws that place a limit on general damages such as a maximum recovery of $250,000. Even when this has not been applied to all tort cases, statutes may limit how much can be recovered from a governmental agency. Figure 14.3 shows a statute that restricts how much can be recovered.

Attorney Fees

Most plaintiff's attorneys handle tort cases on a contingency basis. This means that the attorney agrees to accept a percentage of the verdict as payment for the effort expended on the case. If the jury rules in favor of the defense, the plaintiff's attorney receives nothing; therefore attorneys refuse to take cases if they believe the chance of

Limitations on Recovery in Suits against the Government

Based on Texas C.Pr. & R. 101.023

(a) Liability of the state government under this chapter is limited to money damages in a maximum amount of $250,000 for each person and $500,000 for each single occurrence for bodily injury or death and $100,000 for each single occurrence for injury to or destruction of property.

(b) Except as provided in Subsection (c), liability of a unit of local government under this chapter is limited to money damages in a maximum amount of $100,000 for each person and $300,000 for each single occurrence for bodily injury or death and $100,000 for each single occurrence for injury to or destruction of property.

(c) Liability of a municipality under this chapter is limited to money damages in a maximum amount of $250,000 for each person and $500,000 for each single occurrence for bodily injury or death and $100,000 for each single occurrence for injury to or destruction of property.

Figure 14.3

winning is too low. This serves as an informal screening device for frivolous allegations. The percentage the attorney receives is usually set in the contract that the injured party signs when hiring the attorney. This contract may require the plaintiff to pay expenses incurred during the suit, such as filing fees and the cost of having a court reporter at the deposition, separate from the contingency agreement. It is not uncommon to have a contract that allows the attorney to keep 30% of the recovery if the case is settled before trial and 40% if a trial is required. Some states have enacted laws restricting the amount that the lawyer receives.

The defendant normally pays his/her attorney an hourly rate. In tort cases, the losing party is normally not required to pay the opposing side's attorney fees. Some states have modified this rule, particularly if the judge finds the suit to be frivolous.

Representation by the City

It is common for a city to provide an attorney to represent officers who are sued for acts performed in the line of duty. If the officer decides to hire an attorney in addition to the one provided by the city, the officer must pay for it. Many cities also have a policy of paying any judgment entered against its officers for acts done in the line of duty. False arrest insurance may also cover the judgment and attorney fees. Most states have policies that prohibit cities from paying punitive damages assessed against their employees. Punitive damages cannot to be assessed against a city or governmental agency in many states.

14.2 Suits Under Federal Civil Rights Act

The Civil Rights Act of 1871 provides redress for violations of constitutional rights by state, county and city employees. The Act provides both civil and criminal penalties; Section 1983 of Title 42 of the United States Code is the most commonly used civil section. Its full text is shown in Figure 14.4.

Due to the historical context in which it was enacted, the Civil Rights Act was originally intended to protect former slaves against

Civil Rights Act of 1871

42 United States Code Section 1983

Every person who, under color of any statute, ordinance, regulation, custom, or usage, of any State or Territory or the District of Columbia, subjects, or causes to be subjected, any citizen of the United States or other person within the jurisdiction thereof to the deprivation of any rights, privileges, or immunities secured by the Constitution and laws, shall be liable to the party injured in an action at law, suit in equity, or other proper proceeding for redress. For the purposes of this section, an Act of Congress applicable exclusively to the District of Columbia shall be considered to be a statute of the District of Columbia.

Figure 14.4

oppressive state action. Federal courts were given jurisdiction in order to avoid the hostility of some state courts toward minorities and abolitionists. Section 1983 specifically applies to: (1) deprivation of constitutional rights; (2) under **color of state law**. Since the statute makes no reference to racial discrimination, it can be used to vindicate any constitutional violation. Section 1985 prohibits conspiracies by two or more people to: prevent someone from holding office; interfere with court proceedings by intimidating parties or jurors or otherwise obstructing justice; or deprive any person of equal protection of the laws or voting rights. This section does not require that the actions be done by government employees. In the 1960s and early 1970s, the Supreme Court took an expansive approach to the coverage of the Civil Rights Act. Since that time, the trend has been toward a narrower construction.

Congress has never expanded the Civil Rights Act to cover actions by federal officers, but in 1971 the Supreme Court created what is called a **"constitutional tort"** to provide protection in these circumstances. *Bivens v. Six Unknown Named Agents of Federal Bureau of Narcotics*, 403 U.S. 388, 29 L.Ed. 2d 619, 91 S.Ct. 1999 (1971), established the right to sue federal agents for violating Fourth Amendment rights. A wide variety of constitutional deprivations is now covered. There is no corresponding right to sue a federal agency unless sovereign immunity has been waived by statute. Federal agents have qualified immunity for making arrests if a reasonable officer would have believed that the arrest was lawful in light of the established law and the evidence available at the time of the arrest. This form of immunity applies when the officers had a reasonable but mistaken belief that probable cause existed. The question of immunity is normally determined by the judge.

Actions Covered by Civil Rights Act

The Civil Rights Act covers all forms of violations of constitutional rights. Suits against criminal justice personnel most commonly focus on violations of the Fourth, Fifth, Sixth and Eighth Amendments, Due Process and Equal Protection. The Act imparts no rights itself: the plaintiff must show that a specific constitutional right has been violated. Actions taken by the police are covered whether done during a criminal investigation or while assisting in civil matters such as evictions.

The first step in the analysis is to determine the constitutional standard involved. For example, if the suit is based on violation of *Miranda* rights, the Fifth Amendment standards for confessions will be reviewed to determine if there was a constitutional violation. The second step is to determine the standard of conduct that is covered by the Civil Rights Act. Generally, this will require intentional misconduct or reckless disregard of the plaintiff's rights; negligence is not sufficient for recovery.

In cases regarding destruction of personal property, the Court noted that the due process clause is satisfied if the state provides adequate civil or administrative procedures to recover the value of the item lost. If such remedy exists, there is no violation of due process even if the property was destroyed intentionally. Federal courts also abstain from intervening if there is a criminal prosecution pending in state courts. The plaintiff must wait until the prosecution is completed and then file the case in federal court. Cases involving only the possibility that someone's rights might be violated in the future cannot be litigated.

A growing array of acts is covered by the Civil Rights Act. For example, excessive force by any state or local government employees falls under the Fourth Amendment. Many of these cases could also be filed in state court but the plaintiff files under the Civil Rights Act in hopes of more favorable results in federal court. As mentioned in Section 14.1, the credibility of the officers involved and their prior history for respecting the rights of others are frequently key issues. Prior incidents of inappropriate force are particularly damaging.

Acts motivated by race, ethnicity, gender, religion, sexual orientation, etc., violate Equal Protection. Juries charged with deciding these cases must look both at the objective evidence of what occurred and at the subjective reason for the officers' actions. Both on- and off-duty conduct can be introduced to demonstrate that the officer was racist, sexist, antagonistic toward gays, or in some manner demonstrated animosity toward people based on their membership in a protected group. Officers' memberships in organizations that promote or tolerate these attitudes can be used persuasively by the plaintiff. The officer's use of racial epitaphs in private conversations is another example of conduct that is extremely damaging to the officer's credibility when denying improperly motivated on-duty acts.

Defenses to Civil Rights Act Suits

The main defense is that no constitutional violation occurred. This analysis is based on an objective review of the evidence. The fact that an officer had subjective bad faith does not alter the conclusion that no violation occurred. The second line of defense is that the defendant is entitled to some form of immunity. A historical approach is used to determine who has immunity: those who had tort immunity in 1871, when the legislation was passed, generally have immunity under Section 1983. The Supreme Court also uses this approach to decide whether the immunity is absolute or qualified.

Most actions of local and state law enforcement officers are covered by qualified immunity which means they are immune from civil damages if they meet all of the following criteria:

(1) the officer acted in good faith;

(2) the officer made reasonable efforts to learn current constitutional rights; and

(3) a reasonable officer would have acted in a similar manner under the same circumstances.

This immunity does not apply if the rights violated were clearly established by law at the time of the incident or the officer acted maliciously. Prison officials, including those who act as hearing officers for disciplinary procedures, also have qualified immunity. While testifying in court, all witnesses, including police officers, enjoy absolute immunity: they are not subject to suit under the Civil Rights Act even though they commit perjury.

Judges have absolute immunity from monetary damage awards for their judicial actions even when acting in bad faith. This immunity does not prohibit issuing injunctions against a judge's prospective conduct nor does it extend to personnel decisions relating to courtroom employees. It also does not prohibit awarding the opposing party attorney's fees if a successful suit is brought against a judge.

Prosecutors have absolute immunity for actions taken within the scope of their court-related duties. Qualified immunity applies when legal advice is given to assist police conducting an investigation. Qualified immunity is also applied if the prosecutor is accused of fabricating evidence during a preliminary investigation of the case or prejudicing the defendant's case by making false statements at press conferences. Public defenders and appointed attorneys do not have immunity for intentional misconduct.

Municipalities are not exempt from suits under the Civil Rights Act. To establish liability, a policy of disregard for constitutional rights must be shown. Merely the fact that the city employed the offending police officer or a single act of misconduct occurred is not enough. The city is responsible for failure to train if this results in deliberate indifference to constitutional rights.

A city cannot be held liable for the actions of its officers unless the offending officer was named as a party to the suit and found to have violated a constitutional right. On the other hand, a city cannot claim qualified immunity for its unconstitutional policies by asserting the good faith of the individual police officer. Municipalities are immune from punitive damages. Release-dismissal agreements, in which a person agrees to forego filing a civil suit if the criminal charges are dismissed, have been upheld.

States are immune from suits in federal court under the Eleventh Amendment. State officials, such as the Director of the Department of Corrections, can be sued in their individual capacities. When an individual capacity suit is brought against a state official, the state cannot be required to pay attorney's fees of the prevailing party.

Types of Recovery

The same types of monetary awards are possible in Civil Rights Act suits as in torts: compensatory damages, general damages, and punitive damages. The qualified immunity afforded police officers results in cases ending with defense verdicts unless bad faith is involved. Reckless and intentional misconduct usually result in compensatory and general damages as well as punitive damages. Most cases successfully alleging denial of constitutional rights due to racist conduct result in punitive damages. This also applies to sexist and homophobic conduct. Officers usually pay punitive damages out of their own salaries and savings because most governmental agencies will not pay them. Figure 14.5 shows a jury instruction used to help jurors in a Civil Rights Act case determine if punitive damages should be awarded.

Other types of relief can also be granted in these suits. An **injunction** (court order regulating future conduct) can be issued in civil rights cases only if there is an established pattern of violations that leads to the conclusion that constitutional violations will continue unless the court takes action. It is rare that a court will find that this standard has been met.

Consent decrees are entered in some Civil Rights Act cases, particularly class actions. A **consent decree** is a document agreed to by both sides which states an agreement for future action. Once it is approved by the judge, it has all the legal effect of a judgment at the end of a trial. If it is not complied with, the opposing side can go to court to enforce it. Consent decrees are common in litigation regarding discriminatory hiring practices. Class actions in several cities alleged denial of equal protection because police departments did not arrest batterers in domestic violence cases. Some of these cases ended in consent decrees that established new patrol policy.

Section 1988 allows the prevailing party in a civil rights suit to recover attorney's fees. To qualify as a "prevailing party", the plaintiff

Sample Jury Instruction for Punitive Damages under Civil Rights Act

The following questions, known as "special interrogatories," lead the jury through a process that could end with a monetary award.*

(a) Did John Jones violate the constitutional rights of Paul Q. Plaintiff?

If yes,

(b) Did John Jones act with malice or in reckless disregard of Paul Q. Plaintiff's rights?

If yes,

(c) In your discretion do you find punitive damages are appropriate?

If yes,

(d) What amount of punitive damages do you award to Paul Q. Plaintiff against John Jones? $____________.

* John Jones is a police officer but the jury instructions would not refer to him as Officer Jones.

Figure 14.5

must have received at least some relief on the merits of the claim. Monetary damages qualify; so do injunctions, consent decrees and out-of-court settlements. Establishing the violation of a right is not enough if the defendant successfully pleads immunity as a defense.

The Supreme Court has rejected the theory that Section 1988 is a form of contingency-fee agreement which limits attorney fees to a percentage of the amount recovered. Instead, the fee is based on the complexity of the case, total hours devoted to the litigation, and the value to society. For this reason, sizable attorney's fees have been awarded for the vindication of constitutional rights that had limited financial impact on the individual plaintiff. Class actions, due to their complexity, frequently result in large awards for attorney's fees.

In some cases, defendants can recover attorney's fees from the plaintiff. Successfully having the case dismissed is not enough: the case must be shown to be frivolous. The courts have been reluctant to award fees to the defendant unless there is a showing that there is no possible basis for the suit. Judges have been reticent to make such awards when the plaintiff is a *pro per* inmate because the lack of merit may be the result of poor draftsmanship rather than the facts of the case.

14.3 Forfeiture Proceedings Against Defendant's Property

Forfeiture laws first became popular during Prohibition, but have re-emerged in the last decade as a valuable tool in the war against drugs. Civil forfeiture laws permit the seizure of property used to commit crimes. Forfeiture laws cover several key issues: what types of property are subject to forfeiture; under what circumstances property may be seized; what court proceedings are required; and disposition of seized items. It is important that law enforcement officers be knowledgeable about what is authorized in the jurisdiction where they work because there is considerable variation between the states.

Some states, such as Utah, have forfeiture laws which only apply to the manufacture and sale of drugs and related activities. Others, such as Indiana, cover a much wider range of crimes. The laws usually cover items used to commit the crime (equipment, vehicles, etc.); some also apply to cash and items purchased with the profits of criminal activity. In 1993, the Supreme Court held that seizure of real estate without prior notice and hearing did not comply with the Fifth (federal cases) and Fourteenth (state cases) Amendments' protection against deprivation of property without due process. The Court noted that there was no danger of the land being taken out of the jurisdiction, destroyed or hidden prior to a court hearing. Other civil remedies, including obtaining a restraining order and/or filing ***lis pendens*** (a document which makes it impossible to transfer title to real estate until litigation has been completed) can be used to protect the property until the hearing is complete. The Court approved a 1974 case permitting seizure of moveable property prior to a court hearing. The potential for removing the property from the jurisdiction creates an emergency which justifies seizure based on a court order issued at an *ex parte* hearing without the defendant being present or represented by counsel. Final proceedings to determine if the items should be forfeited require notice to the owner and a trial where there is an opportunity to refute charges.

Items Subject to Civil Forfeiture

Based on Indiana Statutes 34-4-30.1-1

(a) The following may be seized:

(1) All vehicles used or intended for use by the person or persons in possession of them to transport or in any manner to facilitate the transportation of the following: (A) a controlled substance for the purpose of committing, attempting to commit, or conspiring to commit any of the specified drug offenses; (B) any stolen or converted property if the retail or repurchase value of that property is $100 or more; (C) any hazardous waste in violation of IC 13-7-13-4.

(2) All money, negotiable instruments, securities, weapons, communications devices, or any property commonly used as consideration for a violation of IC 35-48-4 which is furnished, or intended to be furnished by any person in exchange for an act that is in violation of a criminal statute; or used to facilitate any violation of a criminal statute; or traceable as proceeds of the violation of a criminal statute.

(3) Any portion of real or personal property purchased with money that is traceable as a proceed of a violation of a criminal statute.

(4) A vehicle that is used by a person to commit specified serious felonies.

(5) Real property owned by a person who uses it to commit any of the following as a Class A felony, a Class B felony, or a Class C felony involving specified crimes related to dealing cocaine, marijuana and other controlled substances.

(6) Equipment and recordings used by a person to commit fraud under IC 25-43-5-4(11).

(7) Recordings sold, rented, transported, or possessed by a person in violation of IC 24-4-10.

(8) Property or an enterprise that is the object of a corrupt business influence violation.

(b) A vehicle used by any person as a common or contract carrier in the transaction of business as a common or contract carrier is not subject to seizure under this section, unless it can be proven by a preponderance of the evidence that the owner of the vehicle knowingly permitted the vehicle to be used to engage in conduct that subjects it to seizure under subsection (a).

(c) Money, negotiable instruments, securities, weapons, communications devices, or any property commonly used as consideration for a violation of IC 35-48-4 found near or on a person who is committing, attempting to commit, or conspiring to commit any of the following offenses shall be admitted into evidence in an action under this chapter as prima facie evidence that the money, negotiable instrument, security, or other thing of value is property that has been used or was to have been used to facilitate the violation of a criminal statute or is the proceeds of the violation of specified felonies involving dealing cocaine, marijuana or other controlled substances or possession of cocaine or narcotics.

Figure 14.6

Some states permit forfeiture even though there was no conviction, while others make conviction a prerequisite to these suits. Another variation is the burden of proof: some states require proof beyond a reasonable doubt while others use the civil standard of a preponderance of the evidence. A few have applied different standards depending on the value of the items and the alleged crime. Many states try to protect innocent third parties by requiring that there be proof that the owner of the property knew, or should have known, that his/her property was being used in the commission of a crime. This type of provision provides a defense for a person who loans a car to a friend not knowing that the car will be used to transport drugs. Protection is frequently given to banks and other institutions that hold mortgages on property that is seized for forfeiture.

The ruling on forfeiture is made at the conclusion of a civil trial. Two dispositions are usually available if the government meets its burden of proof: sell the property at auction and divide the proceeds between the governmental agencies involved in the case; or keep the items for use by a governmental agency. Some states, such as Indiana, permit the government to use the property for a limited time but ultimately require it to be sold.

For years it was assumed that civil forfeiture laws did not raise double jeopardy issues. The Federal Court of Appeals for the Ninth Circuit and a few other courts have recently held that a criminal defendant can plead a forfeiture judgement as double jeopardy. The Supreme Court will have to settle this issue.

SUMMARY

Civil tort suits are filed by the aggrieved party to collect monetary damages and other relief from the person who inflicted the injury. A tort is a wrong that did not arise out of a contract. Torts can be either intentional, negligent or based on strict liability. The most common tort suits filed against law enforcement officers are: assault and battery, trespass to chattels (property damage) and false imprisonment (false arrest). At common law, governmental entities had sovereign immunity which protected them from civil suits; most states have statutes which abolish this immunity and permit suits for damages occurring during specified types of activities. A city is liable for actions of its employees if it hires unsuitable personnel or if it fails to adequately train or supervise them.

Compensatory damages can be awarded in tort suits; these damages pay the plaintiff's expenses for injuries and property damage caused by the tort. General damages are awarded to pay for pain and suffering. Punitive damages are imposed for intentional bad conduct; these damages are based on the defendant's financial resources in order to punish him/her and deter future tortious conduct. Wrongful death actions enable the family of someone killed due to a tort to recover the income the deceased would have earned if he/she had lived. Some states impose limits on how much can be recovered in tort actions.

The Civil Rights Act of 1871 permits civil suits in federal court for deprivation of constitutional rights. The most commonly used section (42 U.S.C. § 1983) applies to actions of state and local government employees which deprive people of their constitutional rights under color of state law. The conspiracy section (42 U.S.C. § 1985) applies to actions of two or more people, whether or not government employees, who act together to deprive someone of specified civil rights.

Most law enforcement officers have qualified immunity for their actions as long as they act in good faith in a way a reasonable police officer would react and have taken necessary steps to learn current rules protecting constitutional rights. Testimony on the witness stand is covered by absolute immunity as are acts of the judge and prosecutor in presenting the case in court. The plaintiff can recover compensatory, general and punitive damages in Civil Rights Act cases for actions not covered by immunity.

Injunctions are also available. These are only given if there is an established pattern of conduct; the injunction orders the plaintiff to stop unconstitutional conduct. Failure to comply can be treated as contempt of court. Consent decrees, which are out-of-court settlements reached by the parties, also serve the function of judicial orders. New policies can be imposed as the result of a consent decree.

Civil forfeiture proceedings are authorized in many states. Items used to conduct criminal activity can be seized under these laws; typical examples are cars, boats and houses used by drug dealers. Portable items may be seized based on a court order issued at an *ex parte* hearing; both notice to the defendant and a court hearing where both sides can present evidence are required prior to seizing real estate. A civil complaint is filed and a trial held to determine if the items are forfeited. Most state laws provide protections for innocent third parties whose property was used by someone else while committing criminal acts. If the judge orders a forfeiture, the property can be sold or retained for use by the agencies involved in the case.

Study Questions

1. Check your state statutes to determine under what circumstances sovereign immunity has been waived to permit civil suits against a police department:
   a. For what actions can a police department be sued?
   b. Does a claim have to be made to the city prior to filing a civil case in court?

   c. Are there special time limits on filing claims? If so, what are they?
   d. Are there limitations on the amount of money that can be awarded to a person making a claim against the city? If so, how much?

2. Look in recent newspapers for information on a tort case against a police department. Identify:
   a. plaintiff(s)
   b. defendants
   c. facts alleged by plaintiff(s)
   d. type of torts involved
   e. defenses
   f. if case went to trial:
      1) verdict
      2) damages awarded, if any
      3) was the verdict appealed?

3. Look for a Civil Rights Act suit against a police department. Write a report identifying:
   a. plaintiff(s)
   b. defendant(s)
   c. constitutional violation alleged
   d. facts showing violation
   e. immunity that applies
   f. if case went to trial:
      1) verdict
      2) damages, if any
      3) attorney fees, if any

4. Check the Federal Reporter, Federal Supplement, or ask a librarian or an attorney to help you find a class action that resulted in a consent decree. Prepare a report:
   a. plaintiffs
   b. defendant(s)
   c. issue in case
   d. facts supporting plaintiffs' allegations
   e. defense(s)
   f. consent decree

g. if plaintiff later went to court to enforce consent decree:
    1) What violation of consent decree was alleged?
    2) What action did the court take?

5. Check your state forfeiture laws. Identify:
    a. property subject to forfeiture
    b. types of criminal activity that must be involved
    c. procedures used to seize property subject to forfeiture
    d. types of court documents that must be filed
    e. maximum time limits for starting trial on forfeiture
    f. burden of proof
    g. disposition of forfeited property

6. Check court decisions and statutes to determine if a defendant in your state can claim double jeopardy if criminal charges and forfeiture proceedings are both filed.

Index

R

S

T

U

V